DIVERSITY RESEARCH IN ACTION

DIVERSITY RESEARCH IN ACTION

TEACHING WITHOUT TESTING
BY DENNY TAYLOR

NEGOTIATING A PERMEABLE CURRICULUM
BY ANNE HAAS DYSON

TIME IN EDUCATION
BY CATHERINE COMPTON-LILLY

EDITED BY
BOBBIE KABUTO

GARN PRESS
NEW YORK, NY

Published by Garn Press, LLC
New York, NY
www.garnpress.com

Book and cover design by Ben James Taylor

Library of Congress Control Number: 2020950244

Publisher's Cataloging-in-Publication Data

Names: Taylor, Denny | Dyson, Anne Haas | Compton-Lilly, Catherine | Kabuto, Bobbie.
  Title: Diversity Research in Action / Denny Taylor (author), Anne Haas Dyson (author), Catherine Compton-Lilly (author), and Bobbie Kabuto (editor).
Description: New York : Garn Press, 2021.
Identifiers: LCCN 2020950244 | ISBN 978-1-942146-82-7 (pbk.)
Subjects: LCSH: Critical pedagogy. | Teaching--Principles and practice. | Literacy. | Effective teaching. | BISAC: EDUCATION / Education Policy and Reform / General. | EDUCATION / Teaching Methods & Materials / General.| EDUCATION / Multicultural Education.| EDUCATION / Philosophy, Theory and Social Aspects. | EDUCATION / Aims & Objectives.
Classification: LCC LB2822.75.T23 2021 (print) | DDC 370.107--dc23.

Library of Congress record available at https://lccn.loc.gov/2020950244.

TABLE OF CONTENTS

Dedicated
With Admiration and Respect
To
Public School Teachers
Who Opt-Out of Commercial Standardized Tests

INTRODUCTION

BOBBIE KABUTO

In 2016, Garn Press published its first book in the Women Scholars Series *Negotiating a Permeable Curriculum: On Literacy, Diversity, and the Interplay of Children's and Teachers' Worlds*. I was excited to undertake the project and viewed it as a means of acknowledging the voices of women scholars who have made seminal impacts in literacy education within a higher education setting. I also viewed this series as a way to spotlight women scholars who are researching and teaching within an educational context that is defined by the many inequalities between men and women in higher education (Berg, 2020). According to Berg for instance, women faculty are disproportionally hired at community colleges and less prestigious colleges when compared to Research I institutions. Strikingly, women earn almost $13,000 to $20,000 less than men in higher education (Johnson, 2017). While women are making strides in the higher education system, there is still a long way to go to combat the systemic inequity built into the higher education system that privileges men over women in salary negotiations, scholarly production, promotions into leadership positions, and receiving tenure and promotion (Berg, 2020; Johnson, 2017).

The world has certainly changed since 2016, which has caused me to rethink and revisit the potential impact of the Women Scholars series. The year 2016 marked the year that Donald Trump took office in an unprecedented election. His divisive rhetoric and bombastic and incoherent leadership style have taken us down a path that has increased racial tensions in the United States. In 2020, we are living in a health pandemic because of COVID-19, a major economic recession following the Great Recession of the early 2000s, and a time of racial tensions. Within this context we find little direction from the members of the federal government and the occupant of the White House, who continues to be dismissive about the language he uses to construct narratives around COVID-19 as the "Chinese Virus", and "Black Lives Matter" as an exclusion that other lives also matter (Degen, Leigh, Waldon, & Mengesha, 2020). The tragic deaths of George Floyd and Breonna Taylor raised issues of police brutality and physical violence, and yet this is only one type of violence that can occur alongside symbolic, linguistic, curricula and pedagogical, and systemic school violence that many students of color face on a daily basis (Johnson, Bryan, & Boutte, 2018). People of color, a term that I will use throughout to refer to people with diverse ethnic and racial backgrounds and to encompass black and brown people, including but not limited to African Americans, Asian Americans, and Native Americans, all of whom continue to experience a range of macro- and micro- aggressions (Nieto, 2015; Jordan, 2010).

As educators, we have the responsibility to respond to and shift the narrative from 'schooling' students of color into the dominant and normalized expectations of what it means to be a student in today's classroom, to 'educating' students (Johnson, Bryan, & Boutte, 2018; Ladson-Billings, 2014; Nieto, 2015). And we can only do this through a diversity, equity, and inclusion (DEI) stance towards education to inform our understandings of pedagogy, curriculum, and assessment.

It is within this context that I decided to reconnect to the trilogy of books in the Garn Press Women Scholars Series: *Negotiating a permeable curriculum: On literacy, diversity, and the interplay of children's and teachers' worlds* by Anne Haas Dyson, *Teaching without testing: Assessing the complexity of children's literacy learning* by Denny Taylor, and *Time in education: Intertwined dimensions and theoretical possibilities* by Catherine Compton-Lilly. At the center of these three selections is the diversity work that drives their research. Placing these works in one volume allows me to re-situate them within a diversity, equity, and inclusion (DEI) framework. The goal is to consider how these combined selections can help educators to make steps (big or small) in teaching for inclusive excellence and educational equity.

Diversity

A modest definition of diversity refers to the dynamic states of being different or having elements or varieties that are distinct (Arce-Trigatti & Anderson, 2018; Faist, 2010). However, a more sophisticated definition of diversity includes the complexity within diversity, and the many ways in which that complexity impacts how we see and interact with the world and how the world, and individuals within it, see and interact with us (Faist, 2010; Nieto. 2015). The complexity within diversity reflects the concept of pluralism, and suggests that there is no single group of diverse people (i.e. all Blacks are African Americans), but rather there are multiple layers of diversity that can intersect, complement, and challenge other layers (Faist, 2010). Through this definition, diversity is not seen as a type of decoration, as often portrayed in some multicultural curricular books (Botelho & Rudman, 2009), but rather as sets of practices composed of intersectional self-identities (DiAngelo, 2011; Oluo, 2019).

To capture a consistent definition of diversity in the literature and in public texts such as speeches, news feeds and articles, is often elusive. Using a critical discourse analysis, Arce-Trigatti and Anderson (2018) analyzed the underlying definition of diversity of public educational speeches, speech transcripts, and press releases by Arne Duncan from 2008-2015. They found that, within these larger public narratives, diversity is connected to, what they described as, economic and democratic inputs. Economic input refers to how diverse skills are needed to compete in the labor force to participate in a global society. Diversity as a demographic input positions diversity as addressing the social injustices of minority and underprivileged students. Arce-Trigatti and Anderson (2018) argued, "However, when linked with either of these two themes, diversity loses its place at the center of the policy initiative, becoming little more than a means to an end: diversity for economic progress or diversity to solve the social woes of American society" (p. 13).

Families who have participated in my study *Revaluing Readers and Families* have articulated similar definitions of diversity as economic and democratic endeavors. Working with a linguistically diverse family, Maria, a mother, made every effort to place her daughter Jenny in a dual language school in a large urban school system because she felt linguistic diversity would benefit her children in finding jobs needed to reach economic stability, both of which Maria did not have (Kabuto, 2015). Placing diversity at the center, however, has illustrated how the families in my study constructed narratives around their families' linguistic diversity that may have very little to do with common terms that connect to societal categories, like *immigrant families, bilingual family*, or *dual language learner* (Kabuto, 2018).

Rather, these categories create binary understandings of self and other. For instance, binary understandings of gender confuse gender as a social construct with the biological definition of sex (and there are even exceptions to this definition). Forcing individuals to select a binary division between male or female perpetuates ideas of "self" and "other" instead of creating inclusiveness through gender neutrality. Similarly, societal categories like immigrant families contrasts with the concept of what it means to be an *American family*. The term *bilingual* is itself a binary term that privileges two different languages. Along these lines, more contemporary terms and models that have been created by researchers and used to advance the education of linguistically diverse students, like dual language education, generate a binary construct that can create separation. Within a dual language model of education, consider some of the structures that I have encountered in my own research with linguistically diverse families:

- Organizing Spanish work and English work on separate days.
- Having classroom teachers specific to each language.
- Different periods of the day dedicated to each language.
- Participating in large school formal activities in English.
- Differentiating students in the class who could speak or read better in one language or the other.
- Assessments like state exams that are conducted in English.
- Separate grading systems for each language.

Notwithstanding how dual language education has positively impacted the education of linguistically diverse students, I argue that we still can do better in breaking down language barriers and organizational structures that have become built-in ideological edifices that undermine linguistic equity and inclusion within educational settings.

Similarly, Compton-Lilly explores systemic inequalities in

Time in Education (this volume) through Marvin's experiences in education over time. Readers first met Marvin in *Reading Families* (Compton-Lilly, 2003). Compton-Lilly described Marvin as a student of color living in a low socioeconomic community that was designated the eleventh poorest city in the United States. Marvin lived within a structure that perpetuated many of the racial inequalities that exist in society: Marvin was removed from his parents' home to foster care to live with his grandparents, he was retained in school by the time he was in first grade, and by the time he was in high school, he had altercations with other students and teachers and was incarcerated for stealing a car. Compton-Lilly wrote, "Being retained in school, failing high stakes tests, falling behind with reading, being placed into special education, and incarceration are all temporal disruptions that defined Marvin as unsuccessful and resulted in his being three years behind at age 18". Marvin's experiences still resonate today, and are illustrative of what Johnson, Bryan, and Boutte (2018) described as racial violence and institutionalized racism that causes many of our urban schools to continue to be underserved.

Marvin's experiences also exemplify "racialized discipline" that can lead to the school-to-prison pipeline and the overrepresentation of Black males in the special education system (Johnson, Bryna, Boutte, 2018; Noguera, 2016). Compton-Lilly) described Marvin's experiences as, "The instructional experiences he experienced – heavy-handed discipline, low expectations, special education placement, retention, and racism – informed his sense of self and the dispositions that he brought forward." By placing diversity at the center of her work, Compton-Lilly explicated how Marvin, as a student of color, made sense of his experiences from the time he was in preschool to dropping out of high school before he was 18 years old. It is through this perspective that we see Marvin as not just a victim of the societal racial injustices, but also, and more importantly, as a complex, nuanced and multifaceted individual. It is within this type of diversity work in which Compton-Lilly explained, "For Marvin, time as context reveals agency, lost opportunities, challenges, strengths, resilience, and hope."

White Privilege and Intersectionality

The three works in this volume illustrate how engaging in diversity research requires recognizing privilege, and how the multiplicity of our identities impacts our roles and responsibilities as teachers and researchers. DiAngelo (2011) used the term "white privilege" to discuss "racism as encompassing economic, political, social, and cultural structures, actions, and beliefs that systematize and perpetuate an unequal distribution of privileges, resources, and power between white people and people of color" (p. 56). Scholars who focus on white privilege and whiteness describe it as a social process, a cultural practice, and a standpoint linked to aspects of domination (DiAngelo, 2011; Fine, 1997). One may wonder what white privilege has to do with teaching and researching.

As educators and researchers, we are in a position of power. As educators, we make curricular decisions, grade assignments, and make recommendations on how students will progress from grade to grade. As educators and researchers, we *are* the data collection tool. We write observational notes, decide what data to collect, and organize and interpret the data for other to make sense of it (Agar, 1996).

Positionality with ethnographic research refers to the multiple and intersectional identities of researchers (Agar, 1996). The concept of positionality is not new. In my early parent-research, I discussed my positionality as a 'parent' and as a 'researcher', and how these identities sometimes conflicted with each other and provided me with an insider's lens into how I collected and interpreted data on Emma's linguistic diversity (Kabuto, 2008). I often talked about how as a Japanese Asian

American, middle class, academic mother researching her Japanese Asian-American daughter's biliteracy aligned or "othered" myself with the research context. In this way, I discussed the different vantage points that I had within the research context, including my shared history with Emma that defines what it means to be a Japanese Asian-American, and the types of biases that go along with researching my daughter's linguistic diversity.

Recent political discourses around COVID-19 that have carelessly used the term "Chinese Virus" have led to increased violence and hate crimes against Asian Americans (Cheung et al., 2020; Phillips, 2020). These reports do not account for the microaggressions that Asian Americans may have faced, such as the one that Emma experienced right before her college closed due to COVID-19. While coming out of the grocery store with her mask on, a white, middle-aged women told her to "get out the of the f--- country" as she walked past her. Cheung et al. (2020) reported in the *BBC News* that one third of the people they surveyed said that they witnessed Asians being blamed for the COVID-19 pandemic. Emma's experience exemplified their point.

I have also seen how racism and biases against Asian Americans can be minimalized by the model minority myth. The model minority myth was coined by William Peterson to describe the socioeconomic success of Japanese Americans (Oluo, 2019). It has since been expanded to refer to a range of stereotypes about Asian Americans to frame them as an ideal minority group (Oluo, 2019). To provide an example, Kirwan Institute (2018) from The Ohio State University highlighted a 2016 report *Implicit Bias and School Discipline*. The 2016 report noted that Black, Non-Hispanic students are more likely to receive out of school suspensions while Asians were the least likely. These data suggest that there are a disproportionate number of Black, Non-Hispanic students who experience disciplinary action and provide an argument for why Asians are part of the "good" minority group. The former finding reflects the idea of racialized discipline and the latter instance marginalizes the racism and violence they can experience when their cultures, ways of understanding and being, and languages are not accepted in schools (Oluo, 2019).

What happens when teachers and researchers do not have shared experiences with their students and participants? For instance, could a white male have also researched Emma's experiences as a linguistically diverse individual and have come to similar insights as I did? Compton-Lilly (this volume) helps to shed light on this question by highlighting how the intersections of her identity and privilege shaped and were also shaped by her work with Marvin as a teacher and researcher.

Intersectionality was coined by Crenshaw (1991) "to denote the various ways in which race and gender interact to share the multiple dimensions of Black women's employment experiences" (p. 1244). Intersectionality has been expanded to consider how the multiplicity of our identities inform how we see and interpret the world and how we interpret our experiences. As researchers continue to argue, intersectionality needs to be at the core of the diversity and social justice work that we do (Brochin, 2018; Núñez, 2014).

Compton-Lilly, who is currently an endowed professor at the University of South Carolina, Columbia, wrote about her path as an educator and researcher through time. She explained how her trajectory afforded her a means in life that was very different than the students, like Marvin, who she taught. Compton-Lilly (this volume) wrote:

> Time haunts me as a researcher. I contemplate the trajectories that awaited my former students and the severe consequences of attending underfunded schools in a high poverty community. I recall my amazing six-year-old students and the potential they brought to my classroom. I consider the parents' unwavering hope for their children's futures. I lament the opportunities

they did not find in school, the stifling instruction that they reported, and the failed tests, low report card grades, and stringent behavioral policies that they recalled. (p.263)

Oluo (2018) argued that intersectionality compels teachers and researchers to confront privilege and oppression in ways that many people are not used to using. Intersectionality also decentralizes individuals who are used to controlling and interacting with groups of people who have been historically placed at the fringes of social justice work. The Black Lives Matter movement is an example of how voices that have been historically oppressed are taking back the conversation. By taking the time to address her trajectory in the context of time, Compton-Lilly identified deep rooted societal differences between her as a researcher and Marvin, a student of color. More importantly, Compton-Lilly does not use her position to argue what is best for Marvin. Rather, she listens to Marvin and his family, gives them a voice that is different from her own, and shifts the power from her privilege to Marvin and his family so they can speak out.

Inclusion

If diversity is defined as a range of dynamic states and characteristics, then inclusion can be defined as a way of engaging with diversity. Within an educational context, the term "inclusion" is mostly connected with special education settings. Inclusion in this context should not be conflated with integration and the idea of "including all learners." My work with Christie (this volume) illustrates how students who have been placed in "inclusive" classrooms can leave with stigmas of being educationally classified as "learning disabled." Contech (2013) argued that discussions of inclusion in curriculum and pedagogy are paradoxical to notions of diversity and often promote an "'idealized primary pupil' with a notional set of qualities that enables her or him to perform to a fixed and absolute standard of success" (p. 344).

In addition to addressing diversity and inclusion in special education settings, linguistically diverse students who are learning English are overwhelming placed in classrooms with students who speak only English, as they receive English as a Second Language (ESL) or English as a New Language (ENL) instruction. In the United States, very few school districts offer dual language instruction. In fact, some states, like Arizona, do not permit *any* form of dual language instruction. At the same time, the linguistic diversity of students who are proficient in English, like Emma, are ignored. In my work with Emma, I found that there was little engagement with her language and linguistic experiences, or any teaching to the language and cultural experiences and competence that Emma brought to the classroom, in spite of the fact that Emma's teacher knew that she was linguistically diverse in speaking, reading, and writing. Taking these ideas into consideration, inclusion is better defined by eliminating the barriers and structural inequalities that have oppressed different ways of knowing and learning.

Anne Haas Dyson in *Negotiating a Permeable Curriculum* (this volume) provides an illustrative example of inclusive excellence in curriculum and pedagogy through her concept of a "permeable curriculum". Underlying how diversity work gets done in a permeable curriculum is the idea that schools and teachers serving students of color from diverse sociocultural backgrounds need to feel connected their students, rather than relationships being impaired by differences in race in class. Dyson proposed that students are social actors whose "culturally patterned ways of using language are evident in stories, jokes, prayers, arguments, and other genres through which people construct their social lives together" (p.203). Dyson called these cultural ways of using language and ways of knowing that are embedded with their social lives as students' "unofficial worlds", and she distinguished these unofficial worlds with those of schools where teachers work within official worlds.

Gee's (1996) seminal work in sociolinguistics, discourses, and identity highlighted how children have "ways of being in the world," or learn to be types of "culturally-specific" people. Gee provided an example of a common classroom experience with "share time" when students were permitted to bring in an item to share with the class. Gee compared the discourses of a white, middle class 7-year-old girl with that of a Black 7-year-old girl from a low socioeconomic background in the same class. In that comparison, Gee noted that the discourse from the white student was aligned and deemed appropriate by the teacher (who was also white), while the Black student's discourse was not and resulted in interruptions and corrections by the teacher. This finding led Gee to argue that students learn social languages that have a history deeply rooted in culturally specific ways of using language that are not valued in schools.

Supported by a body of research that focuses on the discord between home and school literacies (Compton-Lilly, 2003; Heath, 1983; Taylor & Dorsey-Gaines, 1988), one would argue that the white student learned discourses and ways of acting that aligned with school-based literacy practices, while the Black student did not. The result was that the white student was more successful than the student of color. Success and failure had little to do either with cognitive abilities, or with notions of inclusive understandings of how students are culturally specific people who use language to construct meaning. In this volume, Compton-Lilly, Dyson, and Taylor suggest that it is time that schools stop insisting that students conform to the ideals of school, and that we educate students as social and cultural individuals who are part of learning communities connected to both home and school.

Dyson in *Negotiating a Permeable Curriculum* challenges that there is one acceptable way to be a student. Dyson shows that when students are acknowledged as being capable language users and when negotiation occurs between students, teachers, and curriculum, teachers and schools can create inclusive pedagogy and curriculum. Notable in Dyson's research is the idea of intersectionality and how it played a role in pedagogical inclusion. Dyson illustrated how a white, middle class teacher Louise teaching in a school with a majority Black student body in a low socioeconomic classroom viewed her students as cultural and social actors. Louise drew from her students Eugenie, Lamar, and Jameel and their cultural ways of communication. Dyson explained:

> Louise took advantage of the diversity of cultural material the children brought to the rug. In the presented examples, the genres included horror stories and pop songs, but they could have been cartoons or raps, "true stories" filled with hyperbole, or expressive "love stories". In response to the children's inclusiveness, Louise worked to help children name their efforts, to place their work in the social landscape of discourse. (p.219)

Expanding to assessment practices, Denny Taylor in *Teaching without Testing* (this volume) placed assessment within a humanistic perspective that views students as learners and social actors. In *Teaching without Testing*, Taylor provided a framework through the development of Biographic Literacy Profiles for capturing "the complexity of the richness and diversity of children's literacy experiences in classrooms that encourage the self-organization of problem-solving activities" (p.123), as teachers constructed "biographic profiles based upon observations of children's literacy behaviors" (p.135). These profiles drew from systematic observations to capture students' literacy manifestations, or the ways in which children used and interpreted print to create patterns of literacy behaviors.

In turn, Biographic Literacy Profiles provided powerful portraits of children from an advocacy perspective that challenged standardized assessments that did little to consider socioeconomic class, educational histories, race, and language backgrounds. Taylor wrote, "To 'move' beyond the debate, it is essential that researchers and educators reexamine the 'scientific' assumptions on which testing (irrespective of whether the tests emphasize word-recognition or comprehension) is based" (p. 148). Taylor continued by arguing that standardized tests promote an "objective reality" and reductionism, and that "our interpretations of language (and life) cannot be reduced to a series of competing logical structures or linear stage-theories" (p. 148).

While the standardized, high-stakes testing that resulted from No Child Left Behind (NCLB) in 2001 was exacerbated by Race to the Top (RTT) in 2009, public education entered a new phase of legislation with the Every Child Succeeds Act (ECSA) in 2016. While the act made small steps in recognizing the overemphasis on testing, it has done little to reduce the amount and frequency of testing in schools, the dependency on commercialized testing vendors, the use of test scores for student and teacher accountability, and the needs of linguistically diverse students (NCTE Standing Committee on Literacy Assessment, 2019). Rather than allow teachers to engage in diversity work, standardized assessments 'norm' that data so that some students fall out of the 'norm/al' to promote an ideal performance that defines success and failure.

Equity

Equity is the goal of inclusive excellence. If educational inclusion involves breaking down barriers, educational equity happens when barriers are removed and remain absent. This definition is not to be confused with 'equal.' Equal treatment or access to materials, goods, services, and funds is not necessarily synonymous with equity. Jordan (2010) explained this point when he wrote:

Equity is not about providing the same education to all students regardless of race, social class, or gender. In fact, because of increasing cultural and linguistic diversity it is advantageous to define educational equity in terms of providing knowledge, skills, and worldviews which would enable social mobility. (p. 148)

While educational equity has been the goal of educational reform in the United States, it has also been elusive (Jordan, 2010). Scholars have argued that federal legislation like NCLB, RTT and the ECSA have resulted in a new form of segregation and structural inequity within education (see Jordan for a more detailed discussion). These inequalities have been further magnified during the COVID-19 pandemic when state governors began calling for public schools to close and pivot to distance learning. This pivot brought attention to the lack of technological access and infrastructure for students of color and low socioeconomic status. Dorn et al. (2020) found that only 60% of low-income K-12 students regularly logged into online instruction compared to 90% of high-income students. Students of color (Latinx and Black) logged in at a rate of 60-70%. In other words, 30-40% of students of color did not participate in online education. The authors attributed these findings to the fact that lower income students are less likely to have stable internet connections, appropriate devices at home, and space in the home where they work. The move to online learning virtually segregated students and their educational experiences by social class and race.

The works of Compton-Lilly, Dyson, and Taylor presented in this volume come together in a climate that is dominated by state learning standards, commercialized curriculum, and high-stakes, standardized testing, and when educators feel that they have little control over their own pedagogy. The year of 2020 (and possibly 2021) will be defined by two crises: COVID-19, and the tensions resulting from racial and systemic inequalities. These twin 'pandemics' have caused disruption. But we do not have to let this disruption lead to more problems. Rather, educators can view these disruptions as potential opportunities – opportunities to learn, grow, and challenge our ideas, assumptions, and beliefs. In recent months, I have had educators from diverse backgrounds and with a range of teaching experiences ask me, "How do I teach in the backdrop of a pandemic and the Black Lives Matter movement?" The works in this volume inspire us to take one step forward and give us 'small wins' as we modify and challenge our own histories and understandings of pedagogy and assessment while reaching for the goal of educational equity.

The first step forward begins by recognizing that we are all diverse, cultural individuals and must address our intersectionality. Researchers have argued that white individuals see themselves as outside of culture, or of not having culture (DiAngelo, 2011; Nieto, 2015). Nieto (2015) contends that white individuals "lament that they do not have 'culture'" in the same way that other groups, like Blacks, Latinx, and Asians "have it" (p. 47). The consequence is that whites develop an "unracialized identity" which results in the "inability to think about whiteness as an identity or as a 'state' of being that would or could have an impact on one's life" (DiAngelo, 2011, p. 66). Just as we see in the works in this volume, we should not only acknowledge our position and intersectional identities and how they impact how we see students and how students see us, but confront them. This first step in teaching can help educators to realize they are also co-constructors in the successes, as well as the failures, of students of color.

Educational equity is, then, espoused on the notion that curriculum, pedagogy, and assessment can take a humanistic perspective in which learners are viewed as social actors. Along these lines, notions of ability in all its various forms – cognitive, reading, writing, and communicational, are all socially constructed. Taylor in particular illustrated the ways in which students' abilities in reading and writing can be viewed as successful or not, depending on how standardized tests or teachers define reading and writing and what it means to be a reader and writer. In my own work, I continue to build on notions of ability, and on how ability is constructed through common classroom assessments like miscue analysis, running records, and reading inventories, creating sometimes contradictory profiles of readers (Harmey & Kabuto, 2018; Kabuto, 2017).

By acknowledging the socially constructed nature of ability, educators can act by locating students at the center of curriculum and assessment, as both educators and students traverse the official and unofficial social worlds and classroom curriculum. Dyson in this volume showed the power of breaking down those invisible barriers to make the boundaries permeable. Removing barriers means removing singular ways of knowing, teacher- or commercial- led curriculum, and objectivity to make room for multiple ways of knowing, a teacher and student constructed curriculum, and the subjectivity and viewpoints that come along with social, cultural, racial and linguistic diversity.

Finally, educators need to see disruption as a time for transformative change to challenge how educational institutions have overly depended on and used high-stakes, standardized state testing. Due to the COVID-19 pandemic, many states around the country canceled their testing for the 2019-2020 academic year. With the uncertainty of how schools will reopen for the 2020-2021 school year, states may continue to forgo testing. Colleges and universities are making the move to go test-optional, which will allow students to choose whether or not to take and submit their scores for Advanced Placement (AP) exams, the SAT, and the ACT. The College Board showed its vulnerabilities, its privileging of higher socioeconomic students, and the "big business" of testing, when it was unable to provide testing to students after a series of test cancelations over the spring and summer months (Adams, 2020), and in its attempt to provide online AP exams in the spring (Jaschik, 2020).

The collection of papers in this Women Scholars edition shows the timeless nature of their works and how they speak to today's educational climate. In this moment of turmoil and disruption, Taylor, Dyson, and Compton-Lilly inspire educators to talk back to standardized testing, and to advocate for a major shifting of resources away from the big business of testing and state standards, to the professional development of teacher knowledge and school and classroom resources for students attending schools in urban settings and areas that are underfunded with little access to technology. Educators can make the shift to culturally responsive assessment practices that build on the knowledge, literacy manifestations and discourses, as well as the sociohistorical, cultural and linguistic identities of students of color in ways that capture human diversity.

REFERENCES

Adams, S. (2020, July 27). ACT is struggling to give its college admissions tests during the pandemic. *Forbes*.

Agar, M. (1996). *The professional stranger: An informal introduction to ethnography*. Academic Press.

Arce-Trigatti, A. & Anderson, A. (2018). Defining diversity: a critical discourse analysis of public educational texts, Discourse: Studies in the Cultural Politics of Education, *40*, 3-20. DOI: 10.1080/01596306.2018.1462575

Berg, G. A. (2019). *The rise of women in higher education: How, why, and what's next*. Rowman & Littlefield Publishers

Botelho, M. J., & Rudman, M. K. (2009). *Critical multicultural analysis of children's literature: Mirrors, windows, and doors*. Routledge.

Brochin, C. (2018). Assembled identities and intersectional advocacy in literacy research. *Literacy Research: Theory, Method, and Practice, 67*(1), 164-179.

Cheung, H., Feng, Z., & Deny, B. (2020, May 27). Coronavirus: What attacks on Asians reveal about American identity. *BBC News*.

Compton-Lilly, C. (2003). *Reading families: The literate lives of urban children*. Teachers College Press.

Conteh, J. (2013). Multilingual Literacies in Mainstream Classroom Contexts. In D. Martin (Ed.), *Researching Dyslexia in Multilingual Settings: Diverse Perspectives* (pp. 136-156). Multilingual Matters.

Crenshaw, K. (1990). Mapping the margins: Intersectionality, identity politics, and violence against women of color. *Stanford Law Review, 43*(6), 1241-1299.

Degen, J., Leigh, D., Waldon, B., & Mengesha, Z. (2020, June 23). A linguistic perspective: The harmful effects of responding 'All lives matter' to 'Black lives matter'. *Interactive Language Processing Lab Stanford.* http://alpslab.stanford.edu//blog.html

DiAngelo, R. (2011). White fragility. *International Journal of Critical Pedagogy, 3,* 54-70.

Dorn, E., Hancock, B., Sarakatsannis, J., & Viruleg, E. (2020). *COVID-19 and student learning in the United States: The hurt could last a lifetime.* McKinsey & Company.

Faist, T. (2010). Cultural diversity and social inequalities. *Social Research: An International Quarterly, 77*(1), 297-324.

Gee, J. P. (1996). *Social linguistics and literacies: Ideology and discourse* (2nd ed.). Routledge-Falmer.

Harmey, S. & Kabuto, B. (2018). Metatheoretical differences between running records and miscue analysis: Implications for analysis of oral reading behaviors. *Research in the Teaching of English, 53*(1), 11-33.

Heath, S. B. (1983). *Ways with words: Language, life, and work in communities and classrooms.* Cambridge.

Jaschik, S. (2020, June 1). Testing turmoil. *Inside Higher Ed.*

Johnson, H. L. (2017). *Pipelines, pathways, and institutional leadership: An update on the status of women in higher education.* American Council on Education.

Johnson, L. L., Bryan, N., & Boutte, G. (2019). Show us the love: Revolutionary teaching in (un) critical times. *The Urban Review, 51*(1), 46-64.

Jordan, W. J. (2010). Defining equity: Multiple perspectives to analyzing the performance of diverse learners. *Review of Research in Education, 34*(1), 142-178.

Kabuto, B. (2008). Parent-research as a process of inquiry: An ethnographic perspective. *Ethnography and Education, 3(2)*, 177-194.

Kabuto, B. (2018). Family narratives of biliteracy. *Literacy, 52*(3), 137-144.

Kabuto, B. (2015). The construction of biliterate narratives and identities between parents and children. *Global Education Review, 2*(2). http://ger.mercy.edu/index.php/ger

Kabuto, B. (2017). A socio-psycholinguistic perspective to biliteracy: The use of miscue analysis as a culturally relevant assessment tool. *Reading Horizons, 56*(1), 25-44.

Kirwan Institute. (2018). *Race in conversation: Equity in Practice.* The Ohio State University. Ladson-Billings, G. (2014).

Nieto, S. (2015). *The light in their eyes: Creating multicultural learning communities.* Teachers College Press.

NCTE Standing Committee on Literacy Assessment. (2019, September, 20). Key takeaways from a survey of NCTE state policy analysts. *National Council of Teachers of English.* https://ncte.org/blog/2019/09/key-takeaways-survey-state-reps/

Noguera, P. A. (2016). Race, education, and the pursuit of equity in the twenty-first century. In P.A. Noguera, J.C. Pierce, & R. Ahram (Eds.), *Race, equity, and education* (pp. 3-23). Springer.

Núñez, A. M. (2014). Employing multilevel intersectionality in educational research: Latino identities, contexts, and college access. *Educational Researcher, 43*(2), 85-92.

Oluo, I. (2019). *So you want to talk about race.* Hachette UK. Phillips, K. (2020, May 20). 'We just want to be safe': Hate crimes, harassment of Asian

Americans rise amid coronavirus pandemic. *USA Today.*

Taylor, D., & Dorsey-Gaines, C. (1988). *Growing up literate: Learning from inner-city families.* Heinemann.

BOOK ONE

TEACHING WITHOUT TESTING: ASSESSING THE COMPLEXITY OF CHILDREN'S LITERACY LEARNING

INTRODUCTION

BOBBIE KABUTO

In his early writings, Walter Benjamin, a writer of literary and cultural analysis, wrote "We are living at a time when it is impossible to open a newspaper without running into the word 'school,' at a time when the words 'coeducation,' 'boarding school,' 'child,' and 'art' are in the air" (p. 26). While written sometime between 1910 and 1917, this critique certainly has not changed much. Today, newspapers such as the *New York Times* dedicate entire sections to education and words such as "charter schools" replace "boarding schools" and "Common Core State Standards" replace "art." Education is a political enterprise, and more recently, an overtly commercial one. This point has been consistently reified through the political endeavor to privatize public education through the evaluation system of both students and teachers.

Established through No Child Left Behind in 2001 and exacerbated with Race to the Top in 2009, standardized testing has been deemed the key instrument in determining educational accountability. Through federal regulations, assessing students and evaluating teacher effectiveness are about building data systems and adopting standards in the form of the Common Core State Standards (CCSS). Researchers have painstakingly demonstrated how the movement towards national standards and assessment data systems create data-banks of student and teacher evaluation data. These databanks connect to and directly benefit special interest groups and business companies, who profit from the use and development of national standardized tests for K-12 public school students across the nation (Cody, 2014; Spring, 2015; Strauss, 2005).

The direct result is the overemphasis on testing, and students in the United States are tested more than students in any other developed nation. Grassroots resistance, however, continues to grow in the form of Opt-Out movements nation-wide. Opt-out movements evolved as the implementation and adaption of the CCSS connected to assessment and evaluation systems gained ground across the United States. States began to scramble to find ways not only to develop curriculum around the CCSS, but also to assess students on whether they met the new standards and evaluate teachers on their effectiveness in teaching them. Parents, community organizers, and educational researchers raised concerns over the assessment and evaluation of their children, the time taken away from classroom instruction as children sat for test after test, and the true purpose of the tests. They questioned as to how the tests could help improve instruction for their children when they were evaluated in the spring and the results were provided months later in the fall, when their children had new teachers and new classes. The Opt-Out movement was born from the concerns of these stakeholders, who have direct vested interests in their children's mental and educational well-being. Opposing the marketization of education and the over testing of children solidified the strength of the movement. Parents, community organizers, and researchers argue that children are not data points, and learning cannot be standardized if we are make education an equitable enterprise.

Public education entered a new phase of legislation with the Every Child Succeeds Act, which, in 2016, was signed as a reauthorization of the Elementary and Secondary Education Act of 1965. The act makes small steps in recognizing the over-emphasis on testing. The new act requires states that receive federal grant money to audit their assessment system (Sect. 1202). States must report timelines for the release of the assessment data and the amount of time teachers spend on assessment preparation and administration. There are also provisions that allow states to allocate small sub-grants to local schools to hire instructional coaches outside or within the school to support teachers in the development and implementation of classroom-based assessments and developing instruction. The most notable section of the act is Section 1204, which proposes the implementation of "innovative assessments" that include competency-based assessments, instructionally embedded assessments, interim assessments, cumulative assessments, or performance-based assessments. While on the surface this new legislation appears to tackle the increased level of testing in schools, it is still a far cry from amending the woes that testing and commercialization have placed on public education.

It is within this context that I introduce *Teaching Without Testing: Assessing the Complexity of Children's Literacy Learning* by Denny Taylor. Originally published by the National Council of Teachers of English (NCTE) as a special edition of *English Education* (Taylor, 1990), and later as a chapter in her book *From a Child's Point of View* (Taylor, 1993), *Teaching Without Testing* illustrates how we can assess children in meaningful ways that do not depend on testing. The second book in the Women Scholars Series, *Teaching Without Testing* is as relevant today as it was in 1993 through the revisiting of Taylor's *Biographic Literacy Profiles Project*. Taylor wrote, "We are expected to be accountable, and accountability is built into the system. We use standardized tests to make sure that teachers teach and children learn" (this volume, p. 132). She questions the connection between standardized testing and teacher evaluation by asking, "How does this contingency affect teaching and learning? What pressures does such policy put on teachers? How does it affect opportunities for them to teach and children to learn?" (p. 132).

Taylor challenges the scientific assumptions of standardized testing in developing effective instruction to meet the literate lives of all students in the classroom. Arguing that standardized tests promote an "objective reality" and reductionism, Taylor contends that "our interpretations of language (and life) cannot be reduced to a series of competing logical structures or linear stage-theories" (p. 148). The *Biographic Literacy Profiles Project* highlights how teachers can base their instruction on observations of children and what can happen when "teachers and administrators try to view teaching, learning, and schooling from the perspective of the learner" (p. 50).

Biographic literacy profiles provide powerful portraits of children from an advocacy perspective, a perspective oftentimes lost in the standardization of teaching and learning but which needs to be reclaimed by students and their families. There is no better example of this than Christie, who was a participant in a larger study *Revaluing Readers and Families* (Kabuto, 2015) that was built on the very premise of biographic literacy profiles: understanding the social organization of children's everyday lives from the child's point of view. I have followed Christie's literacy learning experiences over ten years, between the ages of seven and seventeen. Over this time frame, Christie's case continually adds to the complexity of what it means to be a "special education student" in today's climate of testing and accountability. Her profile unveils the hidden tracking structures that special education students involuntarily enter into as they move from elementary to middle school and then to high school, as well as how a social classification system shapes the literate identities of students like Christie in special education settings.

In the following, I will introduce biographic literacy profiles through Christie's learning biography to explore the connections between learning and identity, and to problematize global definitions of literacy learning that privilege the standardization of education and accountability measures reflected in corporate management models (Spring, 2015). I argue that biographic literacy profiles provide a humanistic perspective to assessing learning and focus on an advocacy model of learning.

Learning Biography

Biography involves the telling of a life story, whether it is our own through personal biographies or autobiographies, or of another. Regardless, the telling of a life story involves the presentation of events that may serve many functions, such articulating turning points in one's life experiences and presenting unresolved conflicts and concerns that are emotionally charged. Listening to Christie's mom Carole, and then later Christie, tell Christie's learning biography over ten years epitomizes how "the telling of the story is born out of experience and gives shape to the experience" (Ochs & Capps, 1996, p. 20).

I met Christie when she was a first grade student in the public school system. Although she was seven years old at the time of our first meeting, she already had a long history of educational testing starting at 18 months when she started receiving speech and language services because, as her mother Carole described, she "stopped talking." Upon entering kindergarten, Christie received an Individualized Educational Plan (IEP) and began receiving a variety of classes, including a special integrated class daily for 5 hours, occupational therapy, physical therapy, and speech and language therapy. Carole talked about Christie as an "enigma" and that Christie's school described her as an anomaly because the slew of testing that she underwent could not place her in some nice, neat category.

Carole's comment was in fact not just a comment about

Christie. It was also part of a Carole's learning memoire. One day as Carole and I walked to her car, she stopped and pointed to a building and said to me, "I remember coming here for reading classes. And I remember reading *Gone with the Wind* and getting it and understanding what I was reading." Carole continued by describing how she thought that she had dyslexia, which she self-prescribed, and knew that while she could not have read every word, she understood what she read. As Carole compared Christie's experiences with her own, Carole began to self-fashion particular identities for her family. These self-fashioned identities developed through Carole's and Christie's learning biographies. Attending resource room classes and Committee of Special Education (CSE) meetings, and writing and rewriting IEPs reified these self-fashioned identities as they became packaged and embodied by a label: *learning disabled.*

Although Carole played less of a role in talking to me about Christie's learning biography over the course of time, she unwittingly discussed how Christie's school interpreted that "teaching" Christie really meant "reducing the requirements." Carole said that she refused after-school tutoring for Christie and extra homework help because the offerings were a disguise for additional test preparation. Carole forlornly talked about how Christie's self-esteem began to take a turn downward, which she said happens when one "robs a child of their specialness."

Christie, however, played more of a role in storying her learning experiences. In telling her story as a third year high school student, Christie discussed unresolved, personal conflicts that took an emotional toll on her over the years as a child identified within the special education system. In addition to losing her home during Hurricane Sandy and being displaced for a year, Christie felt the social pressure from her classmates. She described how she felt "traumatized" by others because of her "learning disability." Christie said, "[They say that] I'm ugly and start bullying me, people [are] bullying me." She described how some students said, "You should not be in this school."

Christie also discussed particular events as turning points in her educational experiences. One particular turning point happened when Christie started attending her CSE meetings in 8th grade. Christie said that she realized that she needed to take more control and be more vocal in her CSE meetings because the school's tracking system would have placed her in "life skills classes" rather than in college preparation classes. Christie said:

> I told everyone [that] I don't want to be in life skills, end of story. I don't belong there, I don't do like XXX does, I don't do like YYY does. I'm different. You don't see how much different I am. Like I socialize a lot and I catch my speech delay and my dyslexia, my reading problem and my math problem. So I know I have another couple of years [before I graduate] and I told them [that] you're not going to change anything about what I want.

Christie did not see herself like the other students who participated in the life skills program and said, "I don't want to have their, like their disability [passed] onto me." By attending her CSE meetings, Christie gained a voice and agency in determining her future trajectory. After discovering that the school had placed her in the life skills track, she attended her next CSE meeting and demanded that she take college preparation classes. Christie further elaborated, "So this year was a real opportunity to put me in that normal class, but I know now I've realized that I have to have a couple of more years, because I'm really graduating [at] 20, 21 or 19."

One of Christie's educational concerns that endured over time in her learning biography related to the challenges that her "dyslexia" presented in her educational progress. When I asked Christie about the bullying, she replied that the bullying was the result of her learning disability. I then asked Christie to talk a little more about her learning disability, and she replied,

"My dyslexia you know?" While Christie used this term to describe and characterize herself, particularly at the age of 17, nowhere is the term used in any of her educational or medical documents over the years. Christie and Carole are adamant that Christie is dyslexic, but lack any official claiming of the term.

Learning Biography and Identity

Learning biographies are enactments of identity, or self-fashioning a sense of who we are in relation to other people, places, and things (Coffey & Street, 2008). Over time, Christie's learning biography evolved and changed. Some aspects were conserved over time, as in her identification by others and her self-identification with deficit-oriented views of her learning experiences, which became bundled in the label of a *learning disability*. Other aspects changed, particularly Christie's action towards advocating for herself to challenge the tracking systems in place for students such as herself. Christie engaged in meaningful human action to oppose how she was positioned as someone who was "not capable". Christie came to see herself as different from how the label narrowly defined her as a learner.

Christie's learning biography also demonstrated how identity reflects multiplicity. She saw herself as struggling by claiming the term *dyslexic* for herself. Christie recognized how her speech often interfered with her orally expressing her thoughts. She described, "I catch my…like some verbal [words], because I have a speech delay also. So I know that by now. I catch it myself from my brain and I'll just mix up the words and try to understand." While she defined that part of herself, she questioned what it means "to struggle." Christie felt that she should not be boxed into a category of being "incapable", which she felt that being placed in life skills meant. Consequently, she used terms like "normal" to describe classes outside of the life skills program. Christie described:

English [is] doing simple work like [reading] a little passage, like two sentences, fill in a questionnaire. That's easy enough [because] it's level two reading and I don't want to do that. And for science, they don't have a science class for it, or social studies. They don't do that. I take four other courses and go out to the workforce.

Christie has dreams of going to college. She developed a proclivity for photography, photographing beach sunsets near her home and talking about being a photographer or a makeup artist. In addition to sunsets, she talked about photographing her "creations." Christie has aspirations that were not recognized by the school in her IEP, and certainly not by the CSE team.

Teacher as Biographer

Christie's learning biography provides a glimpse into her reality and how she views the unfolding of the events around her. As Ochs and Capps (1996) remind us, the telling of our stories "are embodiments of one or more points of view rather than objective, omniscient accounts" (p. 21). Christie's learning biography was made up of fragmented memories of her experiences, worries, and dissatisfactions, resulting in incomplete self-understandings. Her learning biography developed because "the tale…lies beyond the telling" (Ochs & Capps, 1996, p. 21), and the telling involves not only the speaker but also a listener, both of whom come together to create a shared understanding or perspective of the teller's experiences. This statement has major implications for understanding the role of the teacher in developing biographic literacy profiles: the role of the teacher is the role of the biographer.

Teacher as biographer reframes the idea of assessment by placing a critical responsibility on documenting not only what students can do with reading and writing, but also students' learning biographies, in a manner that captures their own version of reality. Just as the role of ethnographers is to observe and document the everyday, lived experiences of individuals, groups of individuals, and communities, "teachers as biographers" suggest that teachers observe with the idea of capturing students' actions as well as their words. Observation means listening as much as watching, and organizing the past and present events with future possibilities. Taylor writes that through observation, teachers "'capture' a brief glimpse of the complexity of the symbol-weaving that takes place in the problem-solving situations as children reconstruct the functions, uses, and forms of written language" (p. 149).

Through the development of students' learning biographies, teachers question more profoundly. As Taylor describes, teachers attempt "to study and teach from the perspective of the learner" (p. 149). They not need to solve all of the problems and predicaments that students present to them, but instead teachers help to find and relocate life and learning trajectories for students. Teachers as biographers humanize students and their learning by highlighting a more "authentic sense of life" (Ochs & Capps, 1996, p. 23).

Literacy Profile

Definitions of literacy run far and wide. While literacy involves the inclusion of the physical and cognitive acts of reading and writing, it also includes the ranges of practices that *use* reading and writing. As Gee (2002) argues, the study of literacy is to investigate the ways in which certain practices give rise to different forms of reading and writing. Literacy viewed as social and cultural practices is, of course, composed of different written language forms and functions. However, a social and cultural perspective challenges the view of literacy as a universal practice. Rather, a social and cultural perspective highlights how language forms are privileged in certain social and cultural environments, part of semiotic and textual meanings within activities, and tools used to gain access and power into social structures. As Bomer and Maloch (2012) remind us, "There is nothing natural about a school report, an expository essay about a text, or a test; they're practices that are native to a special bureaucratic institution – school" (p. 44). The social and cultural environments within schools privilege these types and forms of reading and writing, and use them as a means of determining who is successful and who is not.

Historically, the definition of literacy in schools has taken a predictable, linear, unimodal view of reading and writing. Reading and writing are studied as codes to be taken apart and made sense of, often in that order.

For example, Christie's educational documents articulated a narrow, standardized view of reading and writing. In one document that Christie received when she was 17 years old, her reading progress was described as follows:

> Christie is able to read simply worded sentences. Christie struggles with her pronunciation of unfamiliar vocabulary terms. When Christie is asked to explain or reword what she has read she experiences great difficulty. Her reading comprehension is below average as well as her decoding skills. Christie struggles with her inferential and interpreting skills.

These types of conclusions about Christie's reading and writing were reflective of the numerous and repeated testing that she underwent throughout her years in the special education system. Based on these conclusions, the following recommendations were noted,

> Christie needs to identify the main idea of a given story or text and identify supporting details. After being presented with a reading assignment, Christie needs to describe the major events in the text and sequence events from the story or text. When

presented with unfamiliar words in context, Christie needs to decode multisyllabic words.

When I met with Christie when she was 17 years old, I asked her to read aloud the picture book *The Sweetest Fig* by Chris van Allsburg, a book with foreign words, such as *francs*, and multisyllabic words, such as *appointment*, *toothache*, and *whispered*. The book, which is full of complex sentence structures, is about a dentist who received magical figs from a woman for payment. When the dentist realized the power of the magical figs, his dog Marcel, who the dentist does not treat very well, stole the last fig. After reading the story, Christie provided the following retelling:

A person who was a dentist…was like taking care of an old lady that had toothache. Once they were like done, the old lady gave the dentist a fruit. And it started to not go well because he was like having it at night and he got his dreams, and it came true. And once again he had the last one, he was sort of being sad about it, because the dog ate it and he got so mad. He [the dentist] was mad and all he wanted to do is have another dream and be happy about it. It is not coming true, because the dog ate it and had his [the dentist's] dreams.

While Christie did have difficulty with orally reading parts of a story that some might consider below what she would be expected to read for her age and grade levels, her retelling demonstrates the knowledge that she constructed as she read. She comprehended the story, retold the story in a chronological fashion, provided major events, read multisyllabic words, and clearly read beyond simply worded sentences. This picture of Christie shifts away from *what she is not able to do* to *what she is able to do*.

At the same time, Christie engaged in a variety of reading and writing practices on a daily basis. When I asked Christie what she liked to read, she replied that social media was a major outlet for her reading and writing. Christie talked about reading different social media sites, particularly Facebook, and keeping connected with people (including me) through social media. When I asked her whether she felt herself to be a good reader, Christie said that she felt like an average reader, but also felt she struggled when reading aloud. In turn, the school's evaluation of Christie's reading was based on her reading aloud, and was judged on her reading performance rather than what she was able to do within her learning biography.

A Humanistic View of Literacy

Sharing Christie's learning biography extends the enduring impact of *Teaching Without Testing* that will be presented in this volume. Through biographic literacy profiles, *Teaching Without Testing* presents a humanistic perspective both of students as learners and social actors, and of teachers as biographers. It places advocacy in the forefront through careful observation and the listening of stories. Bomer and Maloch (2012) write, "Living things can't really be standardized that way – they require a focus on the local" (p. 44). Attempting to standardize Christie's knowledge and learning experiences dehumanized her through a social classification system that produced a taxonomy of student categories, such as special education, mainstream, English Language Learner (Foucault, 1975; Wortham, 2006). She became a number and was placed within a tracking system that Christie herself saw as "not normal." Biographic literacy profiles capture what Taylor describes as, "the complexity of the richness and diversity of children's literacy experiences in the classrooms that encourage the self-organization of problem-solving activities" (p. 123).

While the global view focuses on standardization, the local view focuses on uniqueness and diversity. A shift from the standardized, global view to a local perspective could well have positioned Christie differently over the years. She may then have been viewed as a symbol weaver or a story teller, rather than someone who lacked ability. She may have been recognized as someone who was as an advocate for herself but felt excluded from the daily activities of her school and peers, rather than someone "who needs to increase her understanding of her limitations and educational needs."

At the center of creating a humanistic perspective is the teacher as biographer. Taylor writes of the shifting perspective of the teacher in the development of biographic literacy profiles:

> The difficulty has been that they have needed a way to clearly articulate that the children that they teach are learning in far more complex ways than would be possible if they have been using the simulated teaching/learning activities that are presented in packaged programs. Building biographic profiles based upon observations of children's literacy behaviors has helped the participants in the project to become more confident in their abilities to explain. (p. 135)

Not only do teachers learn to explain, they also celebrate and recognize the local and diverse forms of knowledge that students have both inside and outside of the classroom. Teachers become committed to their students' learning biographies, and they aim at what Bomer and Malcoh (2012) describe as, "maintaining an open, curious, listening stance toward their students' lives for their own sake" (p. 48). In turn, they take this perspective and use it to construct multiple and diverse visions of students' learning experiences, while challenging a global, standardized model of learning. As Taylor argues, "To 'move' beyond the debate, it is essential that researchers and educators reexamine the 'scientific' assumptions on which testing (irrespective of whether the tests emphasize word recognition or comprehension) is based" (p. 148).

Teaching Without Testing encourages readers to consider the detrimental effects of testing on children, and the de-professionalization of teachers because of test driven, corporate led accountability practices. Taylor urges us to "push beyond our own training in the 'objective' reality of the present educational system" to develop "the professional expertise and specialized knowledge that will enable us to work with every child" (p. 143) in humanistic ways. Reflecting on the work of Taylor's biographic literacy profiles, Cochran-Smith (1991) contends that the use of descriptive observation enhances assessing and teaching by offering "opportunities to construct curriculum, to plan and reflect on teaching strategies, and to raise questions, collect data, and analyze particular aspects of children's learning and their own teaching" (Cochran-Smith, 1991, p. 112). In this sense, instruction is based on *observable literacy behaviors*, an important premise and consequence of teaching without the mandate of standardized testing.

Taylor wrote, "There is a continuous interplay between our past and present experiences as we try to place ourselves in the much larger arena of what is happening in education both at the national and the local level." (p. 49) Reading these words seventeen years later, I am reminded of the words of Walter Benjamin in the opening of this introduction. *Teaching Without Testing* is a reminder that educational reform movements that address standardization and accountability through testing have a long history that educators, parents, and stakeholders continue to challenge as we create humanistic teaching practices at the local classroom level. It is with this in mind that I invite readers to challenge their own assumptions about teaching and learning to rethink the role of assessment and teaching in the lives of the students in our classrooms.

REFERENCES

Benjamin, W. (2011). *Early writings (1910-1917)*. Translated by H. Eiland. Cambridge, MA: Belknap Press of Harvard University Press.

Bomer, R. & Maloch, B. (2012). Diverse local literacies and standardizing policies. *Language Arts, 90*(1) 44-50.

Cody, A. (2014). *The Educator and the oligarch: A teacher challenges the Gates Foundation*. New York, NY: Garn Press.

Coffey, S. & Street, B. (2008). Narrative and identity in the "Language Learning Project." *The Modern Language Journal, 92*(3), 452-464.

Gee, J. (2002). A sociocultural perspective on early literacy development. In S. Neuman & D. Dickinson (Eds.), *Handbook of early literacy research* (pp. 30-42). New York: Guilford Press.

Foucault, M. (1975). *Discipline and punish: The birth of the prison*. New York, NY: Random House.

Kabuto, B. (2015). Transgenerational learning within families. *Journal of Family Diversity in Education*, 1(4). Archived at: http://familydiversityeducation.org/index.php/fdec.

Spring, J. (2015). *American education: Sociocultural, political, and historical studies in education*. New York, NY: Routledge.

Strauss, S. (2005). *The linguistics, neurology, and politics of phonics: Silent "E" speaks out*. Malwah, NJ: Lawrence Erlbaum.

Taylor, D. (1990). Teaching without Testing: Assessing the Complexity of Children's Literacy Learning. *English Education*, 22(1), 4-74.

Taylor, D. (1993). *From the child's point of view*. Portsmouth, NH: Heinemann.

Wortham, S. (2006). *Learning identity: The joint emergence of social identification and academic learning*. Cambridge, MA: Cambridge University Press.

TEACHING WITHOUT TESTING: ASSESSING THE COMPLEXITY OF CHILDREN'S LITERACY LEARNING

DENNY TAYLOR

On the last day of the 1989 Summer Institute for new teachers and administrators in the *Biographic Literacy Profiles Project* everyone participated in a literacy "dig." Mary Yates, a teacher participating in the project, had brought into the institute a voluminous collection of her daughter's early explorations of written language. Mary spread Katie's work across several large tables and explained that the books and papers had been done between November and May of Katie's kindergarten year. Mary told us that while she was teaching Katie went home from school at lunchtime and spent the afternoon with her grandmother who lived with them. Mary said that it was in November, during the time that Katie spent with her grandmother, that she started making books out of everything from brown paper grocery bags to brightly colored wrapping paper. Some of these books were displayed on the table; the other pieces of writing represented the various books and papers that Katie had brought home from school during that year.

Together the teachers and administrators began their "dig." At first it seemed like an overwhelming task. We had been talking about the ways in which young children figure out problems and reinvent the forms of written language as they learn to problem-solve and reconstruct the functions and uses of print. We had explored our own "literacy configurations," emptying briefcases and pocketbooks, and sharing with each other the ways in which we ourselves use literacy in our everyday lives. "Literacy configurations are like thumb prints," I had said, somewhat flippantly, "no two are quite the same." So what of Katie's literacy configuration? Did she already have one in kindergarten? Was it possible to describe how the ways in which she was using print produced a unique patterning of early literacy behaviors? On the surface, her discoveries appeared lost in the chaos of her crumpled papers, but a pattern slowly emerged as Mary took the pieces one by one and talked to us about her daughter's writings. Gradually, as we discussed the writing that Katie had done in November and then December, the teachers started to respond and make notes about the personally distinctive features of Katie's writing that were beginning to be identified. For as they wrote about the ways in which Katie reconstructed the functions, uses, and forms of written language, forming in their own minds was a changing order that they could now describe.

Over lunch and into the early afternoon, the participants began to develop their own biographic profiles of Katie's early literacy behaviors. For several hours the teachers and administrators examined Katie's writing and tried to create a systematic account of what appeared on the surface to be a disorderly confusion of erratic discoveries.

Marcy Mager, a principal, wrote:

> In November Katie spontaneously began writing books. She had an understanding of the construction of a book which included the binding, cover,

ordered progression of pages and the combination of pictures and texts. Katie had a sense of authorship and ended her books with "by Katie Yates." Even her earliest books contained complete thoughts related to a theme. The themes she focused on from November to May included the girl and her animals, rainbow stories, and adventures and travels from her life. Often she would elaborate on a theme as she continued to write. ... Katie's sight vocabulary included the words "the," "cat," and "dog," and by May it also included "of," "book," "day," "to," "today," "mommy," "daddy," and the names of some friends. She experimented with the spelling of many words that she uses, such as "dear," and "journal." Katie's invented spelling uses consistent rules. She has the initial consonant-vowel-consonant in "rab" (rabbit), and both syllables of "spr" (supper). She uses vowels as markers and often uses an initial vowel but not always the correct one. She occasionally represents long vowel sounds with letters such as: *o* in "om" (home) and ramb*o* (rainbow); *e* in at*e* (auntie) and pt*e* (pretty). Most consonant sounds are represented. The format in which she writes includes horizontal and vertical placement. ... Katie can write complex sentences with prepositions and prepositional phrases. Katie uses pronouns and matches them correctly to her verbs. Her nouns and verbs also match. ... Katie writes to convey information (i.e. addresses and events), to keep a personal record, to entertain herself and others, and to communicate with others about her feelings ...

Marcy's first draft of a biographic literacy profile for Katie provides us with some insights into the potential of such an approach to assessment. Marcy knew Katie because the little girl attends the school in which she is principal. However, she had not spent the year observing Katie's literacy behaviors and she had no notes from the time when Katie had worked on the construction of these texts. Marcy relied solely on Mary's descriptions of Katie's writings and upon the examples contained in the portfolio of work that Mary had brought into the institute. But what Marcy knew, as did the teachers in her school who had already begun recording their observations of children's literacy behaviors in their classrooms, was that this was still a "thin" account. If they had been able to base the process of portfolio analysis upon their own disciplined, first-hand observations of Katie as she reconstructed the functions, uses, and forms of written language, then the detail (thick description) generated by such observations would greatly have increased the possibility of providing relevant support and instruction for Katie as she learned to read and write in school.

However, there were many other teachers in the institute that summer who had not yet begun to systematically observe and keep notes on the early literacy behaviors of the children in their classrooms. For them, the opportunity to construct a "first draft" of a biographic profile made them want to meet Katie and observe her as she used print "to convey information ... to entertain ... and to communicate her feelings." For it made visible to them that although the profiles they were constructing might be idiosyncratic in their form and expression – highly dependent in fact upon their own education and training – the patterns in Katie's writing reoccurred in similar ways across their own individual, "archeological" reconstructions of her early literacy development. The following excerpts illustrate how four of these teachers created recognizable images of Katie as a young reader and writer:

1. In November, at home, Katie spontaneously wrote a series of four books about a girl and her pets. She wrote the words one per line, from top to the bottom of the page. The first book went back to front, the next three went conventionally front to back. Each book was a story written in complete sentences.

Kate has a strong sense of theme. Her books focus on a single topic: "The girl walking with her cat, her dog, and her rabbit." When she writes in a different genre she writes in a consistent fashion. She uses her writing for varied purposes.

Katie can carry a theme through several individual pieces, each time she does, she elaborates on her ideas (e.g. stories about a girl walking animals).

She uses one word per line, complete thoughts per page with pictures describing text.

2. Over the course of seven months Katie has composed in a variety of genres. Personal narratives, journal entries of daily events, and fictional stories are examples of these collected from home and school.

    Katie is using a different style for her journal. She tells events of the day, using herself as the protagonist and she writes from her own point of view.

    Katie writes about important people and animals in her life. She writes an autobiographical sketch in her journal.

3. When Katie composes she uses a combination of illustrations and words. Her illustrations mirror her text and are integral to it. When she writes, "The GRL WT TO BAD The CAT WT TO BAD TO The DOG WT TO," she has each of her characters in their beds smiling from the page.

    Drawings correspond directly with the text.

    Katie writes with meaning and her illustrations mirror her text.

4. Katie uses rules that she has learned, that she has

access to, and that she has invented.

> In December and January Katie often wrote her stories left to right across the paper. She is using vowel markers: *a*, *o*, and *e*. She is including complex critical features in her invented spelling: ram*bo* for rain*bow*, *A TE MNA* for Aun*ty* Mo*n*ica.

> Katie attends to dominant (critical) sounds in words (e.g. SPR for supper). Her spelling is rule governed by her own set of phonetic rules.

> Katie knows about vowels and uses them as markers ... Katie seems to be aware of some critical features of words e.g. *RAMBO* for rainbow, *SPR* for supper.

At the end of the day the teachers and administrators shared the profiles that they had written and, as they listened to each other, they made further notes. No one had a "complete" picture, and no one ever would, but between them they had created a "sketch" of Katie's early literacy development that no "diagnostic" or "standardized" test could ever achieve.

The impact of having written such biographic literacy profiles is clearly evident in the statements made by the teachers and administrators who are beginning their second year in the *Project*.

Recently, Brenda Eaves, who is teaching an entry class, spoke in clear terms about the difference the profiles are making, "I've been taking notes in my classroom for years, but when you don't put them together, you don't get the whole picture. The notes are not enough. You just miss so much." Then she added, "We don't need to accept tests anymore and we can articulate why we don't need them." As we talked, Brenda said that for her one of the most important differences that the profiles were making was not one that she had anticipated. "I'm feeling a whole lot better about communicating with parents," she explained, "The profiles really help me to communicate what kids are actually doing."

In another conversation, Mary Benton, who is the reading coordinator in the school in which Brenda teaches, talked about the "spill over" into her school. While Brenda had spoken of the effect of the *Project* on parent-teacher communication, Mary talked about some of the other effects that the *Project* was having on the daily lives of both teachers and children. She said that as the teachers entered their second year of participation in the *Project*, many of the conversations that she was hearing were about the changes they were making *across the curriculum*. "The *Project* has created a forum," she said, "for us to discuss kids beyond the profiles. We're talking about how we've changed. How we're looking at kids differently. *The more you look, the more you see*. The math committee is talking about developing math profiles. We're no longer just looking at reading and writing. I think what we're moving towards are biographies of children's learning in school."

Essentially, what was happening in this conversation, and in many other conversations that are taking place as we meet to discuss the *Project*, is that we are changing minds – *our minds*. We are the ones who are changing. We are "playing" our experiences of working in holistic/process classrooms in which instruction is based upon our assessment of *children's observable literacy behaviors* against a backdrop of our own and other educators' experiences of using standardized and diagnostic methods of assessment and teaching.

There is a continuous interplay between our past and present experiences as we try to place ourselves in the much larger arena of what is happening in education both at the national and the local level.

In Washington, President Bush speaks of the need for more "accountability" within the system, and at the same time, in a local paper, there is a report of a school district in which "*all of the student population* has been tested for special education needs" (Gospodarek, 1989). The newspaper report states that children have been "earmarked," "coded," and "segregated," placed in "modified" classrooms, "resource" rooms, or in "rainbow park" so that they can receive the special services, the various kinds of "therapy," that their "conditions" require. The article also states that children whose needs cannot be met by the district are to be sent to a place called "Children Unlimited Inc." An apt name it seems, for within our medicalized education system there are an unlimited number of children whose needs are not being met by "the system."

The major question driving the *Biographic Literacy Profiles Project* is "What happens when we base instruction upon our observations of children?" In the October 1989 issue of the *Anthropology Newsletter* Jeffrey Shultz writes:

> We have focused on societal and cultural influences on schools and processes of classroom interaction without knowing a great deal about what role the learner plays in all of this. More needs to be known about teaching, learning and schooling from the *perspective of the learner*. [emphasis added]

Shultz then adds:

> [I]t is important to examine what our knowledge of classrooms, schools, culture and society has to say about the preparation of teachers. Specifically, how would a teacher education program based on this knowledge differ from more traditional programs? (p. 10)

Without any grand plan, but through reflexive research and teaching (Barnes, 1976), and by asking ourselves how we can base instruction upon our observations of children, I think we have gained some understanding of what happens when both teachers and administrators try to view teaching, learning, and schooling from *the perspective of the learner*, and we have also gained some insights into the ways in which teacher education programs based upon this knowledge would differ from the more traditional programs that are presently offered in most colleges of education.

TEACHING, LEARNING, AND SCHOOLING FROM THE PERSPECTIVE OF THE LEARNER

To understand schooling from the perspective of the child it has become essential for us to try to understand the social organization of children's everyday lives. Their lives, in other words, need to be viewed within the larger social, cultural, and political contexts, both visible and invisible, that determine what and how they learn both in and out of school. We must be "side-by-side" as we think of children. It means beginning with individual children, metaphorically standing next to them, trying to imagine the world from their individual and shared perspectives. It means asking:

- What's happening?
- What's going on?
- How do these children, create order out of the complexities of their everyday lives?
- How does this child construct and use language?
- How does this child learn to generate problems as well as solutions?
- How does this child become a member of a community of learners?
- How does this child theorize about doing?

- How does this child lead others in problem solving situations to arrive at workable solutions?

When teachers ask these questions, their classrooms change. Even holistic/process teachers with years of experience notice the difference.

At the second institute that took place in the summer of 1989, teachers and administrators who had been participating in the project for one year met to share their experiences, advance their own training, and begin the training of a new group of teachers from their respective schools. Much of our time was spent in observing ourselves in complex problem-solving situations – observing the ways in which we, as learners, generate and reconstitute problems through the use of the social, symbolic, technical, and material resources at our disposal, and then go on to invent new procedures and arrive at instrumental solutions. Some teachers and administrators participated in the collaborative problem-solving situations, while others observed and took notes which were later shared and analyzed by all those who participated in the institute. In this way, we advanced our own understanding of the social construction of cognitive tasks, while at the same time the teachers new to the project had an opportunity to think about the possibilities of establishing classroom environments in which they could observe children engaged in *solving the problem of problem-solving literacy*.

Later that day, the second year *Project* teachers, who had been observing, note-taking, and writing profiles for the past year, met in small groups with the first year *Project* teachers. As they looked at portfolios of children's work, they talked about *teaching from the child's perspective*. Listening to them talk provided another level of verification for the legitimacy of the direction that the *Project* had taken through the previous year. Each month, as I had visited these teachers in their classrooms, specific concerns (based upon actual experiences) had been discussed, and later these concerns became the focus of the afternoon group meetings that we held in each of the schools. Our experiences in working together "troubleshooting" problems and developing clearly thought-out practical solutions have eventually led to the emergence of what we have since come to regard as the "objectives" of the *Project*. In presenting these "objectives," I will try to include some of the questions that were asked and the answers that were given at the second institute, which was recorded for me by Helen Schotanus of the New Hampshire State Department of Education, so as to document the "processes of change" that all the teachers participating in the *Project* experienced.

SEEING THE PROJECT THROUGH ITS OBJECTIVES

One: Learning to Observe Children's Literacy Behaviors

"It's a change of mindset," a teacher explained. "I notice different things – what children can do rather than what they can't do." The only "rule" – one that I have jokingly said is carved in granite – is that we focus upon children's *observable literacy behaviors*. We are watching children as they develop personal understandings of literacy that are both socially constructed and individually situated in the practical accomplishments of their everyday lives. There are no linear, predefined, or artificially isolated skills to be ticked-off on some reductionist "scope and sequence" chart or checklist. The teachers and administrators participating in the project have made what is essentially a paradigmatic shift. They are making the connection between the ways in which children in their classrooms both *learn* and *use* language. Their observations are providing them "with insights into not only the complex and seemingly chaotic ways in which individual children's reconstructions are encoded and processed into coherent patterns of symbolic relationships, but also the equally complex and chaotic ways in which their symbolic inventions are transformed into functional forms that they use in classroom and everyday settings" (Taylor, 1989, p. 193).

The paradigmatic shift that has taken place in the ways in which the teachers and administrators think about literacy is creating "new perspectives on reality" (Doll, 1989, p. 65) which require that we learn to look at children's literacy behavior in different ways, and this, in turn, affects what we see. Our task is to try to describe children's personal understandings of the forms and functions of written language that they develop as they participate in the problem-solving environments that we create for them. To achieve this aim, it is essential that teachers are supported in their own explorations of the many functions, uses, and forms of written language, for we cannot observe what we have not learned to see.

Characteristics of Family Literacy

In the *Biographic Literacy Profiles Project*, we began by examining the multiple interpretations of literacy that have been generated by ethnographic studies in family, community, and school settings (Heath, 1983; Taylor, 1983; Taylor & Dorsey-Gaines, 1988; Taylor & Strickland, 1988).

The following are characteristics of family literacy:

1. Some rituals and routines of written language usage appear to conserve family traditions of literacy, while others appear to change the patterns of the past.
2. Patterns of family literacy are constantly evolving to accommodate the everyday experiences of both parents and children, and the introduction of a younger sibling can lead to the systematic restructuring routines.
3. Many of the literacy experiences that occur at home take place as parents and children go about their

daily lives.

4. On many occasions, the act of reading is not the focus of attention, and the print has no intrinsic value. The "message" is embedded in some other event, useful within the context in which it was written or read, but otherwise appearing to be of little importance.

5. Many of the deliberate uses of literacy found in family settings occur when "moment-to-moment" uses of literacy are in some way lifted "out of context" to become specific events that are the focus of attention.

6. There are times when reading and writing become deliberate acts, when the text becomes as important as the message that it contains.

7. At any one time multiple interpretations of a literacy event are possible, and the possibility of different interpretations are created over time.

8. For each family member participating in a literacy event, the occasion is both socially constructed and personally interpreted through the "inter-play" of the family members' individual biographies and educative styles.

9. Both moment-to-moment and deliberate uses of literacy can be social events or solitary endeavors.

10. Whether solitary or shared, deliberate or momentary, literacy is a complex multi-dimensional phenomenon.

11. When both parents work or when there is a single working parent and time is at a premium, the moment-to-moment and specific uses of print that occur when a parent is at home full-time with a child will diminish.

12. However, literacy can become a key element in the ability of some families as they attempt to juggle

all of the schedules, rituals, and routines, and time constraints that are a part of their daily lives.

In our explorations of the functions, uses, and forms of literacy, these characteristics of family literacy have become directly relevant to our observations of literacy in classroom settings, for although none of the participants would suggest that literacy in the one setting is the same as literacy in the other, there are characteristics that are common to both. The notion of conservation and change in the transmission of literacy styles and values is directly relevant, as is the idea that many of the ways in which we use literacy in classroom settings occur at the margins of awareness, in moment-to-moment uses of reading and writing that only come to our attention when for some reason the act of reading or writing becomes a deliberate act, and therefore a specific event. Sensitivity to such "patterns" of literacy have become immensely important as the teachers in the *Project* have tried to create collaborative learning environments in which, if we stand "side-by-side" with individual children, there are multiple meanings for any literacy event that occurs in the classroom setting.

Similarly, in such classrooms, it is essential that teachers learn to observe the "dynamics" of both shared and solitary literacy experiences. Thus we have become comfortable in talking about a plurality of literacies of practical complexity, chaotically patterned into personal and shared configurations, and even though no two "configurations" are exactly the same we can describe the social organization of the configurations and also the types and uses of literacy that form the patterns that we observe.

Types and Uses of Reading

The following list describes the different types and uses of reading, one form of literacy:

1. *Confirmational* – Reading to check or confirm facts

or beliefs, often from archival materials stored and retrieved only on special occasions.

2. *Educational* – Reading to fulfill the educational requirements of schooling; reading to increase one's ability to consider and/or discuss political, social, aesthetic, or religious knowledge; reading to educate oneself.

3. *Environmental* – Reading the print in the environment.

4. *Financial* – Reading to consider (and sometimes make changes to) the economic circumstances of one's everyday life; reading to fulfill practical (financial) needs of everyday life.

5. *Historical* – Reading to explore one's personal identity; reading to explore the social, political, and economic circumstances of one's everyday life; reading conserved writings that create a permanent record of one's family life history.

6. *Instrumental* – Reading to gain information for meeting practical needs, dealing with public agencies, and scheduling daily life.

7. *Interactional* – Reading to gain information pertinent to building and maintaining social relationships.

8. *News related* – Reading to gain information about third parties; reading to gain information about local, state, and national events.

9. *Recreational* – Reading during leisure time or in planning for recreational events.

10. *Scientific* – Reading to gain information about or develop new understandings of the natural or physical sciences.

11. *Technical* – Reading to gain information using the different symbolic forms of technological communications (computer, fax, virtual reality); reading

to advance one's understanding of the functions of such technologies.

12. Other.

Types and Uses of writing

Similarly, writing has many types and use. It can be:

1. *Autobiographical* – Writing to understand oneself; writing to record one's life history; writing to share life with others.
2. *Creative* – Writing as a means of self-expression.
3. *Educational* – Writing to fulfill the educational requirements of school and college courses; writing to educate oneself.
4. *Environmental* – Writing in public places for others to read.
5. *Financial* – Writing to record numerals, to write out amounts and purposes of expenditures, and for signatures.
6. *Instrumental* – Writing to meet practical needs and to manage/organize everyday life; writing to gain access to social institutions or helping agencies.
7. *Interactional* – Writing to establish, build, and maintain social relationships; writing to negotiate family responsibilities. (The writer envisions or knows his or her audience and writes to the addressee.)
8. *Memory Aids* – Writing to serve as a memory aid for both oneself and others.
9. *Recreational* – Writing during leisure time for the enjoyment of the activity.
10. *Scientific* – Writing to develop new understandings of the natural or physical sciences.
11. *Substitutional* – Reinforcement or substitution for oral messages; writing used when direct oral

communication is not possible or when a written message is needed to create a record (e.g. for legal purposes).

12. *Technical* – Writing to gain information using the different symbolic forms of technological communications (computer, fax, virtual reality); writing to advance one's understanding of the functions of such technologies.

Thinking about the types and uses of reading and writing enables us to focus upon the social processes through which individuals and groups of children create literacy configurations that are functional in their everyday lives. Observing children as they use reading and writing in classroom settings has emphasized how important it is that we gain some understanding of literacy as a problem solving activity and so we have incorporated into our "observational framework" recent research on problem-solving in the work place and other everyday settings (Carraher, 1986; Carraher, Carraher & Schliemann, 1985; de la Rocha, 1985; Lave, 1985; Lave, Murtaugh & de la Rocha, 1984; Scribner, 1984).

Literacy in Problem-Solving Activities

When we use print in classroom settings there is a continual interplay between the activity and the setting. The activity and setting are mutually dependent – the one does not exist without the other. Using social, symbolic, technological, and material resources, students and teachers can:

1. Recast (reconstitute) problem-solution relationships.
2. Examine variations in procedural possibilities.
3. Discuss contradictions in interpretations of problem-solution relationships.
4. Depart from literal formats through the reorganization of tasks.

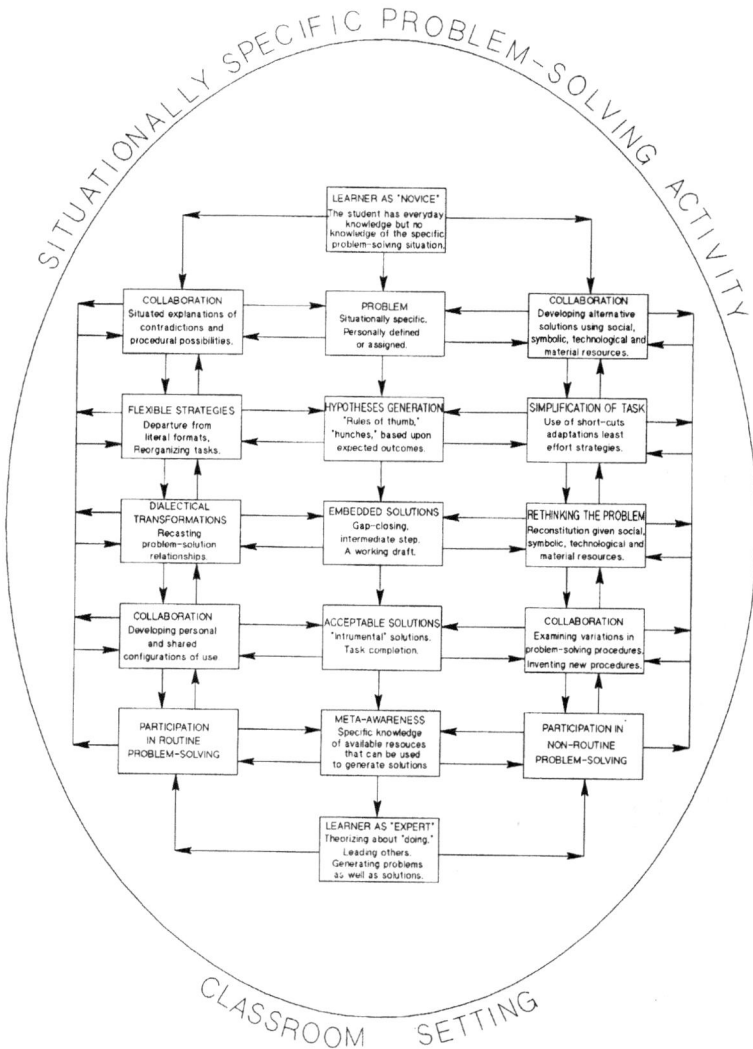

Figure 1: Problem-solving activity chart

5. Develop least-effort strategies.
6. Arrive at "instrumental" (purposeful) solutions.
7. Theorize about "doing."
8. Lead others in problem-solving situations.
9. Invent new procedures.

10. *Generate problems as well as solutions.*

From this perspective, the problem-solving context exists in the dialectical relationships that are established between the activity and the setting. This proposition is both consistent with and supportive of the idea that children's personal understandings of literacy are both socially constructed and individually situated in the practical accomplishments of their everyday lives.

The visual representation in Figure 1 allows us to imagine how such complex processes might interact. It is designed to suggest a kaleidoscope of patterns and shifting formations of such infinite variation that they cannot be depicted in "fixed" form. It is not a model in the tradition sense of the word. Instead, it is presented as a frozen image of the possible global patterns of the locally chaotic problem-solving relationships inherent in learning to use written language in everyday life (Taylor, 1989, pp. 191-2).

The characteristics of effective problem-solving presented in Figure 1 lead us to the proposition that learners learn by solving situationally specific problems through the intellectual use of social, symbolic, technological, and material resources at their disposal. Thus, teachers need to construct environments which support such activity. This is done by providing opportunities for children to create multiple solutions to a problem. In this way children come to rely on nuanced judgments made in situations where there is often a high degree of uncertainty. Awareness of such complexity is essential if teachers are to observe and support children as they learn to organize their own problem- solving activities and become successful participants in non-routine problem-solving situations.

If we pause for a moment and reflect upon the first three ways in which project participants are "learning to look" at literacy, it is evident that *the kinds of information that we are obtaining from such observations bear little resemblance to the kinds of information currently assessed using traditional stan-*

dardized measures. This paradigmatic shift is demonstrated, for instance, in how a child uses, in a complex back-and-forth matter, a reference text to construct her own book about dinosaurs (See Taylor, 1989, for an in-depth analysis). Rather than repeat that story, let's step lightly and "play" with the "Tuck-In Service" flyer (Figure 2) that was found taped to the glass door of a dormitory at a nearby college.

When's the last time you were tucked in your bed, given cookies and milk, and read a bedtime story?

Your right ... too long ago!

Sign Up Now ... For only $2.⁰⁰ you can have this luxury service!

SIGN-UPS ... Wed thru Friday
October 19th - 21st
Lunch : Dinner at Prospect!
What a deal... what a Treat!!

Figure 2: "Tuck-in Service" Flyer

Undoubtedly we could fill up several pages describing the insights into literacy that this flyer represents. The writer assumes a shared history with the students who might read the flyer, and she or he is hoping to capitalize upon (conserve) the rituals and routines of family literacy experienced by other students in the dorm. Thus, if we were present, we would be able to observe and describe some of the ways in which the event of storybook reading in the college dorm appeared to be socially constructed and personally interpreted through the "interplay" of the participants' individual biographies and educative styles.

We could also analyze the information presented in the flyer to gain some understanding of the types and uses of literacy that were utilized by the writer in the construction of the text. We could state that the flyer was a substitute for an oral message, and was written to fulfill instrumental as well as work-related needs, and to fulfill financial requirements. It is an example of environmental print that we can imagine reflects the autobiographical experiences of a writer who in turn appears to assume the biographical experiences of the readers.

We could continue musing on the types and uses of reading and writing reflected in the flyer, but let's move on and consider what it tells us about this situationally specific problem-solving activity. Since students are perennially short of cash, we can imagine that the writer has examined many procedural possibilities for stop-gap solutions to alleviate this problem. In this particular situation, it is easy to appreciate the mutual dependence of the problem-solving activity and the setting. The writer needs money, students are away from home and miss their families, and thus the writer, as problem-solver, arrives at an instrumental solution.

These descriptions of the dynamics of the "Tuck-In" literacy event are mostly inferential. But imagine the information that could have been gained if this activity occurred in a classroom with a teacher observing the event. This is essentially what is happening in the *Biographic Literacy Profiles Project.* Teachers are observing children in complex problem-solving situations, and they are using their understandings of a plurality of literacies to describe the interrelated complexity of such events.

Characteristics of "Symbol-Weaving"

We could add another level to the analysis of the "Tuck-In" flyer by discussing the "symbol weaving" (Dyson, 1986) that is taking place as the sad-eyed, thumb-sucking, teddybear-clutching person at the top of the flyer invites the reader to respond to the question, "When's the last time you were tucked in your bed, given cookies and milk, and read a bedtime story?" Exploring the "connectedness" of multiple symbolic forms is an important feature of our observations of children's reading and writing behaviors, as we try to describe the many forms of symbolism used by children as they engage in situationally specific literacy activities. Newkirk's (1989) explorations of the interrelationships between pictures and texts has proved particularly helpful, and we are trying to counter the currently dominant way of thinking about other forms of symbolic representation as subservient to text. Newkirk states:

> Although we pay lip service to the idea that a picture is worth a thousand words, we don't really believe it. It's the thousand words that really interest us. Once the golden age of drawing has passed (around the second or third grade), art gives way to a predominantly, if not exclusively, word-centered school culture, and children no longer allocate informativeness between the two systems. (p. 65)

Newkirk questions this "word-centered" approach to symbolic representation, and we in the *Project* share his concern. Our world is filled with graphic images, different ways of knowing, that we must learn to describe. A book that has become an important symbol of this need for a broader perspective on print is *Show Your Tongues* by Gunter Grass. In this diary, "a stunning document in words and drawings," Grass recorded his experiences of living in Calcutta.

What is so extraordinary about this achievement is that the words Grass wrote are integral to the visual images portrayed in the illustrations that appear at the beginning and end of the book. His writing forms the landscape, gives depth to the drawings, adds shadows to the faces and cracks to the walls. For me, it is one of the most socially significant examples of symbol-weaving that I have so far encountered, just as the illustrated poems of William Blake are artistically/linguistically significant and Benoit Mandelbrot's *The Fractal Nature of Geometry* is scientifically significant. In the *Project*, we have used *Show Your Tongues* to legitimize the importance of creating environments in which children have the opportunity to use multiple forms of symbolism in the learning situations that they encounter. Our observations of print in everyday settings support the need we feel to extend the ways in which we think about the symbolic representations constructed by children. The more we focus our attention upon their productions, the more convinced we have become that our classrooms must be multimedia centers which encourage the exploration of complex symbolic systems.

Yesterday, when I had finished writing this section of the report, I telephoned Mary Benton and read to her what I had written about the characteristics of family literacy, the types and uses of literacy, and problem-solving literacy. Then we talked about the beginning of the *Project* when teachers often focused almost exclusively upon sound-symbol relationships. They were familiar with the patterns, and they were comfortable describing the variations that they saw in the ways in which children invented their own patterns of the relationship and then reinvented the more traditional forms. Their detailed understandings of the ways in which children reconstruct sound-symbol relationships and invent the syntactic structures of various forms of texts are tremendously important, but there is so much more to literacy than these traditional skills. As the teachers spent more time observing children, they became increasingly aware of some of the more complex relationships that children are establishing as they problem-solve literacy. "Is this what's happening?" I asked Mary. "What about sound-symbol stuff? It's certainly one of the important ways in which we're looking at children's construction of written texts, but where does it fit? What happens when you observe a child?"

Mary was quiet and after a few moments of silence I jokingly asked her if she was "still there." "I'm thinking," she said and then hesitated, "I don't know how to say it." But after a few more seconds of silence she explained that for her it was crucial to have a solid understanding of grapho-phoneme concepts, but not let that be the focus.

"It's all there," she continued, "but not in the sense that I am consciously pulling it apart. I'm trying to leave behind me all that training that views sound-symbol relationships as a linear progression of skills that all kids acquire in the same way. I'm not looking for what children can't do with some checklist in my head." Mary laughed, as she tried to explain, "I'm going for everything, letting what I see take on it's own shape, watching until I see. Understanding how each child learns and uses grapho-phonemic concepts comes only after seeing how these are used in combination with other concepts and strategies." She paused again and then concluded, "I think if I went in with a structure broken down into types and uses, or grapho-phoneme patterns, I just wouldn't see what was happening. I'd be too busy trying to find specific things. Going back and looking at what I was writing at the beginning of last year – it's incredible what I see now that I couldn't see then. The way in is to look at sound-symbols and then it goes beyond – I think it's even gone beyond any notions of literacy. Observing kids is about us changing our thinking."

Two: Learning to Develop Note-taking Procedures to Record Observations of Children Reading and Writing

At the second Summer Institute in 1989, many of the discussions that Helen Schotanus recorded for me were of the conversations about note-taking that took place between teachers who had participated in the *Project* for a year and the teachers who were just beginning to participate in the study. When one new teacher asked if there was "a system for note-taking?" she was promptly told that "there is no one way to do it. No cut and dried how-to." Teachers talked about "catching what is happening as it happens – otherwise you may lose it" or "writing exactly what a child is doing over a longer period of time – up to ten minutes." In one conversation a teacher said, "Writing is easier to take notes on than reading because with writing there is a product. How do you see reading?" In another conversation a teacher talked about "reaching all the children" in her class: "Some children demand more of one's time. Others demand very little and are easy to overlook."

Similar interactions have taken place in seminars when *Project* participants have talked about the research. Teachers ask, "Don't you have a note-taking system?" "A set number of children that you observe each day?" "Specific times when you observe and write?" or "A list of skills that you write about?" At such times there is usually a *Project* teacher who jumps in and says, "We are each developing our own note-taking system. A system that works for me might not work for you. It depends on how you organize your classroom, and on your own literacy configuration – how you use print." The underlying assumption on which the *Project* is founded is that teachers are professionals in their own classrooms and that they do not need pre-packaged ways of writing down what they see as children work together reconstructing the functions, uses, and forms of written language. In fact, we do not believe that observational teaching and instructional assessment can be packaged, for this is problem-solving teaching. On many occasions I have heard teachers say that the observations that they make and the notes that they write, as they work side-by-side with the children, cannot be separated into "strategies" and then added to the ways in which they teach. The observations they make and the notes they write are constitutive of ways in which they teach. For them teaching is learning about children as they develop original and authentic ways of using print to solve problems on their own and with friends, and use their creativity and ingenuity as they develop insights and learn to theorize (talk about) the construction of invented and standardized forms of written language.

This fall (of 1989), during my visits to the classrooms of the *Project* teachers, I have been particularly interested in furthering my understanding of the note-taking procedures that they are developing. For just a few short minutes I watched Martha Dahl take notes as she worked with one of her kindergarten children. They were quick jottings, small things to remember, from the moment she talked with this particular child. What fascinated me were the many different types of notes that she was unobtrusively constructing and how the different types of notes that she made actually became a part of the instructional context in which she was working. I asked Martha if she would share some of her notes and the following are examples that she sent to include in this report.

Several of the notes are written on an observational form that I put together at the beginning of the *Project*. Martha uses just the top section of these forms and, like other *Project* members, she has adapted the format to suit her own particular needs. Indeed, some teachers have never used the form, while others have combined reading and writing – a change I would make myself if I was using the form today. Here is the first example of some of Martha's notes:

Writing: Journal   Kitty (10-11-89)

Comment: Story Language!

Anecdotal Description: "Suddenly a leaf fell right into her hand. It was a yellow leaf – and she took it into her Mom." (Picture has a girl, apple tree, dog (?) and *yellow* leaf coming down.)

Martha is particularly interested in the language that her students use as they talk about their writing, produce an invented reading, or give a standard reading of the texts that they construct. From the comment that Martha made on this record it is clear that what she wanted to remember was the language Kitty was using as she produced an invented reading of her text.

The next example was written on a post-it note. (Most of the teachers use post-its as they are easy to carry in a pocket and can be pulled out and used at a moment's notice.) Martha wrote a verbatim account of Kitty's personal narrative mentioned above.

Once upon a time I cut my toe some blood came and daddy came to see what was the matter. He called our next door neighbor and they came with Melanie and they took me to the doctors where they had to give me stiches and Aunty Betsy came and I slept on the way home. The End.

Martha attached to her notes a copy of Kitty's written account of this oral rendition, an important step, for Kitty was able to read this text (Figure 3). Further, this allowed Martha to learn not only about Kitty's use of written language to create a personal narrative but also about how she reconstructs sound-symbol relationships.

At a group meeting, Martha showed me how she could reconstruct the text and she talked about the illustration in which the child had drawn herself crying and her toe being cut.

Today, on the telephone, Martha said, "The thing that impressed me was that she had written the piece at home and she brought it into school to share with me. She knew exactly what she had written and a lot of the text was right there. She could make sense of her invented spelling as she read." We talked for a while about the writing Kitty does and Martha said that based upon her observations she thought Kitty "was in transition. Sometimes what she says goes along with what she writes and sometimes it doesn't. Sometimes it seems really important to her that the sounds go with the writing but not always."

Figure 3: Kitty's written story

Another note was short and to the point. On a post-it Martha had written: "HSO [house] from another's journal. Then she said, 'This is my journal.'" The post-it was left in the journal so that Martha could refer to it when she was conferencing with a parent or working on her biographic profiles. "Most of the children don't mind if I leave a note in their journal. Some children would prefer that I didn't, so then I date and keep them."

Another type of note occurs on one of Martha's writing forms:

Writing: Journal   [Child's Name] (10-11
                                      -89)

Comment: Had written: A I LOY
                                      EV

Anecdotal Description: Reading what she had written
"I love you"
[Child]: "But I don't know how to write you"
MD: "How could you?"
[Child]: Thought for a while – "U!" – wrote U

Here was another form of note talking: Martha recording small snatches of her conversations with the children in her class. This gives her some idea of the ways in which she is creating opportunities for them to problem solve language as well as how they actually go about it. When I read this section to Martha she added, "It also gives me an idea if the action taken was self-initiated or taken as a result of working with me." Martha is clearly trying to learn more about the "grey zone" between what individual children can do on their own and what they can do with the support of a teacher (Vygotsky, 1978).

This approach to note taking allows us to understand the different ways in which the children in Martha's classroom are constructing texts as they write in their journals and the ways in which Martha is learning about each child's reconstruction of written language during the time when the children work in their journals. In other words, the notes point to global patterns that are locally unpredictable.

> *Writing*: Journal   [Child's Name] (10-11-89)
> *Comment*: Writing – "Someone is riding a motor cycle"
> *Anecdotal Description*: Stuck
> MD: "Maybe you could write about part of it? How about motorcycle?"
> [Child]: "Okay"
> MD: "What do you hear?"
> [Child]: "T? How do you make a T?" (Looking through alphabet cards) Found I – "I think this is a T."
> MD: "Is it?"
> [Child]: (Ask Martha)
> MD: "See if you can find a T?" Looked thru and found Ii and Tt
> [Child]: "One of these is a T"
> MD: "Which one is it?"
> [Child]: Pointed to T. Then wrote T and said – "that's all I hear in motorcycle"

> *Writing*: Journal   [Child's Name] (10-11-89)
> *Comment*: Looking at letter cards to see how to make letters N and K – can spell words beginning/ending sounds unsure of how to make letters, enjoys looking thru cards for letters – says all letter names.

We could describe this last brief jotting as an analytic memo in which Martha collects together an observation with some of the characteristics of this child's writing that she has identified in some of her other observations.

In the following example Martha produces a similar kind of note when she includes some of her own problem solving in the "comments" section as well as the problem solving of the child which is written in the "anecdotal" section:

Writing: Journal   [Child's name] (10-11-89)
Comment: [Child's name] puts the letters in the space where he hears them in the word. Doesn't necessarily write from beginning to end – but gets them in the right space.
Anecdotal Description:
[Child]: "I'd like to write the whole word of snake."
Had written [Martha didn't have time to finish]
MD: "What else do you hear?"
[Child]: "A *T*"
MD: "Where?"
[Child]: "In the middle – is this the middle?" – moved over a space – "No it's at the end!" Then wrote a *T* at end of space.
MD: What else?
[Child]: "*A*"
MD: "Where?"
[Child]: "In the middle"
Final writing: T iRTA SAT (I saw a snake)

In this note Martha presents an interpretation (working hypothesis/ informed opinion) of the ways in which this particular child is reconstructing the form of written language and then backs it up with a detailed description that illustrates how she arrived at the interpretation that she presents in the comments section.

In all of these ways Martha adds to the information that she has collected about each of the children mentioned here and, over a period of days, notes are written about every child. Keeping detailed notes provides Martha with an opportunity to learn more about the many complex ways in which each child in her classroom is learning to reconstruct written language. She is convinced that it is worth recording when a child draws a picture of her baby sister, writes her name from right to left *N L T K*, and then reads "Kaitlyn." And Martha also feels that it is worth recording the conversation that followed the event in which she said to the little girl, "I don't know how to write Kaitlyn," and the child responded "Just look up here. I wrote it – see" and reading the letters from right to left she reads, "K–T–L–N." At this point, as I am reading the draft of this report to Martha on the telephone she interjects, "What I thought was so wonderful was her confidence in her own ability to write. I was feeling that I didn't know how to spell Kaitlyn and she felt confident enough to show me how she had spelled it."

Martha uses other kinds of note-taking in her classroom to capture a wide range of activities, however let's look at the note-taking procedures developed by another second-year *Project* teacher. Kathy Donovan began her teaching career in special education and now teaches a class of first- and second-year children. When I visit her classroom it always takes me a few seconds to find her. The children work in small groups or on their own. There are invariably many activities taking place in the classroom and Kathy is usually working with a few children on one project or another. Kathy uses a variety of note-taking procedures to "capture" the many ways in which the children participate in the daily life of the classroom. In a large binder Kathy keeps a separate section to record each child's particular ways of becoming literate.

Last year, during the writing workshop, Kathy wrote her notes on labels that she transferred to each child's page in her binder. The following examples are taken from one child's writing workshop record:

> 11-30 "My birthday" added *a* while oral rdg. "I had – chocolate cake" "Oh I forgot the *a*, can I put it in?"
> 1-18 *A–N–D* spells *and*
> Don't forget D [child's name] – conversation between D and K. D seeking correct spelling.
> 1-18 "When I'm done with all my little stories I can put [them] in a chapter book."

1-26 "I want all my stories about *The Princess and The Mitten* published into a chapter book."
3-3 *she* consistently spelled *sey*
– word boundaries established
– sight words: *I my me* and *to*
– beginning, medial final sds
– short vowels present
– story sequenced
– working on not starting sentence with *and*

Kathy continues by recording a series of stories that K wrote and the comments that she made as she worked on them, such as "This is true! I'm going to put non-fiction on the bottom!" Other comments that Kathy makes focus upon K's writing strategies: "involves reader as audience 'and you would too I bet'"; upon the language K uses, "'good gracious' expression used"; and the way in which the writing activity was accomplished, "collaborated with A. Read orally and each took character part. Will be writing chapters. Discussed next events."

Kathy also keeps a "Log Sheet" for the writing workshops on which she records the "key words" that are taken from each child's writing and logged in their dictionaries. Thus at a glance Kathy can see the words that a particular student is using in his or her writing:

	A	J	R
10-2	toad	climbed	chameleon
10-3	fabulous	wanted	seaweed
10-4	super	policeman	tooth
10-5	spider	sign	roller coaster
10-6	animal	Halloween	home run

The books that each child reads are noted on a "reading group conference record sheet." Kathy keeps a separate sheet for each child so that during the course of the year both Kathy and each of her students have a pretty good idea which books have been read and what progress has been made. When conferencing with Kathy the student summarizes the story and then chooses a page to read to Kathy. Then the student is asked to rate the book *E* for Easy, *M* for Moderate or *C* for Challenge. Kathy circles the response and then she underlines what she feels is the level that the book represents. This allows her to check whether her own perception is "side-by-side" with the child's perception of the book. Kathy also has a section called "Response/Comments." Here she writes a description of the discussion with a particular child or the child's verbatim comments, for example, "I picked it because I thought it was funny. I liked the monkey part."

Kathy also collects information about the individual children in her class as they organize their daily life in school. For example, there is a "Lunch Count and Attendance" form that the children fill in themselves and then one child is given the responsibility of checking the information. Children sign up for their lunch and also for snacks, and the names in the various categories (hot lunch, snack juice, snack milk) are counted and the numbers entered at the bottom of the form. Kathy says this particular form provides her with a wonderful opportunity to observe the children in her class as they work together. She can make sure that everyone has what they want for snack and lunch and, because there is a category called "All Set," where every child writes their name, the form then doubles as an attendance record.

At group meetings the teachers often compare note-taking systems and procedures and adapt their own system to accommodate variations on some of the other forms that they encounter. Some ways of collecting information come from texts such as *In the Middle*, in which Nancy Atwell describes taking the "Status of the Class." Sue Caswell, a third grade teacher, who has just joined the *Project*, uses this procedure during reading and writing and she has encouraged other teachers to experiment with this quick way of recording the reading and writing activities of every child in the class. Sue says, "It only takes two to three minutes and then you have a record that you can use as you're working on a profile. You know immediately how long the child spent working on the project and it gives you a good idea of the topics that interest them." And Lee Proctor said she thought she would try this approach in her first grade classroom as she wanted to find a better way of keeping track of her student's work.

While there are many different ways in which information is being collected, the process continues to evolve and changes are constantly being made as each teacher tries to find his or her own way of capturing the information that they need to construct biographic profiles of the children in their classes. For those teachers having difficulty incorporating note taking into their daily routine, often a simple adjustment is all that's necessary. When I first visited Bob Magher, who teaches third grade and joined the project this year, he quickly mentioned his problem with note-taking and then was off to be with his class talking about their writing and arranging to meet with children who were ready to conference. Bob sat at a table with a group of students who took turns in reading and discussing the stories that they were writing. Bob took notes as each student read their text and then he used his notes as a basis for his contribution to the discussion that followed. He then gave his notes to the student on whose work he had been commenting and the student was free to use the comments (or not) in constructing a further draft. "What happens to the notes when the student has finished using them?" I asked. Bob smiled and said that once the student had used them they were probably thrown away. We talked for a while about the importance of the notes and of stapling them, plus any written comments made by other students, to the draft that had been discussed. Then once the piece was finished the stapled draft and the final version could be kept in the student's portfolio and used later by the student and by Bob as they reviewed the progress the student was making. Bob has adopted this way of collecting the notes that he was already making and as the year progresses he will modify the procedure so that he can use this important information when he is writing biographic profiles.

Three: Learning to Write Descriptive Biographic Literacy Profiles

The notes that Helen Shotanus wrote at the Summer Institute begin with a comment by one of the teachers who was joining the *Project*: "It was scary seeing what a person in the *Project* did last year." Leigh Walls responded by stating that "writing and composing, just thinking and pulling thoughts together took time." Leigh qualified what she had said by adding, "It took two hours each time I wrote about a child." The excerpts from some of the biographic profiles that are presented here reflect the amount of time that teachers are taking to write them. Disciplined and systematic observation and note-taking procedures create opportunities for teachers to construct detailed ethnographic accounts from the perspective of the learner. Such in-depth analysis requires slow and deliberate consideration on the part of the teachers who are writing them. The profiles that follow illustrate the developing literacy configurations of children from kindergarten classes through fourth grade, while at the same time they are suggestive of the particularity of the ways in which the teachers are working to construct these profiles. All of the profiles were written during the 1988-1989 academic year except for the one written by Bruce Turnquist, who just joined the *Project* this year. Katerina's profile is the first biographic account that Bruce has written.

Leigh Walls: Excerpts from Tom's Biographic Profile

May/June: Tom's high interest in books has continued. He has clear favorites, especially among our "big books" and he requests those often. He listens carefully at story times and his predictions of what might happen next are always reasonable in the context of the plot, and frequently accurate as well, even when he has never heard the story before.

Tom understands that written notes are a way of communicating with those who are not close by. A month or two ago, he demonstrated concern for a classmate who was ill by asking an aide to write "I hope you are better soon" so that he could copy it and send it to his friend. More recently (5/12) he attempted to write (independently) a letter to his Aunt Pat. He brought a paper on which he had written: "V F M T" and said, "I want to say '*I hope you come soon*'" We sat down together and he wrote: "I H O P U K M S(backwards) N," needing help only in identifying the letters which made the "h" and "u" sounds. When he was writing, he reached the end of the line so he returned to the left side of the paper to finish his sentence, showing an understanding of left-right progression in written English:

V F M T

N

I H O P U K M S(backwards) N

He then addressed the envelope, writing: "T O" from memory and "P A T" with a little help with the short "a" sound.

In his journals, Tom continues to draw many houses and trees. However, many of his pictures have become more involved. He demonstrates an understanding of perspective in these pictures; when his house is in the foreground, his school is small and in the background. As he explained to me, "That's the school. It's so little because it's so far away!" (5/19). He spent more than a week on a single page, making black line drawings of each kind of monster (ghosts, vampires, etc.) in a book about "monsters from the movies" which a friend had taken out of the library (Figure 4). He was intrigued with trying to draw every single monster and concentrated more on the art than the writing; however, he was willing to label some of the pictures when asked to do so. He wrote "M N S T r S" for "monsters" (with the help of a friend on the form of "r"), "V M P" for "vampire" and "K q" for "grandpa" from the tv show, "The Munsters" (6/1 and 6/6).

Figure 4: Tom's monster drawing

He is very "tuned in" to his own writing. The day he wrote "S S M Δ B B S S" for "This is my babysitter's" he commented, "There's 1, 2, 3, S's!" (5/26). Another day, when he wanted to write "house," he said, "I hear *s* but that's at the end." So he wrote "A" followed by "S", showing an understanding of the importance of the sequence of individual letters if they are to properly represent the sounds of spoken language (5/25). Left on his own to write his page of our book about riding the horse, Big George, on our trip to the Owens' Farm, he wrote: "I L K B G J" for "*I like Big George.*"

Sharron Cadieux: Excerpts from Vanessa's Biographic Profile

September. Vanessa loves to write in her journal. She hears many sounds and can record them as labels on her own if asked to do so (B–butterfly; bPL–little puppy dog, in reverse order). However she is not satisfied with labels. She loves to tell stories. She adopts a story-telling voice and uses story language (Another little puppy caught a butterfly, snap, snap, in his paws.) She wants her stories to be written down but is not yet able to use invented spelling to write a sentence on her own. If I repeat her sentence for her one word at a time, she will write a beginning sound for each word (L P S N L L i A b ! – The little puppy was in love with an angel dog.) She is aware of punctuation. (She added the exclamation mark on her own.) Every page in her journal was concerned with the puppy so she can carry an idea over several pages. Each page was a different episode or unrelated adventure in her puppy story.

November. Vanessa did not choose to write in her journal often this month. She preferred to draw separate pictures on a variety of paper types, often cutting them out. She wrote very little except for "B O O" and "M o M." Once she pretended she was a nurse and prescribed rest for me. At my suggestion, she wrote her recommendations in a booklet she had made. She used scribble lines in a left to right motion to represent cursive writing.

March/April: Vanessa wrote a great deal during these two months for a variety of purposes. She wrote books about a duck, a sheep, an owl, a bunny, and a house where animals come and visit. Animals, the sun and the moon, and comments about the weather often appear in her stories (T X E R A N A W S A G O N A A O A A – which Vanessa read as "The rain was going away"; S M A A N L M L S W T P T O T X E A H S A – which she read as "Some animals went up to the house"). More complex sounds such as vowels and "sh" are beginning to appear (H E W S S A D(backwards) – He was sad; W L E W S W K W L E   F A D W L E A B S H – which she read as "While he was walking, well he found a bush"). She has a strong sense of story language as indicated by her story introductions (W S A P N A T M W R W S A b K – which she read as "Once upon a time there was a duck"; A F N L T A N A M O O M S N A A N A L M A – which she read as "In the light of the moon the owl sat on her branch." She had likely written something similar). She also wrote about learning to ride her bike. (I R D M E B K L B E E S F W S b D A D S D, added N b I T O R M B K – which she read as "I rode my bike all by myself. 'It was good,' Dad said." Added – "and tipped over my bike.") She wrote notes – "I LOVE MOM + DAD; I LOVE U O U." She wrote about getting a new tooth. She then added O N A V in front of M i E T O T (my tooth), and went on to revise my tiny printing on the bottom of the page the same way. She drew a very detailed drawing of a tree (with green leaves) with sap buckets and dotted blue lines indicating the sap running from the tap to the bucket which she labeled "M P L S E A P" – maple syrup.

May/June. Vanessa wrote a long story about a baseball game which represented a totally different subject for her. There was a clear sequence of simple outline drawings which very effectively showed the actions and detail. She wrote many signs for the science area describing an item she had brought in and explaining if the kids should touch it or not.

One day she came in and asked for a picture of a monarch butterfly. I showed her a book that might have a picture. She took the book and went off to find it on her own. She is clearly comfortable with books. Looking at the picture, she drew an incredibly detailed butterfly and wrote I S O A A M N N K B R F L I – I saw a monarch butterfly.

She wrote several notes about teeth including T XE T O T X F R E G V M M E P A N E S A – The tooth fairy gave me pennies; A N O T O T X K M N A T O A O L E T O T X A K M A – a new tooth coming in, an old tooth coming out. She then wrote her name followed by an exclamation mark.

Vanessa knows a great deal about books and print. She can write. She can use most consonants to represent sounds she hears plus "sh" and "th." She is aware of the uses of vowels and can use long vowels correctly sometimes. She can use print for a variety of real purposes with great confidence. She has a wonderful sense of story and story language which she uses very effectively.

Brenda Eaves: Excerpts from Donna's Biographic Profile

In September Donna's writing was of favorite things that she had seen with her family, often her grandmother. She quickly sketched out her idea and then explained what it was. Her pictures were of pets, flowers, and rainbows. They were usually all in one color. She did not seem comfortable in writing any accompanying text though she could tell you parts of the words she "would use if she wrote it down."... Donna was focused on the charts and books during shared reading time. She would join the reading when there was a word or phrase that she recognized.

In October Donna's writing became more detailed and she had a definite purpose for the things she was putting on the page. Some of her stories were several pages long and she talked of realizing that writing could "save" things for you.

In April Donna has worked to write one story. It is called *MY BAST FANSE*. What began as a simple story about having a few friends come over to visit has grown until most of the children in the class are coming to visit in succession throughout the day. To organize this Donna made a list of all of her friends and asked them if they would like to be included in her book. Once that was done she set up a girl-boy pattern and began writing. "ONE DAY SAME OND KAM AND NATK ON MY DOOR. IT WAS MY BAST FRIEND ..." At this point there is a little door in the page that opens to reveal the friend. The next page tells what they do until another friend comes and the process begins again.

Donna continues to read in her choice time. She uses

books and charts that she is familiar with and she has been attending more to the details of words. As she reads she talks about recurring letter combinations like "ing," "ea," and "tion."

In May Donna has continued to work on her best friend book. It has been a very difficult project to include all of the children but she has stuck with it. At first she wanted each child to follow the same pattern of activity (come to her house, play, eat dinner, and go home). Then she said that she felt that this would get boring for the reader and so she tried to think of different things for each child to do – eating lunch, playing ball, playing with dolls or sleeping over.

In between adding friends to her book Donna worked on pieces about animals and looked back at her other pieces. She wrote a book called *Book of the Week* in which she combined her love of animals and an idea to make our weekly paper folder funny. She wrote "BOOK OF THE ShEEP SHEEP ARE NISE PEKAZ THEY GEVE YOU SOADRES." Each animal was written about using a similar format and once the text was written Donna planned the publishing so that each page would look just right.

Lori Bresnahan: Excerpts from Sam's Biographic Profile

In December, Sam continued to swing back and forth between fiction and non-fiction, with a story about good guys and bad guys turning into a piece about why Indians had wars over land. His written vocabulary is growing, and he is making use of rhyming patterns to spell words (cat, hat, fat, that, bat, mat). This makes sense, as he has been reading and re-reading *Hop on Pop*.

In January, Sam began a story (which continued through February and March), "James and the Big Thing". This is his own version of *James and the Giant Peach*, which had been read to the class. He wrote his title on the cover of his new journal (commenting on having written all of the words correctly), and announced that the story was going to fill up the whole journal (which it eventually did). He wrote a dedication, ("To JaMes My FREND"). He talks a lot as he works on his illustrations, seeming to try his ideas out on the others in the group before he writes them down.

During his library time, he returns to read the charts and books that we have read during shared reading sessions. He has also spent a lot of time reading through the *Hop, Skip, and Jump Book*, which is a word book filled with verbs and pictures to illustrate each. When he read this aloud, he used much expression in his voice. He has also read *Bony Legs*, again providing a very expressive reading, proceeding word by word, self-correcting as necessary.

In February and March, the illustrations seemed to dominate the pages of Sam's journal. He still added text, but not to every page, and sometimes it was quite small, being hidden by the picture. He did plan ahead what would happen in the story though, commenting "I'm almost to the part when –." He added pages to his journal to be able to complete his storyline the way he wanted it, drawing the illustrations first, with the text added afterwards.

Mary Benton: Excerpts from Alex's Biographic Profile

March: Alex varies between a text then picture and a picture then text approach to creating his stories. He has a clear sense of what is going to happen next in his story. The pictures are used to support the text. Alex's revisions have changed from ones which were only for him as a writer (not being able to reread his own text changing a character from a wife to a mother because he could spell the latter) to ones which concentrate on expanding the details of the story ("He kicked and kicked and kicked" revised to "The soldier kicked and kicked and kicked at the door"). While writing he uses a great deal of information from his printed and verbal environment. He sometimes overhears an editing conference between a teacher and another student and then spontaneously finds appropriate places within his own text where he can apply the skill discussed. After reading several *Frog and Toad* stories, Alex began structuring his own writing with a lot of dialogue so that he would have an opportunity to use quotation marks. Alex's self-selections now include non-fiction and chapter books. He is choosing books because of their appeal to him not because of the amount of text. When reading fiction he particularly enjoys stories which contain some kind of puzzle or humor. ... When reading he uses a combination of strategies to determine an unknown word. He is less reliant on using the picture as the primary strategy and self-corrects more often. He is more aware of when his miscues interfere with the sense of the story and is willing to stop and reread to see if he can reestablish the meaning of the text.

Kathy Matthews: Excerpts from Chris' Biographic Profile

September. Chris' first entry in his reading journal seems to reflect his feeling about reading: "Reading is okay ... but sometimes I'm not in the mood for reading." Given the chance to read anything he wishes, he generally chooses familiar stories that he has either read or listened to in first and second grade. When selecting a new book for reading, Chris opts for books that are similar in genre to others he has read, have recently been read aloud in class, or are stories written by a familiar author. He often spends quiet reading time searching for a book. Once he has made a choice he looks carefully at each of the pictures in the book before he begins reading the text. Chris' primary strategy for new text is to "sound out the letters." Sometimes he reruns the sentence if what he reads doesn't appear to make sense.

Chris' writing often reflects his interest, and, sometimes, his concerns. His first piece of writing, *The First Day of School*, indicates his awareness of, and his positive feelings about the ways the class is similar to and yet different from last year. He shares his feelings directly with his audience ("There's a new school getting built. It is going to be big. I can't wait until the new school is built. Can you? I can't."), and uses the text as a way to pay compliments to me. Chris' daybook often contains summaries of the day's events, reflections, and speculation about different issues. His entries are sometimes detailed, sometimes sparse. The conversational tone of Chris' reading journal and daybook as well as his occasional revisions for clarity and meaning suggest he is very much aware of his reader audience.

Chris titles the pieces he composes and includes a title page as well. He is careful to put the date on everything he writes. He uses periods with initials and writes with mixed use of upper- and lower-case letters. Instead of crossing out words when revising, Chris prefers to erase what he no longer wants. His penmanship is executed with dark, heavy lines with wide spacing in between the letters within a word as well as the words themselves. He usually skips every other line when writing on lined paper. Chris' spelling development is in the early transitional stage. He uses standard spelling for many high-frequency words and has assimilated structural concepts such as *-ING* endings and plural *S* as well as these phonetic concepts: all regular consonants, final *-MP*, all long, open-syllable vowels, the short vowels *I, E, A*, the digraphs *CH* and *Th*, and the blends *BL, SL, ST, FR, DR, TR, TW, SC*. Chris often writes syllables as separate words.

November. Writing continued to be an expressive outlet for Chris this month. He spent a great deal of time composing a very personal piece entitled "THE CAT THAT CHRIS FOUND IN HIS YARD." Beneath the title he wrote, "Based on a true story." He also included a title page. Chris uses clear, honest language in his dialogue to describe the central conflict of this piece, i.e. naming the cat ("I said to myself, "Na! Na! Na!" and went upstairs."). The piece begins as a third person narrative based on real experience ("One day Chris found a cat in his yard."), quickly becomes a first person account ("It is orange like Chris' other cat, Duncan. I have to come up with a name for it."), and ends with detailed descriptions of the cat's behavior ("When I am sleeping he comes on my bed and lays on my face and bites my nose ...") which convey his fondness for his cat. Chris proofread and edited this piece by himself, adding periods at the ends of sentences and apostrophes to show possession.

Chris used written language for numerous purposes this month. He began writing in a learning log, wrote a brief report about our archaeological experiences, and wrote letters to classmates that included puzzles and jokes. Chris appeared willing to take some risks. He wrote a story with science fiction overtones, humor, and bizarre episodes that seemed intended to simply arouse audience reaction. He shared this piece with the class and was able to be open to their suggestions without abandoning his own point of view.

Bruce Turnquist: Excerpts from Katerina's Biographic Profile

September/Early October. Katerina has worked on three stories: "The Bear and the Mouse", "The Thing in the Forest", and "The Missing Teacher." "The Missing Teacher" has gone through several drafts and is still in the process of revision. Katerina takes conference information seriously. For instance, Katerina's story about the teacher has him losing all his clothes through theft in the night. He goes out to purchase new clothes the next day. Other children pointed out that this would be a problem, and that the teacher might get arrested. Katerina redrafted her work and had the teacher go to bed with clothes and shoes on. Again, the children thought this strange. Katerina placed the shoes on the floor, and eventually in the closet. Katerina also revises on her own. She plays with the details in her stories.

Katerina uses formula language to begin and end stories. Examples include "One day ...", "Once upon a time...", and "They lived happily ever after..." Most of her sentences are straightforward, and make syntactic sense. Many of her sentences are simple in construction, but she is beginning to use compound sentences and dialogue. Katerina's punctuation and capitalization fit to a close approximation of the standard. End punctuation is appropriate. Commas are used for a series of words. Quotation marks enclose dialogue. Katerina's choice of verbs is usually in the passive voice. She's beginning to use more adjectives for effect. ("They were dripping wet.").

Katerina's writing is by no means limited to story writing. She is conscientious about keeping a Reading Journal and writes in it more often than is required. She writes about favorite parts of books, favorite characters, why she picked a book, and her opinion of a book. She often backs these statements up with a reason. ("... my favorite character is Oscar. Oscar is pretty nice because he learns a lesson. The lesson is to stay around where he lives.") ("I thought this book was boring. Because there were words I didn't like in there and I didn't like the picture a lot either") Katerina generally browses through the first page of a book to determine whether or not to pursue it. Her reading choices show variety with a mix from magazine articles on animals, to joke books like *Witcracks*, to folk tales, to favorite picture books. Most of her choices can be read in one sitting. She usually abandons "chapter" books after a couple of days. She enjoys using the listening center, and follows the text as she listens. She is currently using the center to read a "chapter" book, *Stone Fox*.

Katerina's uses of literacy show that she places great value on it. This is particularly true for her as a writer. She uses writing for social interactional purposes. For instance, she became enthusiastic about a Home-School Journal when her sister's class began using one. Having suggested it to her teacher and seeing no results within two days, Katerina created her own Home-School Journal and got her teacher involved in it. Katerina also uses writing for educational purposes. The back of a math homework paper will list the color coding she has used on the front as an explanation of the patterns she found. She has used her *LOGO* Log to do more than list commands. She describes what she has done at each *LOGO* session. ("I made square on the computer and I taught Nat how to use the LOGO and I think Ia'm doing good.") ("I made a double flag. It was neat.") These descriptions are Katerina's own idea. She proudly points them out to her teacher.

It is important to state here that even as I type these biographic accounts into my computer the teachers are changing the ways in which they are constructing them. Some of the *Project* teachers, who have spent a year writing profiles, are in the process of restructuring the task so that their profiles can reflect the multiple layers of information that they are collecting as they observe and take notes about the children in their classes.

Four: Learning to Increase Our Awareness of the Multiple Layers of Interpretation That We Are Incorporating into Children's Biographic Literacy Profiles

"You know at the beginning of last year I rejected your 'categories.' They were confusing to me," Leigh Walls said a few days ago when I was asking her if I could include the profile of Tom in the previous section of this report. "But as the year went on what I was seeing in my notes fit." We joked a bit, remembering. Leigh said that for her the "category" that made the most sense focused upon the interrelationships between children's pictures and their writing, and then she added that she had just read an article published in *Early Childhood Research Quarterly* that examines the social uses of print (Schrader, 1989). Leigh said, "Their categories are similar to the types and uses of print that we are using in the project." I ventured that I thought she was reaching a time in her own development when she would be creating her own categories. Leigh laughed, "I already have," she said, "it's called 'the other' category."

We talked for a while about the way in which she was organizing her profiles this year. "I have to find a way to make it more manageable," she said, and she spoke of the time it was taking to write the profiles. She talked of taking her notes and the other information that she had collected and organizing it so that the biographic profiles would reflect the categories that we were using as we tried to think about the multiple layers of literacy activity that occurred in classroom settings. Leigh emphasized that she did not want to use the categories as a basis for classroom observation and I agreed with her, "Then it would become just another checklist and the theoretical base would change. It would become an 'outside-in' way of looking at children and we would be back into a 'medical model.'"

Like Mary Benton, of whom I spoke earlier, Leigh strongly believes in observing children and writing down her interpretations of what she sees, and Kathy Matthews presented a similar point of view. When I spoke with her earlier this evening she said, "The thinking comes afterwards." Kathy is also trying to find a way to organize the information that she collects into a system of recording and reporting that makes sense within the framework that she has established in her own teaching. Kathy has been taking notes in her classroom for many years but last year was the first time that she tried to synthesize the "data" that she had been collecting into some form of cohesive representation that would inform her own teaching, be given to parents, used by other teachers, and shared with the children themselves.

The problem that Kathy faced when she joined the Project was that she had been teaching the same group of children for two years, and she had too much information about them to produce a short paragraph each month about their literacy learning. The first profiles that Kathy wrote were three pages of single-spaced narrative – just for the month of September. "This kind of teaching is like an escalator," Kathy said. "The more you learn the further up you go and the more difficult it is to get off." For Kathy, Leigh, and Mary, this is the year in which they will "play" with different ways of presenting the information that they are collecting, so that they can both make the process manageable for themselves and provide insights for some of the other teachers in the *Project* who have not yet reached a similar point in their own development. Indeed, for some of the teachers, taking notes is a challenge, and the profiles that they are writing still focus largely upon the development of sound-symbol relationships and syntactic structures.

It is important to emphasize here that the experiential differences that exist among the teachers have created an opportunity for us to establish a dialectical relationship which, through our collaboration, enables us to "play with" our own situationally specific problem-solving activities. These activities include:

1. Creating environments in which children can explore the functions, uses, and forms of written language.
2. Establishing note-taking procedures which reflect the practical complexity of the plurality of literacies occurring in these specific classroom settings.
3. Developing systems of analysis which reflect the multiple layers of interpretation that we are trying to incorporate in the biographic profiles that we are writing.

Consistent with the structure of the *Project*, in presenting objective four I am going to add to and combine the information outlined in the first three objectives described so far. Thus the "layering" will be presented directly (explicitly) and indirectly (implicitly) in order to deliberately "model" the complexities of the process that we are trying to achieve.

1. Creating environments in which children can explore the functions, uses, and forms of written language.

In a chapter entitled "Thinking in action: some characteristics of practical thought," Silvia Scribner (1986) reminds us that "the computer metaphor, dominant today, portrays mind as a system of symbolic representations and operations that can be understood in and of itself, in isolation from other systems of activity" (p. 15). Cautioning us about what I would call the distortions of anonymity which occur in such hermetically sealed studies, Scribner states:

> Researchers adopting this metaphor seek either to model mental tasks undertaken for their own sake ("recall a narrative," "solve this arithmetic problem") or to analyze individual mental functions (e.g., inference, imagery) abstracted from tasks and separated from one another. Whatever may be said about the value of this framework and these research approaches (and their accomplishments are recognized), they offer little possibility for probing the nature of practical thought. (pp. 15-16)

The impact of research that "disembodies mental activity" (see Lave, Murtaugh & de la Rocha, 1984) is clearly evident in the corpus of research studies that have been conducted in the reading field which focus upon eliciting information in totally synthetic laboratory environments or artificially structured classroom environments (see studies reviewed by Chall, 1989; also Taylor, 1989). Less evident are the effects of quasi-normative studies in which "context" becomes just another variable.

And yet, as Lave, Murtaugh, and de la Rocha state:

> There is speculation that the circumstances that govern problem solving in situations which are not prefabricated and minimally negotiable differ from those that can be examined in experimental situations. (p. 67)

Studies in "practical intelligence" (Sternberg & Wagner, 1986) and "everyday cognition" (Rogoff & Lave, 1984) provide convincing evidence that "mental activity" is not "context free" (see also Carraher, Carraher & Schliemann, 1985; Carraher, 1986). Thus we are left asking if the generic teaching of "skills" or the testing of (of what? – I no longer have any idea what "it" is that we test) have any relevance at all, except for the purpose of academic endorsement of what is essentially a political activity. If we shift away from the defective idea of generic teaching and learning that underlies this lucrative commercial enterprise and we localize education and try to think about teaching, learning, and schooling from the perspective of the learner, then we are no longer able to think about separating the activity from the setting.

Indeed, I would argue strongly that such a division has always been an illusion. Even on so-called "normed" tests the child's particular interpretation of the task is dependent upon the dialectical relationship that is established between the activity and the setting. The difficulty that occurs is that we cannot predict the individual child's "response" to the task. An example of a child's reaction to a "standardized" achievement test is provided by Don Graves, who recounts that in the Atkinson Study, a young boy kept putting up his hand, and in keeping with the "standardized" procedures for the administration of normed tests, his teacher kept signaling him to put his hand down. Eventually the child pointed to his test booklet and asked, "Who wrote this anyway? It doesn't have a voice."

Leigh Walls has shared with us another example of the

difficulties that arise when there is no accounting for the perspective of the learner in "standardized" testing situations. Leigh spoke of a time early in her teaching career when she was teaching social studies in a junior high school. She was expected to administer the "standardized" tests used in the school, and that on one occasion she watched as a junior high school boy zig-zagged his way down the page, shading the boxes, without looking at the questions. Leigh said it took him less than five minutes and he scored at the "mean." What bothered Leigh then, and still bothers her today, is that the boy had difficulty reading. "He could not read the items on the test," she told us, and then she asked, "what was he learning?"

It is from this perspective that we have approached the task of constructing learning environments in which children can actively engage in the reconstruction of the functions, uses, and forms of written language. To quote Scribner (1986) again:

> The concept of the environment germane to practical problem solving is not a physicalist notion. Here "environment" includes all social, symbolic, and material resources outside the head of the individual problem solver. In this sense, activities such as seeking information from other people, "putting heads together" to come to collaborative solutions, or searching documents and looking things up in files, may be understood as extended and complex procedures for intellectual use of the environment. (pp. 24-25)

In the *Project* we often talk of the classroom "setting," and we use this term in similar ways to "environment" to mean individual and shared interpretations of the social, symbolic, material, and technological resources that make up the particular classroom. We also use the word "arena" to indicate the larger institutional framework which, in similar ways to the "setting," is made up of people using the symbolic, material, and technological resources at their disposal within the defined space of the physical plant called "the school" (Lave, Murtaugh & de la Rocha, 1984). We do, of course, include family and community as constitutive of both the classroom setting and the institutional arena of the school. In the classrooms described in this section, "family life" takes place in classroom settings.

Our task then has become to gain insights into what Scribner describes as "the specificity of practical knowledge," and to gain some understanding of "the role of thought within a system of activity" from the perspective of the learner. Standing side-by-side children with our "heads together," we are trying to understand their learning based upon what we observe as they use the social, technical, symbolic, and material resources at their disposal. In the next few pages of this report I want to explore what this means specifically for the participants in the *Project*.

Recently during a conversation that took place when the second year *Project* members made a presentation of our work at the Maine Reading Conference, Lee Proctor said that she was keeping the first hour of her school morning "unstructured," and then she said, "the things I'm seeing I couldn't make happen." During this early morning "unstructured" time she sets "them the task of writing their news and many of them start that when they first come in. I think they feel pretty much that they own it." In preparation for writing this section, I talked some more with Lee about what she meant by "unstructured" and she responded:

> I provide the time, and the paper, and I visit with as many of them as I can. I spend a lot of time looking at their work when they've gone home. I look at the books they are reading and I go through their folders just about every night. I find I can't keep that whole ball game going without a good idea about what they're doing. Initially, I'm just checking up on who's starting a book, who's finishing a book. I look at their logs. Their record is my record. It's a shared respon-

sibility between us.

Lee is working with her students to create an environment or setting in which "self-organization" is constitutive of classroom life, recognizing in a similar way to Doll (1989) that the complexity of children's learning cannot be simulated in artificially-structured classroom environments. As Doll explains:

> In retrospect, one aspect of self-organization we might have utilized better was that of the forced grouping of students. We placed them into groups of 2's and 4's because of my belief in the role cooperation and communication play in re-organization. Now I see we could have had cooperation and communication in a more varied, less forced mode. We should have allowed interaction and verbalization to occur, not forced it. Learning occurs on a number of levels and in a variety of manners – this is the nature of complexity. (p. 69)

Thus, in the *Project* classrooms, we are trying to provide opportunities for children to engage in problem-solving situations in which they have participated in the organization of the activity.

In **Sharron Cadieux**'s kindergarten classroom, the physical arrangement of the room is designed to encourage "self-organization." At any one time children may be actively engaged in a variety of learning situations, including playing in the house-keeping area. One day last year, while Sharron was working with some children who were writing in their journals, children from the house-keeping area kept arriving with the telephone. "It's for you," they would say, and Sharron would stop what she was doing and talk on the telephone. As the morning progressed the telephone "rang" continuously and each time a child would tell Sharron that someone wanted to speak to her. Finally, Sharron said, "Take a message." The child wrote a message and gave it to Sharron. Other calls were received and more messages were taken. Sharron put a notice board by the house-keeping area and tacked the messages on it.

When I talked with Sharron about including this example of children's self-organization of a literacy activity being constitutive of the classroom environments that we are trying to establish in the *Project*, we had fun remembering that moment. "Kids would write messages to each other," Sharron said, "and a lot of them could read them back. They took messages for me. Once when we were reading them back a child said, 'It's from Mr. Cadieux.'" I asked how long they continued taking messages. "Eventually they lost interest in the telephone but they had so much news to share that they began using the notice board to write it down. If they had something to share they wrote it down, and then they shared what they had written and that lasted a long time. Some kids used the notice board almost every day. I think it was the sense of sharing information. They announced their important news." Sharron talked about the kinds of messages that the children wrote. She said that many of their messages serialized the events in their lives, "It's almost Julie's birthday party. Two days to Julie's birthday party ... Today is Julie's birthday party." Or, "I might get glasses. I might get glasses. Tomorrow I might get glasses. Today I might get glasses. I don't need glasses." Some of the messages were about events that were worrying individual children. For instance, one child wrote messages when her aunt gave birth to a premature baby, and the family was very concerned about the health of the baby. "When the baby reached 11 pounds that was a big thing, she wrote an announcement and put it on the notice board." Sharron's children wrote notes about learning to ride their bikes, and about when they had fights with each other, and when they gathered together they shared what they had written. If we stand side-by-side with Sharron and her children, we can gain some understanding of how they are learning about the many ways in which print can be used as a substitute for an oral message. Their interest in message-writing and their self-organization of the activity underscores the complexity of the environmental setting that Sharron has established with her children.

Sharon Williams, a first grade teacher, provided us with another example of the ways she is creating opportunities for the children in her class to actively engage in the reconstruction of the functions, uses, and forms of written language. Sharon shared her class list with the teachers attending one of the group meetings which we conduct throughout the year, and she said that she used the class list from the beginning of school in September "since all the children can find their name." Sharon explained that one of the ways in which they used the list was to record lunch and recess milk orders, and she pointed to a list to show us how the system worked. "*H* for hot lunch, *C* for cold lunch, *B* for lowfat milk which comes in a blue container, and *R* for regular milk which comes in a red container." Sharon talked about Sally, who was the first child "to record on our list," and she explained how she had asked Sally and another child to get the information they needed.

In writing up this account of the event that Sharon Williams described, I telephoned her and she explained, "Both children had lists and they figured out how to use them." Then she added, "It's child structured and child figured out, and the task changes according to the children involved. Sometimes another child will join in and add his or her expertise." Going back to Sally, Sharon explained that she had sat across a table from the other child and as the child called out a name Sally would find the name on her list and record the called-out response from the child whose name had been read. The children figured out a system for themselves and it worked. At the group meeting Sharon said, "Sally felt confident and capable of doing this task." Then she laughed as she told us that two weeks later the intern had misplaced the attendance sheet and had gone immediately to the children's records to find out who was absent. "Our list has multiple purposes for both records and problem-solving,"

Sharon concluded. In Sally's biographic profile, Sharon wrote, "Sally is using print to organize and record information. She had the responsibility of recording lunch and recess milk orders for a week and she was able to use the list of class names to accurately record all of the children's requests."

In **Susan Sullivan**'s second grade class, the children gathered together, and two boys moved to the front of the group and sat on chairs facing the class. One of them was carrying a terrarium, and as he sat down he carefully balanced it on his lap. He reached inside and took out a red eft salamander. The boys had two of them. One of the girls in the class had brought into school twenty of them that she had caught in the woods with the help of her dad. The girl had given two of the red efts to the boys who had then made a terrarium for them. "It was totally their own project," Susan said. "They went and collected mushrooms and mosses. I had nothing to do with it except that I showed them some books where they could find out about salamanders."

Susan said that the boys took the terrarium, together with the *Audubon Field Guide to Reptiles and Amphibians*, everywhere with them. The two boys have been studying this book and another entitled *Reptiles* that they now shared. They talked about the red eft for a while, and then the discussion shifted as the boys talked about the book they had been studying, and one of them flipped through the pages until he reached a page about turtles. They read and talked about turtles for a while with the children sitting around them, and then the conversation turned to rattlesnakes. The two boys looked through the book together, somehow negotiating the turning of the pages until they reached the page on which there was a picture of several snakes – including a rattlesnake. They showed the picture to the class. Then one boy read, not straight through the text, but relevant bits of information that they both wanted to share. Susan listened and when he has finished reading she asked, "What does it mean when it says rattlesnakes can strike?" A discussion followed and the boys alternated between looking at the book and talking with the class. Eventually the class arrived at an acceptable explanation, and they went on to discuss where the poison comes from. Children made suggestions. "It comes from the back of the throat," one child said. Others suggested the mouth, the teeth, and the tail. "How can we find out?" Susan asked, and the discussion continued, with most of the children agreeing that the best way would be to go and look in the library.

For a moment Susan talked with them about the library, and then the discussion was back to rattlesnakes, and Susan asked if rattlesnakes were useful. "There was a section in the book on useful snakes. I took it right off the page," she said. The children considered whether rattlesnakes were useful and if there were any positive reasons to have them around. The boy read from the text, and the discussion went back and forth between the information presented in the book and the information provided by the children, as they posed problems, developed hypotheses, and discussed possible explanations.

What happens in Susan's classroom underscores the importance of establishing with children environmental settings that enable them to explore the practical complexity of scientific knowledge. Susan said, "They get everybody interested and talk about it all the time. Right now they have a black-spotted salamander and they are working out what it means to be nocturnal. They took it out with them at recess and put it on some playground equipment and the salamander was distressed. They had a long discussion about why the salamander was not happy and they have been trying to find out more about when they need to sleep and when they need to hunt."

At the beginning of this report we met **Mary Yates**, and I presented the biographic profiles that the teachers in the first summer institute wrote about her daughter Katie's literacy development. Mary is a second grade teacher and the following story was written by one of her second grade children, Vicki. It is a story called "SUPR MOREO Brothrsr." On the cover Vicki had drawn a small person, and inside a "speech bubble" she had written "to mare yats", and in another speech bubble "a good boook." Vicki had also written "by Vicki", acknowledging that she was the author of the book. Inside the story begins:

Moreo and Lawege wint for a wock in wrld one one

It was Hot so Lawege tock a swim

and got in to big trobol and moreo was in bigr

It was a canin but He coud not flut up. in the air.

yaaaww spines are coming done

Lawege is in shock and Moreo is history in world 2 3

The prinses is in trobol. what cinde oof trobol the trolls.

Lawege is in big trobol whth the dragan got [read "can't"] Get bet up.

I'm olmost thare to see the prinses. Get a way big men Dragan.

I Dont want to be Lonch seid Lawege thes fling fish are

Jrving me crasey. Ware is the Prinses

ware Ther

Vicki explained that in the last picture Lawege and Moreo have saved the princess, and the turtle and "the guy who shoots the spines" have been caught. I asked Vicki who was holding onto the turtle and the spines and she said, "just a person."

Mary said that when she talked to Vicki, she explained that she had started her story at world one one and finished it at world two three, because that's as far as she can go when she plays the Nintendo game. Thus we can say that it appears that

Vicki is symbol-weaving as she works to create a story based upon the Nintendo game (Figure 5).

It is interesting to note that when I have shown this story to researchers and educators, the immediate reaction is that they can't comment on the piece because they do not know the game. What we are learning in the *Project* is that such games are a part of the educational environment of the classroom, for children bring their technical expertise of playing video games with them when they come to school. It is clear that from the perspective of the learner, electronic games have both practical significance and theoretical relevance. This is not to suggest that the child has "meta" knowledge of the theoretical and practical significance of advanced technologies, but simply to suggest that from the perspective of the child the technology is functionally important. Vicki provides verification of this perspective when she explains that her story is written in the "worlds" that she has visited when she plays the game.

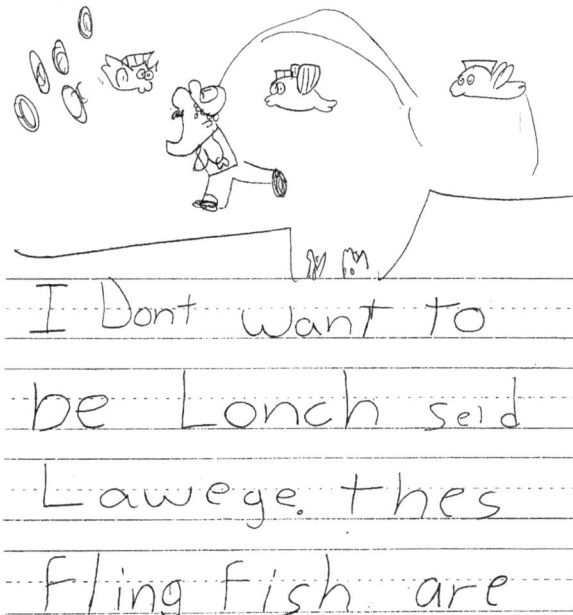

I Dont want to
be Lonch seid
Lawege thes
Fling fish are

Figure 5: Vicki's Nintendo story

Vicki's story could be described as archetypal in its construction, for it is a new copy of an old pattern, with a fairy tale structure that incorporates a new technology, into a traditional form. In the *Project* we are trying to learn from the children about this technology so that we can gain some understanding of the ways in which it has become part of their daily lives. At the second summer institute, for example, we spent several hours discussing with Donna Parmenter a story written by a boy in her class who was being evaluated by the child study team. We knew from observing and talking with him that the "story" was carried by the voice of a race commentator, and that he had incorporated elements from *The Road Warrior* into his text, in which the formation of letters served to illustrate the speed of the cars performing at a raceway as well as giving a verbal rendition of the speed of the Mad Max chase. If you flipped the pages, the writing created the illusion of the increasing speed of the race.

A week after I worked as a participant observer in Mary Yates classroom, I visited **Bob Magher**'s third grade class, and listened to Jeff read another Mario Brothers story during a writing conference with Bob and three other students. I present it here to emphasize that the children themselves are actively engaged in the process of incorporating new technologies into the classroom environment, and that the teachers in the project are sensitive to this development. Jeff gave his story the same name as the Saturday morning TV show, "Captain N The Game Master," and above the title he had written "make-believe." The story was written in script and dated October 3, 9, 10, 12, 16:

> One day I was playing Super Mario brothers with Andrew and Bill when Andrew got hungry so I paused the game and when I came back my game was unpaused and Andrew was gone. Billy was sitting the couch and breathing heavy. I asked him what happed he was talking to him and the game came unpaused and Andrew got sucked into it. Billy and I got up from

the couch and I touched the T.V. I got sucked in too. Billy yelled, "Wait a second Jeff! I'm coming with you"! and he touched the screen and he came in too. I landed in the level 8-4. I saw Andrew then Billy almost fell on my head. I told Andrew and Billy to follow me we had to jump over pits of lava. Billy fell in one of them. He only has 1 guy left now. We made it to King Koopa. I told Billy and Andrew to run under him but not to pick up the ax. I had a case full of fire bombs I killed King Kooper I am going to save the real princess. We went to get her she told us we must save Pricess Zelda. She told us how to get to a warp zone that gets you all of the wepons and triforce and to the 9th palace and to Ganon. It is in the Castle Vania. And there is a warp zone to Castle Vania in the wall of the palce. We went in to the warp zone and ended up in Castle Vania. We saw Madusa I got the whip out of my pocket and whipped Madusa with it good I brought my paddle belt with me. I was tired I paused the game. I jumped out of the T.V. and got a drink then ["then" inserted] I went back in and unpaused the game ["game" inserted]. I kept whipping Madusa. I beat her we got to the warp zone we went through it. Now we are in the nineth level. Ganon is in the room right above us. "O.K. lets go guys'!' I shouted get the sivler arrows out "Who is going to go in'?' I shouted. Billy and Andrew both said at the same time "Not me"! "O.K. fine I will go". I said. I went in to ganon You have to stab im four times then you have to hit him with silver arowws. "Ouch'!' yelled Ganon I hit him with my sword once. "Ouch'!' he said again 'cause I hit him. "Ouch"! he said again. "Ouch"! he said. Now he is brown. I have to hit him with silver arrows "Bang" I hit him once. "Bang" I hit him twice. "Bang" I hit him three times now he is dead. I ran out to tell Billy and Andrew. "Billy, Andrew I beat him"!

"Come in let's go get the triforce"! "And save princess Zelda". We ran in to the room where Ganon used to be I grabed the triforce and ran in the door with Billy and Andrew. There's Zelda guys"! I shouted. "Billy don't go there you'll get killed!" Billy was so excited he ran up Zelda and in to the fire. "I warned him". "Yup, you did", said Andrew. "Well it will be a long time before we see him again. He is dead we won't see him until we die." "O.K. now Andrew you wait here I am going to put out these fires." There finished. "Come on Andrew"! We ran up to Zelda "I gave her one of the triforce. I gave Andrew one too." We held them up above our heads. Then Zelda told us we have saved H – and the whole world of Nintendo Land. The End.

In a way similar to Vicki, Jeff was symbol-weaving the technological quests of video games ("You'll have to think fast and move even faster to complete this quest!" Super Mario Bros. 1985) with the images and stories that result from the transposition of these games into a Saturday morning TV show about Kid Nintendo. In addition, Bill and Andrew are friends of Jeff's. Bob said, "The kids like to do that, they incorporate each other into their stories." When all these elements are combined, the result is something between a child's version of the Canterbury Tales and Bill and Ted's Excellent Adventure. Jeff made his own story, incorporating his friends into a technological adventure that has many of the elements which can be found in traditional, even ancient story forms.

The final example builds upon the questions raised about complexity in the classroom life, and is connected to the ideas of symbol-weaving in problem-solving situations in which the children themselves have participated in the organization of the activity. During the 1988-1989 school year, **Kathy Matthews'** third grade children studied the culture and mythology of ancient Greece. Kathy has written an article about her students' study of mythology (Matthews, 1990); at the beginning of her paper Kathy describes the Greek festival, the culminating event of their year of activity and study:

> In our "amphitheater" that evening, two groups of children performed their own versions of the classic tales of Perseus and Persephone, using the elaborate puppets that they had made. Guests wandered through the exhibits of the children's work, admiring the results of weeks of problem-solving and labor: Aaron's scale model of the Parthenon, Debbie's version of the Minotaur's maze, the wings Mike had built so that he could fly like Icarus, Jenny's life-like Pegasus perched for flight, embroidered tapestries of Athena, Prometheus, and Aphrodite, the twelve dioramas Chad and Amber sculpted in plasticine to symbolize the labors of Hercules, Matt and Nate's relief map of Ancient Greece, and our clay pots painted with classic Greek designs and seeded with Greek herbs. The guests talked with the children about their work, read the reports they had written, and feasted on traditional Greek fare including that classic bacchanalian drink – grape juice. (p. 40)

In her essay, Kathy speaks eloquently of the "significance of the metaphors that myths have provided" and of the importance that mythology has played in the lives of children for thousands of years. During my visits to her classroom I became increasingly aware of the historical connection that Kathy was encouraging her children to make between their own lives and the lives of ancient civilizations. On my first visit to her classroom the students were creating visual representations of their own life histories, and my second visit coincided with the sorting of artifacts recovered during an archeological dig. It took several minutes before I began to see what was happening. The children were working in twos and threes, sorting and classifying the objects that they had collected during the dig. Kathy was participating, clip-board in hand, examining objects shown to her by the children and listening to them, and discussing with them the classification systems that they were developing as they worked to create a record of their participation in the dig.

As a novice or neophyte, there has never been a time when I have visited Kathy's classroom that I have been able to walk in and just take notes. When children participate in the construction of their own environments, the task of the participant observer, like the teacher, is to try to capture some of the practical complexity of the symbolic activity. What are they doing and how are they doing it? What kinds of negotiations are taking place? How do they arrange to work together? What problems are they trying to solve? What are they saying? What are they writing in their daybooks, journals, and learning logs? What are those diagrams? What are they drawing on those large sheets of paper? Is that a mountain that those children are painting? How is it constructed? With cardboard and glue? What books are they reading? Are they studying geometry? Ancient forms of measurement? The origin of machines?

In *Order Out of Chaos*, Prigogine and Stengers (1984) write about the "irreducible multiplicity of representations," and although they are not talking about classrooms filled with children, I am convinced that the description applies. When we provide opportunities for children to participate in the construction of their own learning environments, their activities are complexly structured into temporal patterns of which we can only capture a glimpse of what Prigogine and Stengers refer to as "the wealth of reality, which overflows any single language, and single logical structure" (p. 225).

At the second Summer Institute, as we had gathered together to discuss a problem-solving activity in which we had all participated, Kathy tried to create a visual representation of what the participants said had taken place as they worked together (Figure 6).

"Do you think that the diagram reflects some of what

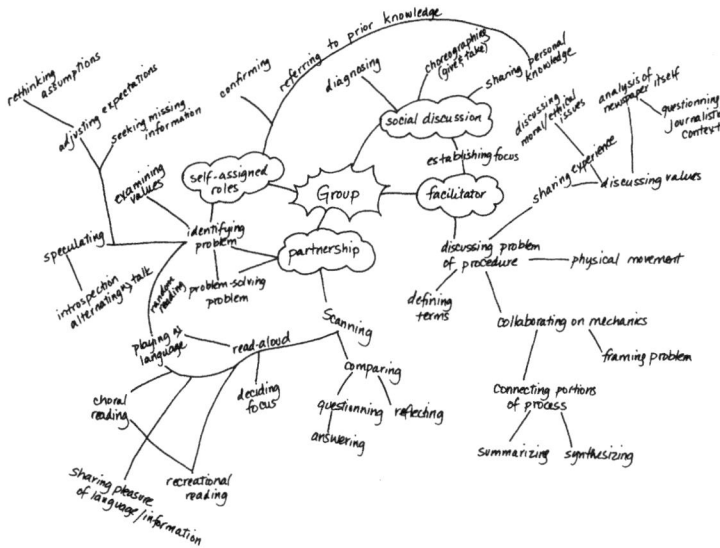

Figure 6: Kathy's problem-solving diagram

happened in your classroom as the children studied Greek Mythology?" I asked. Kathy replied, "I think there was as much depth and breadth. It was certainly that complex." The diagram – and Kathy's written analysis of the activity (Figure 7) – provides us with just one interpretation of the practical complexity of a problem-solving event, but perhaps it will enable us to imagine the multiplicity of interpretations that are possible when self-organization is constitutive of classroom life.

Solving the Problem of Newspapers

Group dynamics – how group worked together
~ partnership   ~ social discussion
~ facilitator   ~ self-assigned roles

Approaches to problem of task
~ identifying problem
~ discussing problem of procedure
    – collaboration on mechanics of procedure
~ framing problem
~ problem-solving problem
    – connecting portions of process
    – defining terms
    – physical movement

Components of Problem-Solving

— reading aloud	~ establishing focus
— silent reading	~ decision-making re:focus
~ choral reading	~ diagnosing
~ recreational reading	~ summarizing
~ re-running text	~ synthesizing
~ introspection alternating w/ talk	~ hypothesizing
~ playing with language	~ speculating
~ innovations on language	~ sharing pleasure/laughter
— comparing texts	~ choreographing (give & take)
~ scanning	~ answering
~ seeking missing information	~ debating moral issues
~ adjusting expectations	~ analyzing newspaper quality
~ rethinking assumptions	~ questioning journalistic context
~ referring to prior knowledge	~ reflecting
~ sharing experiences	~ comparing
~ expressing values	~ questioning
	~ confirming

Note-Taking Issues

~ coping up task	~ ways of note-taking
— defining terms	— running record
— reviewing directions	— categorizing
— group decision-making	— focus on dialogue
— dialogue re: procedure	— inclusion of physical movement

~ personal difficulties
 — removing self (observer)
 — staying in observer's role
 — mechanics of group reading

Figure 7: Kathy's analysis of the activity

2. Establishing "data" collecting procedures which reflect the practical complexity of the plurality of literacies occurring in these specific classroom settings.

Collecting information about children's learning depends upon the classroom environment. If a child copies from the board:

Tab is a sad cat.

Tab has a pal.

His pal is Mac.

Mac is a rat.

The task is curriculum (or basal?) generated and teacher

defined. From the perspective of the learner there is not much happening. The child might passively copy or even "rebelliously" refuse to complete the task. Either way we learn nothing about the ways in which the child uses print in the self-organization of problem-solving tasks, nor of the ways in which the child is problem-solving the construction of written texts. Conversely, as the "Tuck-In" flyer (Figure 2) serves to illustrate, "pieces" of [*** this was the end of the text page in the Heinemann book, Figures 7/8 were placed next] print that were generated in problem-solving situations can provide us with the opportunities to build multiple interpretations of the functions and uses of the text. When we have texts produced by children we can develop detailed analyses of their structural features (sound/symbol relationships or syntactic patterns), but without systematic observation by the teacher we learn very little about the ways in which the individual children collaborated as they worked to develop hypotheses, simplify the task, or to rethink the problem. Did they share personal knowledge? Collaborate on mechanics? Did anyone speculate about the outcomes of the problem? Adjust their expectations or choreograph the discussion? How many drafts were made? Notes or plans? What conversations took place as different symbol systems were incorporated into the text?

Dead tasks (workbooks) or inert texts (print without knowledge of production), neither is enough to create an adequate picture of learning from the perspective of the learner. And, while I would rather have the child's production than some simplistic (asinine is probably a better descriptor) "text" copied from the board, the child's writing without notes written by the teacher still only provides a part of the "picture." Portfolios are not enough. To understand how individual children actively engage in the reconstruction of the functions, uses, and forms of written language we need to observe them at work. The observations that teachers make and the notes that they write are central to the process, and when the information generated through their systematic observation of children is combined with portfolios that contain notes, plans, and first drafts as well as final copies, then we have an opportunity to construct biographic profiles that reflect the literacy development of individual children and we can use these profiles to help us support and enhance the learning opportunities of every child that we teach.

"Take a message," Sharron Cadieux said to one of her kindergarten children, and the rest of the story you know. In her master's thesis Sharron writes:

> I had always encouraged children to explore writing for a variety of purposes (notes, signs, reminders), but did not make a concerted effort to include these in the child's writing folder on any regular basis. If I kept them at all, it was as an interesting glimpse at children exploring written language and its uses, not as an example of one child's understanding of the various functions of language. Taylor encouraged us to save all the little scraps each child wrote, pictures and "letters" they did at home to give to the teacher, examples of environmental print they could read, signs or lists resulting from play ("KEEP OUT" signs, menus, shopping lists), examples of spontaneous writing done at home if we could get them. All of these often indecipherable examples of children's understanding of the uses of print were to be carefully dated and included in each child's folder along with more formal examples of writing and teacher observations. By more formal examples of writing, I am referring to the journals and stories the children write using invented spelling following a writing process model. This is the type of writing I had monitored in the past almost exclusively. The notes, signs, and other products of play were noteworthy and validating examples of each child's writing development, but I did not make a concerted effort to

make them part of the child's record of progress

I now view these writings, which usually find their way into wastebaskets both at home and at school, as indispensable glimpses into each child's understanding about how print works. Such information is essential if we truly seek to begin at each child's level of understanding and provide experiences to encourage growth from an individual perspective rather than education based upon adult assumptions.

Together with the examples of children's writing, and the reading logs that Sharron collects and keeps in each child's folder, she also records what she calls the "supporting information" of actual conversations between herself and a child and between children working together – what she refers to as the children's "explanations" of the work that they are doing.

Sharon Williams was the second teacher whose classroom we visited in the discussion on creating classroom environments in which literacy is used for authentic purposes. Two days ago (October 27, 1989) I received a letter from Sharon with more lists. The multiple uses that her children devise for this simple list of names underscores that the text is not enough. Sharon writes:

Dear Denny,

Here's another use of my class list. Last Tuesday we had indoor recess and the children were playing a game with a score. A number of them got lists to record the game. Here is one I collected. Another girl recorded scores on her sheet. I couldn't find that one. It was a throwing game. Ms. Gurchin and I did not play. Evan won and you can see who all played. ... If I find the other list I'll send you a copy.

Sharon's comment about not being able to find one of the copies is a relevant one, for as Sharron Cadieux notes, much of the everyday writing of children ends up in wastebaskets or as *Project* teachers often remark, the writing is too precious to be given to the teacher. Our task is to try to get representative samples that we can keep in children's portfolios to use in analyzing their literacy development and in building biographic profiles. Very often this means making copies of notes et cetera, so that the communicative purpose of the writing is not interrupted. On the copy of the "game list" that Sharon sent to me one of the children had written "NOPLeYg" by her name and by the name of Ms. Gurchin, and the score had been kept by making X's by the individual players' names. Sharon included another class list with her letter and this one had served to record the children's Halloween masks. "Jack-o-Lantern" and "Frankenstein" together with an "orental princess" and a "O O U O C U U U V" (happy clown) were written by the children beside their names. If we add the way in which Sharon told us Sally used the list to record snack and lunches we have three very different literacy events taking place that require specific explanations of the children's participation (collaboration) in the dynamic construction of a self-organized problem-solving situation.

A single piece of paper might be used for multiple literacy events, and a single literacy event might lead to the production of multiple interpretations of the event. When David, a first grader in Lee Proctor's classroom, read *Cat on the Mat* by Brian Wildsmith, he spent several days making a model of the cat standing on the mat. Then, on October 16, he decided that he would write about it when he wrote his news. David wrote "I LC ROTH CAT/ O N T H M T" (I like reading *The Cat on the Mat*) (Figure 8). Later, on the same day, David wrote, "I L C M C P R t S" (I like making projects) (Figure 9). David shared both the book and the model with the rest of the children in his class and after school he invited his mother into his classroom and she brought his young brother with her and together they looked at the model and the book.

Figure 8 David's "I like reading The Cat on The Mat"

Figure 9: David's "I like making projects"

I had talked with Lee about the ways in which David interpreted Brian Wildsmith's book and a few days later I received a letter with a photograph of David reading to his mother and younger brother. Lee wrote:

I'm really intrigued with the observation of David's

understanding of the Cat on the Mat text. When he looked at the word card "cat" on October 12, he read "Cat Sat on the Mat," and repeated this assertion when I asked him again. He then read "cat" for "elephant," and had no idea about "goat." When I helped him with these, he quickly caught on to the fact that the words on the cards were for the animals in the story, and so he guessed the remaining animal names. (Problem-solving, by using classification skills!)

On October 16, he says/reads "cat" on the card and says, "I know what this is because I can spell "cat"; he then picks out and reads the cards for "sat" and "mat" (the cards are all facing up so he can scan the "universe"). Pointing to "goat" he asks "what's this letter called?" When I tell him "g" he reads "goat." He asks "is this a d?" Then he reads "dog" ... and this says 'cow.'"

When I ask him "what helps you to read?" he says "the first letters." I realize that part of the obstacle for him has been a problem with identifying the lower-case letters – an observation which informs my teaching.

But letter identification is only a small piece of what he is working on. He has figured out something funda-mental about the phonetic aspects of reading between October 10 and October 16, I think. He hasn't needed to do this when looking at the book because here he reads fluently, using the pictures and his memory for the syntax. But the vocabulary cards lead him through a gray area of sound/symbol representations, helping him to both isolate single words from the aural stream, and to figure out what they are.

I guess this excites me because I have the sense of being able to glimpse through a window to "see" his process.

In her letter Lee focused specifically upon the ways in which David appeared to be developing some understandings of how sounds and symbols go together. On an earlier occasion we had also spent some time talking about the model that David had made of the cat on the mat, and so Lee had sent a draft of a chapter she is writing for the book about the *Project*. Lee had marked the following passage with a red pen:

> At one point in the winter, I began to feel that the projects did not constitute a sufficiently "literary" form of response, and the energy level which went into their making seemed pretty high for a reading period. And so I shut down the project operation, and instituted written responses to stories. But with this dictum, every aspect of the process seemed to flatten. The choosing of books did not seem to be as spontaneous. Indecision and wandering increased. Energy went to less constructive actions. Share-times were not as interesting. We needed a Class Meeting to air feeling about my removal of the project option. When we agreed as a group to add written responses, and retain projects also, the zest seemed to return.

These examples of the information we are collecting serve to emphasize the importance of trying to "capture the complexity" of the richness and diversity of children's literacy experiences in classrooms that encourage the self-organization of problem-solving activities. Sometimes it is the "connectedness" of a series of literacy activities surrounding a single event such as reading a book, at other times it might be an odd incident that eventually leads to the discovery of a more general pattern. Since we have discussed Vicki's "Supr Moreo Brothrs" story Mary Yates has become increasingly aware of the use of technology by the children in her classroom. During a telephone conversation Mary talked about a book about aircraft engines that one of the girls in her class had written that day. Mary said that the girl's father was an aircraft engineer and that when she visited his office she played with a computer simulated aircraft engine. Mary said that the student explained that "by pressing the buttons she could move a pulley that pulled parts of the engine back and forth." The book the student wrote describes the differences between several aircraft engines and Mary has made a copy for the child's portfolio and written notes describing the conversation that she had with the child as they discussed aircraft technology.

If we try to synthesize the ways in which we are trying to "capture the complexity" of children's literacy development we can state that among us:

We are collecting as many artifacts as possible of the different types, uses, and forms of literacy that occur in our specific classroom settings.

- We are including examples of "family literacy" (notes and stories written at home), and "recess literacy" in our collections.
- We are keeping daybooks, learning logs, reading logs, and journals as a rich source of information.
- We are ignoring artificial boundaries between scientific, mathematical, and social forms of literacy by paying particular attention to the collection of information that illustrates the ways in which children use the technical, symbolic, social, and material resources at their disposal.
- We are paying particular attention to situationally specific, self-organized situations in which print is constitutive of a problem-solving activity.
- We are incorporating examples of the ways in which children use multiple forms of symbolism in the learning situations that they encounter – both in and out of school.
- We are making sure that the work collected in chil-

dren's portfolios is accompanied by detailed observational notes.

- We are making audio-recordings of children reading (usually self-selected) books. Our aim is to make three recordings for each child (September-October, January-February, May-June).
- We are experimenting with the use of video-recordings to capture specific literacy events – so that we can explore with children "what's happening" as they participate in some self-organized problem-solving activity.
- We are taking still photographs of children collaborating on projects, and generally participating in the literacy life of the classroom,
- We are keeping paintings, graphic productions, and three dimensional structures together with observational notes and photographs of the activities.
- We are including any examples of the above that the children themselves want to add to their portfolios.
- We are making a separate record of each child's comments upon his or her own literacy development, giving special attention to the child's analysis of his or her literacy portfolio.

3. Developing systems of analysis which reflect the multiple layers of interpretation that we are trying to incorporate in the biographic profiles that we are writing.

Describing the first chaos theorists, James Gleick (1989) writes:

They had an eye for pattern that appeared on different scales at the same time. They had a taste for randomness and complexity, for jagged edges and sudden leaps touch, to objects at human scale. Everyday experience and real pictures of the world have become legitimate targets for inquiry. (p. 47)

Although Gleick is writing about physicists and mathematicians he could very well be describing the holistic/process teachers participating in the *Biographic Literacy Profiles Project*, for they teach from the perspective of the learner and of necessity they have developed and continue to develop an eye for pattern which enables them to "see" from multiple perspectives the practical complexity of children's symbolic activity.

When teachers join the *Project* we emphasize that they should "take it easy," learn to look and learn to see, try to make some notes about every child, and begin to collect "data" that can be kept in each child's portfolio. But don't try to write biographic profiles for every child, write one or two, five max. It takes time to build a theoretical framework for observing children and even longer to learn how to observe. Even so, some teachers decide to write profiles for every child in their class. "How could I write them for some and not others?" a teacher will say. So in the end it is a personal decision and it is the teacher who must decide.

This year as we work together at our group meetings we are exploring ways of making the task more manageable. At one of our group meetings Leigh Walls, Sharron Cadieux, and Martha Dahl worked together. Each had brought with them their notes and the portfolio of one child. Their task was to help each other "see" more, to look in different ways, and to "push" each other's thinking. For a while I joined their group and listened to them as they worked. "We're taking notes on the notes," Martha said. They were reading the notes that Martha had written about a child in her kindergarten classroom. Although I never heard their exact questions, what they appeared to be asking each other was: "What's happening?" "How is this child constructing the forms of written language?" "How is this child using written language?"

I listened for a while and at one point Leigh said to me, "Although it seems like an extra step it really does make the process quicker." Then she added, "The structure came at the very end," and she showed me the grid that she had developed. Leigh's grid had ten "categories":

1. Graphics;
2. Oral Description;
3. Sight Words (subdivides into Reading Vocabulary and Independent Spelling Vocabulary;
4. Invented Spelling;
5. Types and Uses of Language;
6. Story Structure;
7. Skills;
8. Problem Solving;
9. Content-Variety (Sources/Inspiration); and
10. As you've probably guessed – Other.

I know that in presenting these categories for Leigh she would want to make it clear that she is not using these categories to look at children in her classroom. They are analytic categories developed to help discover patterns in the notes she has written and the children's work that she has collected. I want to emphasize that such categories are not intended to be used as a "check list." In the *Project* we often talk about the difficulties that arise when ways of studying and teaching children become packaged. I know I speak for many of my colleagues when I say that we are deeply concerned when process writing or holistic reading and writing practices are commercialized. Mass production changes both the philosophical and theoretical foundation of holistic/process teaching and learning and therefore changes the practical intent – it is not possible to commercialize learning from the point of view of the learner.

For me, one of the most exciting developments that has taken place is how the second year *Project* teachers have explored ways to make the process of writing profiles more manageable. Martha and Sharron teach in one school while Leigh teaches in another, Lee Proctor and Kathy Matthews are also in different schools and yet they have all begun to devise ways of analyzing the information that they are collecting about the individual children they teach. Lee Proctor has developed a grid. At the top of the sheet of paper she has written "Information for Literacy Profile," and beneath is a space for the child's name and the date of her analysis – later forms will provide Lee with the opportunity to "compare" her notes with the earlier notes that she has written. The paper is then divided into eight boxes –

1. Type /Use;
2. Content;
3. Graphics;
4. Structure;
5. Problem Solving;
6. Spelling;
7. Sight Words; and
8. Mechanics.

Kathy Matthews has developed a series of "grids" including one she uses to record developmental spelling patterns. She has also added further areas for analysis for reading and writing and these include such categories as "Cueing Systems" and "Self-Evaluation."

At the group meeting when Leigh, Sharron, and Martha explored the possibilities of analyzing the information that they had collected using the categories that we had been using in the *Project*, there was also a whole group discussion that focused upon the same topic. "There is no one way," Sharron Cadieux said. "I've found that whenever I come up with a system there is always an exceptional situation that doesn't fit." Leigh Walls continued, "This works for me but it might not work for you," as she showed the participants the small post-it notes that she writes as she analyzes each child's work. One of the notes that Leigh had written was to encourage a child to begin writing on the left side of the paper rather than the middle of the paper.

"Sometimes I write questions to myself," Leigh explained, "other times I write down things that I want to work on with a particular child."

The variations between the working strategies that the teachers have devised are explored whenever we meet, and teachers often make a note to try a way of working that a colleague has described. But whatever the differences between us, there is unanimous agreement that when we are working out what's happening in a child's literacy development we begin by reviewing all of the information that we have collected.

"Pile it on the table" is something that I have said on more than one occasion. Start in September with the first piece ... Systematically sort the stuff ... Look at the information in the order in which it was collected ... Look for patterns ... Recurring themes ... Significant changes ... Jagged edges ... Sudden leaps ... Pick representative examples of the child's work and use them to illustrate the particular statements that you are making when you are writing his or her biographic profile ... Problem-solve the multiple ways in which individual children are using print and try to reflect upon the complexity of the process ... But whatever I say, the ways in which the profiles are developed depends upon the individual literacy configurations of the teachers who are doing the analysis, their own local interpretations of global patterns, developed intuitively as well as analytically, sometimes with difficulty, sometimes with ease. No two profiles that they write are ever quite the same. However trivial the information may seem on the surface, the details of each child's literacy development are noted, for we learn from their uniqueness, and what makes them special makes teaching them worthwhile.

TEACHING, LEARNING, AND SCHOOLING: WHAT HAPPENS WHEN YOU MAKE A PARADIGM SHIFT?

Crucial Changes in Perspective

In "A New Way of Thinking: The Challenge of the Future," Sam Crowell writes:

> If we are to succeed in creating a new way of thinking, the focus must go beyond teaching practices. The structure of the school will be profoundly affected. The "school" cannot separate itself from learning. It is not merely a place or an organization; the school is teaching and learning. (p. 62)

Crowell's position is consistent with the definition of learning "environments," "settings," and "arenas" presented in the previous section of this report. However, knowing that the school is teaching and learning does not make it any easier for administrators and teachers. The power of teaching from the learners' perspective is that discontinuities between theory and practice are minimized – individual children become central to the educational process and decisions are made to support each child's learning. Betty Marston, a second/third grade teacher, puts it this way, "We are interested in teaching children but we are not interested in teaching them to fit into some mold." But the difficulty is that "the system" (State regulations, Federal laws) is not set up to support teaching from the learner's perspective. At the national level our educational system is driven by what Steven Jay Gould (1989) refers to when he writes about evolution as the "traditional hopes for progress and predictability" (p. 318).

We are not very good at dealing with the "immeasurable contingencies" of life and learning. We are expected to be accountable, and accountability is built into the system. We use standardized tests to make sure that teachers teach and children learn. At a recent conference a researcher told the audience that, in his state, merit pay for teachers was tied to the California Achievement Tests. How does this contingency affect teaching and learning? What pressures does such a policy put on teachers and how does it affect opportunities for them to teach and children to learn? And what about other contingencies?

In a recent report in Science News, Ralloff (1989) reports that:

> Children from low-income families who participate in the federally funded School Breakfast Program improve more on annual achievement tests than do classmates who qualify for the program but skip the school breakfast, new research shows. Though other studies have identified nutritional benefits from the subsidized breakfasts, this is the first to demonstrate the program's statistically significant impact on academic achievement ... (p. 247)

Does this mean that in some states merit pay is tied to whether children are well-fed or undernourished? I apologize if it seems I am making light of a serious matter, but it is essential that, in presenting the "effects" of the paradigm shift taking place in the *Project* (and in many other projects across the country), we recognize that anomalous and paradoxical practices are inherent in the system and that traditional notions of "progress and predictability" might not be in the best interests of the children whom we teach.

To overcome the difficulties that individual teachers face as they try to make changes in the ways in which they work with the children in their classrooms the institutional structure of schools has to change. Larry Cuban (1989) states:

> I fear that further disappointment lies around the corner unless policymakers, practitioners, researchers see that patterns of instruction, uses of technology, and treatment of students are heavily influenced by durable organizational structures that must be fundamentally changed, if neoprogressive notions about schooling are ever to be fully realized. (p. 222)

The adjective "neoprogressive" bothers me but I do agree with Cuban that if we are going to change the way in which we teach then many durable organizational structures must be fundamentally changed. Kathy Matthews said that from her own perspective what the *Project* was really about was "changing the ways in which teachers are allowed to change." In the next few pages through the voices of the teachers, administrators, parents, and children who are making the changes, I will present some of the changes that have taken and are taking place as we continually try to create opportunities for teachers to base instruction upon their observations of children.

Changes Taking Place from the Perspective of the Classroom Teacher

In her master's thesis which focuses upon assessment Sharron Cadieux writes:

> When I first returned to public education, I viewed
> assessment as a threat to how I wanted to teach. I
> wasn't using the school adopted basal reading program
> but had to give the end of the book tests. The first test I
> gave confirmed my fears. My students did not do well
> though I knew they were able to handle the concepts
> and certainly could read the words. Because they had
> not done the workbook pages they were ill equipped to
> take the test which followed the same format exactly.

> So I adopted a more defensive strategy (like any "ratio-
> nal teacher" according to Lorrie Sheppard, 1989). I
> showed my students how to function within the test
> format. If the test expected them to write numbers
> in front of sentences to indicate a sequential order,
> I found a workbook page with that format (one of
> many in a single workbook) and showed them how to
> do it. After that, they had no problem, though I had
> to devote a fair amount of instructional time to the
> process.

In a subsequent section of her thesis Sharron writes:

> In the past I felt that my approach to teaching was at
> risk if my students couldn't make the transition to
> decontextualized assessments. I no longer feel the
> need to "prove" that children can handle tradition-
> ally tested skills. I am moving from a defensive atti-
> tude toward assessment to a more constructive one. I
> feel assessment is valuable only if it provides insight
> into the child's knowledge and understanding of how
> language works. Such information can be used to guide
> a teacher's interactions with each student as well as
> document growth. One might argue that tests should
> be able to do these things, but they can't. The differ-

ence between tests and "assessment from the child's perspective" is both subtle and dramatic. The shift is from negative to positive, from what the child can't do to what she can do, from an adult's understanding of literacy to a child's understanding of literacy. For the first time I am beginning to feel hopeful that schools can move from an emphasis on the test to an emphasis on the child.

The position stated by Sharron is shared by most (I would say all) of the teachers and administrators participating in the *Biographic Literacy Profiles Project.* Like Sharron, many of the participants are experienced holistic/process teachers who have been striving for years to provide authentic learning experiences for children that (by definition) cannot be tied to the standardized programs and standardized tests that so many teachers are expected to use. The difficulty has been that they have needed a way to clearly articulate that the children that they teach are learning in far more complex ways than would be possible if they have been using the simulated teaching/learning activities that are presented in packaged programs. Building biographic profiles based upon observations of children's literacy behaviors has helped the participants in the project to become more confident in their abilities to explain.

Paradoxically, or perhaps ironically, as they have become more comfortable in presenting explanations of their teaching practices they have also become more "accountable" to children, to parents, and to the administrators in the districts in which they teach. In the last year we have shared the *Project* with more than a thousand teachers and administrators through workshops, seminars, and classroom visits, and we have become comfortable addressing the questions that we are asked. Mostly we share our own experiences and, as you have probably already guessed, we try to make sure that we do not suggest that we have the answer or even that an answer, as such, exists.

Changes Taking Place from the Perspective of Educators Who Provide Supportive Instructional Services

Mary Benton and I spent several hours talking on the telephone trying to work out how we could describe the children who receive support from teachers who are members of specialized instructional services. The descriptors used in many schools and in the literature have pejorative connotations that we want to avoid. Mary works in classrooms with children who have been referred because they need a little more support than they can receive from their classroom teacher. Alex was one boy whom Mary worked with (see the biographic profile on pp. 90-91). During the 1988-1989 school year Mary observed Alex and several other children in their classrooms and she also read books and wrote stories with them in a one-on-one setting. The profiles that Mary wrote were used in combination with the biographic profiles that were written by classroom teachers.

Mary explained that her profiles are not really biographic because although she observes in the classroom she is not in the room on an ongoing basis. "If a child has been referred we have to address the reasons for the referral," Mary spoke deliberately, "but in your mind you have to keep it in perspective because if you become too focused on reasons then you are back into the old model." I asked Mary if I could write that on her first day back in school last September she got rid of all the tests that she used to administer. "Sure," she said. "I have committed myself. I don't have any tests so I can't test. I lived with those for too many years. They don't serve any purpose and in the end I didn't know any more than I knew before. All you do is validate the numbers."

Then Mary went on to explain by talking about a child who had been tested. "Before we started using profiles," she said, the child had been given eight different tests: Kaufman ABC,

TOLD-P, EXP.O-WPT, WISC-R, Bender-Gestalt and Recall, PPTVT-R, and a Complete OT. "The recommendations told us nothing," Mary said. "If you use tests they just keep mushrooming. They don't provide the information – supposedly you'll come up with something [but] you don't, so even well-intentioned people get caught into 'Well one more test will tell us.'"

Mary then said she was in the middle of writing up a profile for a boy she had been observing who a doctor said "had" ADD (Attentional Deficit Disorder). "We're hoping that when we show all this other stuff that no one will think the label is applicable. I watched him for forty- five minutes as he wrote a story. He was completely focused on what he was doing. Hopefully we can show his family that. He focuses on lots of different things, listening to the teacher read a story, participating in group activities and in problem-solving situations. All he needs is to write more and to read more and in his classroom he is doing that." Mary finished up the conversation by saying that the "catch 22" was what happened when a student was receiving special services through public law 94.142. "Then you have no option. You have to test."

Terri Apgar works with Mary Benton and she is the one who does the testing for public law 94.142. "You're boxed in," Terri explains, "There's no way around it at the present time." Then she added, "The other problem is that you are time bound. You have forty-five calendar days to complete the evaluation. It's hard to watch the child and engage the child in meaningful activities within the time constraint."

This is the first year of Terri's participation in the *Project* and she is working in Lori Bresnahan's classroom collaborating with Lori. "I've also written a profile of a child who falls under the Federal umbrella," Terri said. She talked of "light weight" testing and of the way she had devoted her energies to observing the child she was evaluating. "Our staff takes real good care of children so basically you know, but you still have to test. I wish I was allowed to do what I can do without all the constraints. I've worked and made lots of notes. I did a lot of observing, watching, trying to catch something. The profile presents a more positive picture and provides tons more information than the test results."

Terri continued by saying, "The classroom teacher also developed a profile. They were very different, but you could see it was the same child." Like Mary, Terri then discussed the differences between the profiles that she is developing and the ones that the classroom teachers develop: "They're much more concentrated, one-on-one situations in both writing and reading." She talked about a child study meeting. "It's so nice to be able to say, 'Now let's talk about what he does when he picks up a book and actually reads it.'"

Changes Taking Place from the Perspective of the Principal

Ed Barnwell is the principal of two schools in the *Project* and you have met several of the teachers who work with him. In preparation for the book that we are writing Ed has written a chapter and with his permission I am going to quote from it here. Focusing upon "Teaching, Learning and Leading," Ed writes:

> In our school's journey, we've been led by the children into new approaches to many aspects of our school from teaching to curriculum development to support services to school leadership. Through our efforts to become more responsive to children, we are fundamentally changing our school.
>
> A multi-billion dollar industry churns out teaching materials and resources. Most of it is norm-referenced according to author and publisher concepts of what can most reasonably be expected of similarly graded kids in Oshkosh, Galveston, Concord, ... I am inher-

ently suspicious of these materials, not that there is necessarily anything wrong with them (many, in fact, are excellent resources), but that they contribute to false assumptions about our student populations. It seems that by adopting normed, graded materials, it can too easily be assumed that there must be an appropriate match between the materials and the needs of most students. More insidious is the built-in expectation that the children should fit into the expectations of the program or leveled material completion of a given set of materials, then we invite testing, screening, or opting children out of that context and into alternative programs with the well-intentioned aim of preventing school failure. If, however, we choose to measure school success in an individualized instead of group way, then we reverse the roles of responsibility – "failure" is then an institutional inability to respond to a child's need, not a childhood affliction. At our school, we are adopting a zero-failure attitude. Children can learn to different degrees, they can explore different interests, but they can't fail. We can fail by not providing the right environment or by not finding ways to reach each child. I think by shifting the burden of succeeding to the school we are becoming more respectful of diversity.

Later Ed talks about the teachers in the *Project*:

They know children can't be counted on to do what is expected based on group norms. They have the confidence and insights to make choices. These teachers aren't driven by test scores or the performance of other groups, including those they've had before children's voices tell them. They are becoming less reliant upon others' notions of what ought to be. They are dedicated to helping all children succeed.

I read this excerpt of Ed's chapter to Peter Sweet, another principal in the *Biographic Literacy Profiles Project*. He said that he agreed with what Ed had written. Although there are some differences in their philosophies, there is much that is the same. Peter shares Ed's deep concern for teachers, and as we talked he voiced some of his own concerns. He spoke of his experiences as the principal of a school in which the teachers have been involved in holistic/process education for many years. Peter said, "As a staff we have set a direction and established a philosophy." He talked about the dedication of the teachers, and then added, "I'm concerned about teacher burn out. One of the biggest difficulties is that teachers as professionals do not have control. They have less control of their professional lives than any other professional group. Everybody is an educational expert." Peter spoke of the steering committee for an upcoming conference on education, "There are twelve people on the committee and only one is a teacher. Change should be teacher initiated, teacher implemented, and teacher controlled. But teachers don't have the power."

We talked about the *Biographic Literacy Profiles Project*, and there is no doubt that both principals and teachers have accomplished many changes in the reorganization of class schedules to provide time for teachers both to work together and to work with me. However, the ways in which the institutions function within the much broader political framework of the system have not changed. Policy makers still require statistical proof that children are learning, as is evident by NAEP's preparations for the 1992 nation-wide testing of "fourth-grade reading." Peter went on to talk of his own concerns about the lack of support from the State Board of Education. He spoke of the different philosophy of the State Board and the effect of the difference on community support (or lack of support) for schools. "It's much easier to get the support of parents than non-parents. But sixty-two percent of the adult population in the state do not have children in school." Peter then added,

"For us it's getting to the point that they could make or break our school."

One more principal's voice adds to the complexity of the issues surrounding administrative support for and participation in the *Biographic Literacy Profiles Project*. This is Cathy Hamblett's second year as a principal in a school which is continuing the process of creating a more holistic approach to education. Cathy said that because she was just beginning her career as a principal, she was probably more "parochial" than Ed or Peter. She said that it has been important to her that we have been "up front" in the *Project* by being clear that what we are trying to accomplish will "take years and years." "What is so important is that it's supporting teachers. Giving teachers legitimacy as well as legitimizing children."

We talked for a while about Peter's concerns and I read to her what I had written. "A lot of the elementary standards are driven by numbers," Cathy said. "Very often the collection of statistical information drives funding. One of the biggest issues is that children have to be identified to receive special services." Cathy then talked about "local control": "In many districts it's a serious issue. Our school board supports process teaching."

We talked for a while, discussing the changes that Cathy and her teachers were making to support more holistic/process approaches to teaching and learning, and then Cathy said, "I think we have to show them that it can work at the local level and then share this with the State. Say, 'Okay, here is an alternative way of collecting information that tells us about kids learning.' We have to show them. Until then the State won't change."

Listening to Cathy I thought about Peter, and I wondered if years ago he would have agreed with her. I think that Cathy is correct when she says that experience separates her from principals like Peter, who for many years have participated in and supported the teacher initiated changes that have taken place in schools. For while Cathy is hopeful that the changes we are making might eventually lead to changes at both the State and

National levels, Peter is not so optimistic. He says, "Teachers don't have the power to institutionalize change."

Complexity Theory and the Reorganization of Schools

The *Biographic Literacy Profiles Project* began with a single child for whom small errors in teaching and testing, followed by repeated retesting had such a catastrophic effect that the school failed – afflicted by what Ed Barnwell refers to as "an institutional inability" to respond to the child's educational needs (Taylor, 1988). The first biographic profile was written for this child, and although the school that he attended did not take the descriptions of his observable literacy behaviors into consideration or use the information as a basis for his instruction in reading and writing, a group of teachers from another school became interested in the profile and asked if it would be possible for them to write literacy profiles for their first grade children. One school participated in the early, tentative steps, which eventually led to the development and implementation of the research project in six other schools. At the present time 47 teachers and administrators and approximately 1,000 children are participating in the project, and so I can write that although we were unable to change the system for a single child, a single child is changing the system. This is important, for at a time when so many of us are overwhelmed by the mass testing of children, which is mandated through Federal laws and State regulations, this young child has taught us that "individual activity is not doomed to insignificance" (Prigogine & Stengers, 1984).

Essentially, the *Project* is about this child and the many other individual children who have taught us to seriously question the notion of "objective" reality by helping us "make visible" the complexity of symbolic activity in their everyday lives. We have learned that "scientific paradigms can exercise a strong influence on prevailing thought" (Prigogine & Stengers, 1984), and that the dominant societal and political educational ideology is driven by traditional hopes for progress and predictability that might not be in the best interests of children. Based both upon my own research experience and upon my participation in the *Project*, I would argue that we are irrevocably altering the lives of young children when we impose upon them our traditional aberrant theories and educational practices. Somewhere along the way we have forgotten that "the playground of contingency is immeasurable" (Gould, 1989), and that in the lives of young children we must learn to look at the ordinary and mundane events if we are to see the remarkably rich and subtle complexity of their symbolic behavior.

In *Seeing Voices*, Oliver Sacks writes, "It is all too easy to take language, one's own language, for granted – one may need to encounter another language, or rather another mode of language, in order to be astonished, to be pushed to wonder, again" (1989, p. ix). This is the purpose of our study. We are trying to push beyond our own training in the "objective" reality of the present educational system in order to be astonished by the irreducible plurality of functions and forms of language that children use in their everyday lives and, especially for us as teachers, in classroom settings. As we push each other to recognize the wonderful complexity and uniqueness of the symbol-weaving behaviors of children, we are also trying to build the professional expertise and specialized knowledge that will enable us to work with every child in ways that ensure "individual activity is not doomed to insignificance" within the classrooms and schools in which we teach. We have learned that to make such a shift in thinking is a slow process, and that we ourselves must engage in the situationally specific problem-solving activity of learning to teach from the perspective of the child. There are no "step-by-step" or "classroom-tested strategies" (as is suggested by a flyer for a writing program that I have just received in the mail) – just teachers and administrators dedicated to professionalism and with in-depth knowledge of the specific social, symbolic, technical, and material resources, the complexly patterned contingencies, that are constitutive of children's literacy learning in classroom settings.

Within this reflexive framework:

1. Teachers are encouraged to explore their own literacy configurations and to share the ways in which they use print in their everyday lives with the children that they teach.

2. Teachers are supported as they work to recognize their own expertise, and their professional opinions are supported when decisions are being made about the education of the children that they teach.

3. Teachers are provided with opportunities to increase their understanding of the ways in which children reconstruct the functions, uses, and forms of written language.

4. Teachers *work together* to explore their own literacy configurations, to share their expertise, to help each other develop new understandings, to share viewpoints on specific issues, and to work together on the construction of biographic literacy profiles for the children that they teach.

5. Principals participate with teachers in the development of organizational structures which support the focus upon teaching, learning, and schooling *from the perspective of the learner.*

6. Principals provide opportunities for teachers to receive on-going support in their classrooms, at *Project* meetings, and in summer institutes.

7. Principals provide opportunities for parents to meet with teachers to learn about the project and to explore the way in which their children are learning about literacy as they learn to *use* literacy.

8. Principals themselves are actively involved in the construction of one or more biographic profiles, so that they have personal understanding of the

practical significance of this approach to instructional assessment.

It is this collaboration – of teachers and principals – that has made the *Project* possible. Credit also needs to go to the local school districts for their financial support of the *Project* for, although the State Department of Education gave their approval, no money has been given to the schools and only limited funds have been made available for two three-day summer institutes and for six seminars to disseminate information about the project throughout the State.

Perhaps it may seem inappropriate to comment on this lack of support within the context of the presentation of the theoretical framework and practical significance of the project. But from the perspective of many of the teachers it is important, for they spend their own time on the *Project* and participants have often stated that much more could be accomplished if monies were made available. We can only hope that eventually as more emphasis is placed upon the reorganization of schools, financial support will be provided at both the state and federal levels. In the meantime, it is important to emphasize that, although State Department support has been limited, Helen Schotanus, the only consultant at the Department with the assignment of early childhood education and reading, has played a major role in the *Project*. She has organized meetings and supported us in many different ways and in such an unobtrusive fashion that I think we sometimes take her for granted. But it is Helen who works, side-by- side with us, and so often reminds us that "a child's first experience in school should not be in a testing situation."

Complexity Theory and the Restructuring of Educational and Political Practice

In a recent article in *Education Week*, Rothman (1989) writes that the governing board of the National Assessment of

Educational Progress is "entering one of the most emotional and diverse debates in education ... [as it is] creating objectives for its 1992 4th grade reading test." Rothman quotes the chairman of the NAEP panel as stating that "getting agreement will take quite a lot of palaver ... [as] primary-grade reading is probably the stage of reading that is most controversial in America (p. 7)." Rothman then illustrates the controversy by quoting the opposing views of two prominent "reading" researchers: should we be testing "word-recognition skills," or using a test which would "minimize the gap between what readers do when they read and what they do on the test (p. 7)." I would argue that this is the wrong controversy, for these two opposing views do not represent the views of many educators, both researchers and teachers, who find the suggestion that "fourth grade reading" can be tested to be scientifically indefensible and, speaking for myself, politically reprehensible. For while we go through the palaver of finding an appropriate reading test, other democratic nations are seeking alternative ways of assessing literacy – based upon scientific evidence (and common sense) that clearly indicates that the complexity of children's symbolic learning cannot be categorized and then encapsulated in some test.

In *Assessment for Better Learning*, the report on assessment presented by the New Zealand Department of Education (1989), the following statement is made:

> In assessment of learning, it is doubtful that numbers or grades can be thought of as anything more than rough estimates of the things they seem to measure. All assessments of learning include subjective judgments and, as such, are inevitably liable to bias and error. The notions, for example, that IQ is an accurate measure of human thought or that a socio-economic index precisely defines the social condition of a family not only ignore this subjectivity but deny human uniqueness. We have no ruler for human thought and must accept the limits forced on us by this fact. (p. 9)

In this country, the *National Association for the Education of Young Children* also supports this position, and although some may say that the following excerpts from the position statement published by NAEYC (1988) applies only to younger children, I would strongly argue that it applies to all children. Childhood is not a coat that kids "take off" when they reach fourth grade. *In Testing of Young Children: Concerns and Cautions, NAEYC* states:

> Mass standardized testing of young children is potentially harmful to children educationally. Testing narrows the curriculum. Inevitably teachers teach to the test. Many of the important skills that children need to acquire in early childhood – self-esteem, social competence, desire to learn, self-discipline – are not easily measured by standardized tests. As a result, social, emotional, moral, and physical development and learning are virtually ignored or given minor importance in schools with mandated testing programs.

> Testing programs also harm children intellectually. Where test scores are stressed, the curriculum is often designed to ensure that children memorize facts and figures that can be easily addressed by a multiple-choice test. More challenging intellectual pursuits such as reading for information, composing stories, problem solving, and creative thinking are given less emphasis. But these abilities will be even more important in the future. Children need to learn how to learn, so that they are prepared to function in an ever-changing American society. ... Standardized testing seldom provides information beyond what teachers and parents already know. The systematic observations of trained teachers and other professionals, in conjunction with information obtained from parents

and other family members, are the best sources of information. (p. 9)

To "move" beyond the debate, it is essential that researchers and educators reexamine the "scientific" assumptions on which testing (irrespective of whether the tests emphasize word-recognition or comprehension) is based. This means reevaluating the existing dominant theoretical framework, which is based upon notions of "objective reality" and inevitably leads to "reductionism," and giving consideration to the development of a theoretical framework that acknowledges that our interpretations of language (and life) cannot be reduced to a series of competing "logical" structures or linear stage-theories. Prigogine and Stengers (1984) state:

> In view of the complexity of the questions raised here, we can hardly avoid stating that the way in which biological and social evolution has traditionally been interpreted represents a particularly unfortunate use of the concepts and methods borrowed from physics – unfortunate because the area of physics where these concepts and methods are valid was very restricted, and *thus the analogies between them and social or economic phenomena are completely unjustified.* (p. 207, emphasis added)

The unfortunate consequences of the plagiarism of physical science paradigms for use in social science research is made evident by Turner (1989) in his re-analysis of the research studies that were used, and are still being used in the reading field's "Great Debate" (see Carbo, 1988, and Chall, 1989). Turner writes of the "patched-up program evaluations," "randomized field experiments," and "laboratory experiments" all of which have severe limitations, and many of which (I would say all) are fundamentally flawed. Again, it is the wrong debate. In taking paradigms from the physical sciences and applying them to the study of complexly structured human behaviors, we have had to resort to complicated simplifications and these have resulted in the creation of pathologies – not in the lives of children as is so often stated in our medicalized textbooks on learning – but in the ways in which we do science and study human learning.

The irony is that while the education field still uses the notion of "objective reality," the physical sciences have long since abandoned the idea (Gleick, 1987; Johnson, 1989). Prigogine and Stengers (1984) write of the "irreducible multiplicity of representations," which they state:

> ... implies a departure from the classical notion of objectivity, since in the classical view the only 'objective' description is the complete description of *the system as it is*, independent of how it is observed. ... No single theoretical language articulating the variable to which a well-defined value can be attributed can exhaust the physical content of a system. Various possible languages and points of view about the system may be complementary. They all deal with the same reality, but it is impossible to reduce them to one single description complementarity, a lesson that can perhaps be transferred to other fields of knowledge, consists in emphasizing the wealth of reality, which overflows any single language, any single logical structure. *Each language can express only a part of reality.* (p. 225, emphasis added)

If we try to study and teach from the perspective of the learner, then the everyday lives of children provide practical demonstrations of the position held by Prigogine and Stengers. The diversity of complex social behavior demands that we acknowledge the multiplicity of representations that, even when combined in complimentary descriptions (biographic profiles) of children's learning, only "capture" a brief glimpse of the complexity of the symbol–weaving that takes place in the problem-solving situations as children reconstruct the functions, uses, and forms of written language. If we look and then learn to see, perhaps at some future date we will come to realize the catastrophic effect that our traditional plans for progress and predictability have upon the lives of children. When we politicize learning and make "state-by-state comparisons of reading achievement scores" (Rothman, 1989), we leave administrators and teachers with no alternative but to teach to the test. Children's lives are altered, drilled, and skilled – the natural rhythm of their learning is changed to a solemn beat.

Writing about recent research on the heart, Browne (1989) reports that scientists have found that "a healthy heart must beat somewhat chaotically rather than in a perfectly predictable pattern." The caption reads, "A 'healthy heart dances,' but a dying one 'can merely march.'" In schools across the country children "merely march," as they try to keep in step with the perfectly predictable patterns of the deadly teach-test beat. But it does not have to be this way. In many schools teachers and administrators are working to keep children's learning alive. Often unrecognized, teachers are providing practical demonstrations that in public schools we can work from the child's perspective, and teachers can create classroom environments which support and enhance the literacy learning that takes place when children participate in the self-organization of complex problem-solving situations. In the *Biographic Literacy Profiles Project*, we have already shown and continue to show that such teaching and learning is disciplined and systematic. We can cope with complexity, and we can use it to ensure that children have the opportunity to participate in an educational community that will prepare them for the complexity of the learning situations they will encounter as they learn new dances and step out to a new beat.

POSTSCRIPT: TEACHING AS A SUBVERSIVE ACTIVITY

On September 16, 1991, I wrote the following memo to the members of the *Biographic Literacy Profiles Project*:

> In the last couple of years I think that we have begun to understand that the *Biographic Literacy Profiles Project* (affectionately known as "BLIPP") is as much about ourselves as it is about children. It is about teachers developing personal theories, about teachers using their practical knowledge and theoretical expertise, and about teachers recognizing themselves, and being recognized by others, as professionals in their classrooms, schools, and communities.

> Our realization that research by teachers is a significant way of knowing about teaching and learning is shared by Susan Lytle and Marilyn Cochran-Smith, who writes in a paper entitled "Teacher Research as a Way of Knowing" of the reconceptualization of *knowledge for teaching* that occurs when teachers are the ones who are doing the research. What follows are some key ideas from the paper written by Susan and Marilyn. They state:

> 1. We are arguing that we need to develop a different

theory of knowledge for teaching, a different epistemology that regards inquiry by teachers themselves
as a distinctive and important way of knowing about
teaching.

2. What is worth knowing about teaching would
    include what teachers, who are researchers in their
    own classrooms, can know through systematic
    subjectivity.

3. In this different epistemology, teacher research,
    currently marginalized in the field, would contrib-
    ute to a fundamental reconceptualization of the
    notion of knowledge for teaching.

Susan and Marilyn go on to write about teacher
inquiry as a way for teachers to know their own knowledge, and they present six cases (stories) of teachers'
explorations. Within this context Susan and Marilyn
write of classrooms as *sites of inquiry.*

When we observe children and write descriptions of
their observable literacy behaviors we are creating
critical sites of inquiry in our classrooms and in our
schools. This is what BLIPP is all about. Learning
to observe children and then learning to construct
descriptions of their observable literacy behaviors
encourages us to look at ourselves and our personal
and shared ways of knowing. It's amazing stuff when
you stop to think about it!

It is now February 1992, and I have been rereading *Teaching
Without Testing* and reflecting on the memos that I have written
over the past few years to the teachers who have participated
in the project. What impresses me most is the optimism of my
writing. I really did believe that there was enough flexibility in
the system for project teachers to work as researchers in their
own classrooms. I know that the teachers believed this too. We
were both disciplined and systematic. We based instruction

on children's observable behaviors, we documented students' progress, and we accounted for the ways in which students were learning to read and write in school. They learned in authentic problem-solving situations that took into account the plurality of literacies that they would need to fully participate in American Society. Ours was a democratic ideal, theoretically grounded and practically situated, an "ad hoc-racy" whose practices were both excellent and equitable. We based instruction on what children could do, on our observations of their learning, and we tried to expand upon their understandings of themselves as learners. Above all we honored diversity, knowing that it was our combined interests, skills, and abilities that would enable children to work collaboratively in ways that would prepare them for the rapidly changing world of the twenty-first century.

If this seems to be a romantic picture, remember that we worked together at the time when the playwright Vaclav Havel became president of Czechoslovakia. It was a brief moment of unexpected opportunity. And so, as the Berlin Wall was chipped away, we chipped away at the dogma of standardized instructional practice and bureaucratic procedure that had ascribed pathological conditions to children and that had forced many young people to drop out of the system. Bathed in the events that were taking place in the world, we began to think that the ideal of democratic education was within our reach. But as I said, it was a brief moment in time.

In every school district in which I am presently working there has been an increased interest in testing students. In one school district, the teachers were told that the Gates-McGinitie reading test would be administered to *all* students beginning with first grade. The teachers were not consulted about the decision. In this same school district, the decision was made that there were too many second-grade teachers, so one of the teachers was "redesignated" as a "permanent substitute teacher" one month after the beginning of the school year. Her students were divided up and sent to the remaining second-grade class-rooms. In another school district, massive budget cuts mean that project teachers do not even know if they will have jobs next year. And in yet another district, the hiring of a new school superintendent resulted in a change in administrative policies and a new emphasis on teaching to prepare students for the California Achievement Tests.

The CATs became an issue for another school district when the State Board of Education denied the request of one of the project schools to continue working a four-day week. The four-day week (students' instructional time was from 8:00 a.m. until 3:30 p.m.) had been in place for ten years. One Friday a month was reserved by teachers for curriculum planning meetings and in-service education: on most other Fridays teachers went to school to participate in ad hoc meetings, to review students' work, and to plan events for the following school week.

Peter Sweet, who is principal of the school, told me that when the State Board of Education was reviewing their request to continue the four-day week, both teachers and parents had reflected on the benefits of the arrangement. Peter said that since 1985, *not one student* who had received the majority of his or her education at the elementary school had subsequently dropped out of high school. Every student had finished school! Teachers found there was more time for collaboration both with other faculty members and with students, parents overwhelmingly approved of the arrangement, and the community was supportive. The State School Board was provided with all of this information, and yet without visiting the school when classes were in progress, and without consulting the teachers (who include Mary Benton, Kathy Matthews, and Bruce Turnquist, whom you have read about earlier in this book), the Board arbitrarily reorganized the school week because of the CAT results, which the Board felt should be higher. No consideration was given to the lack of emphasis placed on these tests by the school. The tests were administered solely as a state requirement that had to be fulfilled. The test results did nothing to enhance any instructional practices, so no emphasis was placed on their administration, and no relevance was ascribed to the test results by the school.

In an article on the school that was published in *Principal* in September 1991, researcher Helen Featherstone asks if the shift to the four-day week transformed the school. She writes, "Is the fruitful use of free time an essential precondition-or a product-of change?" After participating in the Project, my answer is that "free" time is both a precondition and a product of change. Change takes place in schools when teachers work in environments in which they can identify problems and explore solutions. This takes time.

Ironically, as Helen Featherstone's article on the four-day week was published, the teachers and children returned to the school to begin a new year of five-day weeks. The effect on the teachers has been devastating. The day is fractured, and they have less time to meet. As one teacher put it, "People don't get together to talk anymore. The sense of isolation is really strong." From my conversations with the teachers in the school, it would seem that the biggest difficulty is that the State Board's decision (like so many recent decisions in project schools) challenges the teachers' professional identity. Decisions are being made that critically affect the ways in which they teach, and yet they themselves are not a part of the decision-making process.

In project schools across New Hampshire, decisions about the standardization of programs and student assessment are being made without the opinions of teachers being taken into consideration. Their voices don't count, so veteran teachers who have worked all of their professional lives to improve the quality of education for their students are talking about the futility of that commitment. One such teacher spoke of the "uncertainty" and of "feeling threatened." She said, "We are not being supported by the administration, and we've become locked into standardized tests that don't assess what we need to know about children." Other teachers talk of "survival," of "emotional exhaustion," of their "frustration," and of their lives being "out of control." Some schools are more affected than others, but as one teacher commented when she read what I was writing, "the scenarios are different, but the stories are basically all the same."

Like Peter Sweet, most of the principals of the Project have supported the teachers and children by taking an active role in the political decision-making process at both the local and state levels. At the present time, Cathy Hamblett is actively opposing the development of a statewide third-grade testing program. This week she testified before New Hampshire's House and Senate Education Subcommittees. She spoke to them of the ways in which teachers in her school worked with the children in their classrooms, and she spoke of the ways in which they are assessing children's learning. Later, Cathy talked of trying to act as a "buffer" between the teachers in her school and the policy makers who are making critical decisions that affect the ways in which children are learning in school.

The proposed statewide testing about which Cathy testified came to our attention in the summer of 1991. On July 8 of that year the New Hampshire State Board of Education sent a memo to the Commissioner of Education proposing that the reading skills of all third grade children be tested. It is difficult to ignore the coercive language contained in this statement. The Board outlined its intentions as follows:

> Using in-house knowledge, The Governor's Task Force Report and the National Goals as anchors, the Department will be asked to issue a set of *rigorous* objectives. These objectives should identify *concrete areas of knowledge* and detailed description of skills that *must be* mastered by the completion of the primary grades, thereby insuring future academic success. (p. 2)

At the request of the State Board of Education, a task force was created to "develop a detailed plan and schedule of activities for a statewide assessment program" (Marston, 1992, p. 2, emphasis added). There were subcommittees on reporting results, on objectives and standards, and on assessment tools (which in the report of the task force was noted in brackets to be the subcommittee on tests). The task force recommended "mastery and performance tests" in reading, language, and mathematics to be administered to all third-grade children – which was the recommendation of the State Board even *before* the task force was formed. At a meeting held at the legislative offices in Concord on January 29, 1992, members of the task force presented their plan to the House and Senate Education Committees. Among the reasons that were given for the administration of statewide tests at the end of the third-grade year was that the test results could be used by school districts to identify children who needed remediation *before* they took the national tests in fourth grade.

Teachers from the *Project* are writing letters and testifying in an attempt to change the minds of the legislature, which, we are told, is quite likely to support statewide third-grade testing. The teachers know it will be an uphill battle to persuade the committees, because at the local, state, and national level testing has become a national fetish that, Michelle Fine argues, fills public talk, shapes public policy and inhibits public imagination (see Fine, 1990; 1992). Many of the children that have participated in the *Project* will pass the test, but many of the children with whom we work will not. As with other tests that are administered to them, the ways in which they learn will go unnoticed. They will be tested, then remediated, and then retested and re-remediated until they reach a point when they realize that they are excluded from participation in school, so they will drop out, disadvantaged by the social inequality of such a system.

Perhaps it is from witnessing at first hand what happens

to children who do not "make the grade" on standardized tests that keeps teachers from returning to old ways of teaching. In a letter to me one teacher writes, "I don't want to return to the old safe way-the sequential skills taught in isolation, the small pull-out groups [of children] that all need the same treatment to fix their problems. I have been encouraged to think, to learn, and to apply what I have come to know." In a telephone call another teacher says, "Everything has changed, but I can't go back," and then talks about the new emphasis on basals and end-of-unit tests, which she refuses to use. She says, "I'm not afraid. 1 can substantiate what I'm doing. The training and philosophy work."

Last night I telephoned Kathy Matthews and shared what I was writing in this postscript. When I got to the piece about the four-day week, she said that she felt that it was important to add that while no emphasis was placed on the California Achievement Tests by the school, it *had* administered the Stanford Achievement Tests, which was one of the state criteria for monitoring children's progress. "The Board ignored the results of those tests," she said, "and focused on the California Achievement Tests instead." When I reached the end of the last paragraph Kathy commented, "It's hard to undo the thinking about children's strengths and start thinking about their weaknesses." Then, speaking specifically about the project, she said, "It's made a difference for us and it's made a difference for the kids, but given the ways in which educational decisions are made, the reality of making it work is overwhelming." Kathy added, "I'd finally reached a point where I could be the teacher I wanted to be. How can they make me regress? Would they ask a physician to go back ten years?"

At a project meeting that we held last year, one state official who had come to make a presentation commented that we should "go underground." I have often thought about this advice, especially when I listen to teachers and principals who speak of the changes imposed on them at both the state and local levels. There is no doubt that for some, teaching has become a subversive activity. But we still have not "gone underground." Our work continues. We are developing new note-taking procedures, new literacy analysis grids, and new ways of documenting the complexity of problem solving. We have focused our attention on literacy and the mental health of young children, and on developing biographic literacy profiles of children that illustrate the ways in which children who have been sexually and physically abused use print to help them cope with the uncertainties in their everyday lives. As we have focused on children about whom we are seriously concerned, we have found that even five-year-olds in kindergarten have literacy configurations that they use to help them cope with the critical events that have taken place in their young lives.

We are also focusing our attention on developing alternative assessment procedures for children who have entered the special education loop. Working collaboratively, we are collecting information about children as they participate in their regular classrooms. Our observations have become more focused and our note-taking procedures more intensive, but the process is essentially the same. Once these data are collected, decisions are made about other forms of data that may be required. We have made videos of children participating in specific learning activities, and we have made audio recordings of conversations, which provide children with the opportunity to reflect on learning tasks. Most important, we talk with children, we ask them about the ways in which they are learning, and we ask them about what help they themselves think they need. On several occasions, the data we have collected has been used by the school's child study team as they have considered whether or not to code a child. The results of these efforts have been mixed. Sometimes it is hard to convince a school psychologist that the difficulties a child is encountering are socially constructed, especially when the psychologist listens to an alternative assessment presentation and then dismisses it by putting the WISC on the table and saying, "Now let's look at the hard data." But still we have not given up, for on other occasions changes *have* been made that provide new opportunities for children to learn in school. This semester we are continuing to develop new procedures, and we are trying to present our findings in ways that make sense to other professionals who presently don't share our philosophy of children's learning. As Kathy Matthews says, "It takes an audience that is willing to listen."

Fortunately, there are some policy makers and educators who *are* willing to listen. In California, the State Department of Education is developing alternative assessment procedures for special education, and I have been talking with California policy makers about the teacher-researchers with whom I am working in New Hampshire. They have read *Teaching Without Testing*, they are interested in instructional assessment, and they are exploring the possibilities presented by the ideas. In Hawaii, approximately 180 Chapter One teachers participated in an institute that focused on the ways in which we are collecting information about children. At that institute, Dr. Donald Enoki told the teachers that if change is going to take place, it is teachers who will make the changes. Dr. Enoki told the teachers attending the institute that they were "one of the educational system's most valuable assets." He said:

> Your role as teacher-researchers is extremely important. ... No longer can we depend on what others have told us about our children's progress- the test makers, the test publishers, and the psychometricians. We know that only what classroom teachers have developed, taught, and assessed are the true and meaningful measures of what a student knows and doesn't know. (pp. 4-5)

What teachers do actually matters. Their ideas count. They are agents for change in our schools. However tough the situation, however subversive the activity becomes, trying to see the world from the child's perspective has changed our minds.

Our ways of seeing are democratic. Unfortunately, they are not bureaucratic. Except in rare circumstances, I no longer believe that it is possible to be both, because when it becomes bureaucratic the struggle is not about pedagogy, it's about power. About who controls the activities that occur in schools. About who controls who participates in American society. About who controls the power base of the twenty-first century. In a telephone conversation, Kathy said that what is happening is that policy makers are redefining public schools to keep control in a very few hands. The way to tighten this control is to institute more tests that both define the curriculum and restrict innovative practices at the local level (i.e., teacher research). Kathy says, "It's easy for policy makers to talk about innovation, but it would be difficult for them to let it occur." What Kathy says makes sense. To allow innovation to occur, policy makers would have to give up control and share with teachers the responsibility for what happens to children in school. They would have to live with the uncertainty of knowing that it is teachers and children who are the agents of change, who will be working together to create an educational system that is both excellent and equitable. Children who are poor and children of color would have a chance to succeed. Their voices would be heard. Children whose young lives have been damaged by life's circumstances would have the opportunity to recover. *All* children would have the opportunity both to define problems and to solve problems, and they would have the opportunity to work collaboratively with diverse groups of people in ways that would allow them to be a part of the democratic ideal.

It is now December 1992. The New Hampshire State School Board (an appointed, autonomous body) continues to insist on the development of a series of tests to be administered to third-grade students in New Hampshire's public schools. The State School Board has also decided to cut the minimum standards of education in the state. Because of the inequities in school funding (per-pupil expenditures ranges from $2,899 to $9,554), there is no doubt that children living in property-poor districts will suffer because of the Board's irresponsible actions. Project teachers have joined other teachers across the state who are protesting these cuts, but their voices go unheard. Judy Thayer (who was originally appointed by former governor John Sununu and is now the chair of the State Board) has made it clear that she considers teachers nothing more than a special interest group. She said, "They are special interest because they get paid by the system. They are people who have something to gain or lose by this proposal." It is difficult for me to imagine project teachers as a "special interest" group except as a group with a special interest in helping children. To paraphrase Pat Shannon, the struggle continues.

PARTICIPANTS IN THE BIOGRAPHIC LITERACY PROFILES PROJECT

Ten Apgar, Jody Baker, Ed Barnwell, Laurie Barr, Mary Benton, Debbie Boisvert, Lori Bresnahan, Sharron Cadieux, Linda Carter, Sue Caswell, Sally Codd, Martha Dahl, Kathy Donovan, Lisa Drogue, Brenda Eaves, Davita Fortier, Ruthanne Fyfe, Terry Grady, Cathy Hamblett, Betty Jack, Shirley Joyce, Karen May, Marcy Mager, Bob Magher, Betty Marston, Kathy Matthews, Bonnie Mulcahy, Patty Nicols, Joanne Parise, Donna Parmenter, Sue Phillips, Prudence Potter, Carla Press, Lee Proctor, Helen Schotanus, Nancy Shute, Ann Marie Spack, Katherine Sullivan, Susan Sullivan, Peter Sweet, Bruce Turnquist, Mary Yates, Leigh Walls, Linda Walsh, Sharon Williams, Regina Woodland, and Nancy White.

We would like to thank the parents of the children in the six schools participating in the *Project* for their support and encouragement. We appreciate the opportunity we have been given to include examples of their children's work in this report. In presenting the biographic profiles, all names have been changed. However, on some occasions, when particular biographic literacy events are described, first names have been used with parental permission. We would also like to take this opportunity to thank the members of the local school boards for providing the financial support necessary for the schools to participate in the project.

WORKS CITED AND PROJECT BIBLIOGRAPHY

(1989). *Assessment for better learning: a public discussion document.* Department of Education, Wellington, New Zealand.

Atwell, N. (1987). *In the middle: writing, reading, and learning with adolescents.* Upper Montclair, NJ: Boynton/Cook Publishers.

Barnes, D. (1976). *From communication to curriculum.* Middlesex, England: Penguin Books.

Brown, R. (1989). Testing and thoughtfulness. *Educational Leadership*, (April), 31-33.

Browne, M. (1989). In heartbeat predictability is worse than chaos. New York Times, (January 17), C9.

Cadieux, S. (1989). *Assessment in a process oriented classroom: practice, dangers and potential.* Unpublished Master's Thesis, Antioch College, New Hampshire.

Carbo, M. (1988). Debunking the great phonics myth. *Phi Delta Kappan*, (November), 226-240.

Carraher, T. (1986). From drawings to buildings: working with mathematical scales. *International Journal of Behavioral Development, 9*, 527-544.

Carraher, T., Carraher, D., & Schliemann, A. (1985). Mathematics in the streets and in schools. *British Journal of Developmental Psychology, 3,* 21- 29.

Chall, J. (1989). Learning to read: the great debate: twenty years later - a response to debunking the great phonics myth. *Phi Delta Kappan,* (March), 521-538.

Coles, G. (1987). *The learning mystique: a critical look at learning disabilities.* New York: Pantheon Books.

Crowell, S. (1989). A new way of thinking: the challenge of the future. *Educational Leadership,* (September), 60-63.

de la Rocha, O. (1985). The reorganization of arithmetic practice in the kitchen. *Anthropology and Education Quarterly, 16,* 193-198.

Doll, W. (1989). Complexity in the classroom. *Educational Leadership,* (September), 65-70.

Duckworth, E. (1987). *The having of wonderful ideas & other essays on teaching & learning.* New York: Teachers College Press.

Dyson, A. (1986). Transitions and tensions: interrelationships between the drawing, talking, and dictating of young children. *Research in the Teaching of English, 20,* 379-409.

Enoki, D. (1992). Introductory remarks made at a chapter one four day institute. Honolulu (January).

Featherstone, H. (1991). The rewards of a four-day school week. *Principal* (September) 71(1):28-31.

Ferreiro, E. (1984). The underlying logic of literacy development. In H. Goelman, et al. (Eds), *Awakening to literacy.* Exeter, NH: Heinemann Educational Books.

Fine. M. (1990). The public in public schools; the social constriction/construction of a moral community. *Journal of Social Issues* 46(1):107-19.

Fine. M. (1992). Deconstructing the 'at risk' high school

population: public controversies and subjugated non controversies. In R. Wollens, ed. *Children at Risk.* Albany, NY: SUNY Press.

Gardner, H. (1985). *Frames of mind: the theory of multiple intelligences.* New York: Basic Books.

Geertz, C. (1983). *Local knowledge: further essays in interpretive anthropology.* New York: Basic Books.

Genishi, C. (1985). Observing communicative performance in young children. In A. Jaggar & M. Smith-Burke (Eds.), *Observing the language learner.* Urbana, IL: IRA/NCTE.

Gleick, J. (1987). *CHAOS: making a new science.* New York: Penguin Books.

Gleick, J. (1989). Chaos. *Teacher Magazine*, September/October, 46-49.

Goelman, H., Oberg, A., & Smith, F. (Eds.). (1984). *Awakening to literacy.* Exeter, NH: Heinemann Educational Books.

Goodman, K., Shannon, P., Freeman, Y, & Murphy, S. (1988). *Report card on basal readers.* Katonah, NY: Richard C. Owen Publishers.

Goodman, Y, Watson, D., & Burke, C. (1987). *Reading miscue inventory: alternative procedures.* New York: Richard C. Owen Publishers.

Gospodarek, Fran. (1989). Conway school board hears special ed report. Carroll County Independent, (September 20), A8.

Gould, S. (1989). *Wonderful life: the Burgess Shale and the nature of history.* New York: W. W. Norton.

Graves, D. (1984). *A researcher learns to write.* Exeter, NH: Heinemann Educational Books.

Green, J. & Wallat, C. (1981). *Ethnography and language in educational settings.* Norwood, NJ: Ablex Publishing Corporation.

Greene, M. (1978). *Landscapes of learning.* New York: Teachers College Press.

Griffin, D. (1988). *The reenchantment of science: postmodern proposals.* Albany, NY: State University of New York Press.

Hall, N. (1987). *The emergence of literacy.* Portsmouth, NH: Heinemann Educational Books.

Hansen, J., Newkirk, T., & Graves, D. (Eds.). (1985). *Breaking ground: teachers relate reading and writing in the elementary school.* Portsmouth, NH: Heinemann Educational Books.

Harste, J., Woodward, V., & Burke, C. (1984). *Language stories & literacy lessons.* Portsmouth, NH: Heinemann Educational Books.

Hawking, S. (1988). A brief history of time: from the big bang to black holes. New York: Bantam Books.

Heath, S. (1983). *Ways with words.* Cambridge: Cambridge University Press.

Hiebert, E. & Calfee, R. (1 989). Advancing academic literacy through teacher's assessments. *Educational Leadership*, (April), 46, 7, 50-54.

Holdaway, D. (1979). *The foundations of literacy.* Sydney: Ashton Scholastic.

Ianni, F. (1989). *The search for structure: a report on American youth today.* New York: The Free Press.

Jervis, K. (1989). Daryl takes a test. *Educational Leadership*, (April), 46, 7, 10-15.

Johnston, P. (1987). Assessing process, and the process of assessment, in the language arts. In J. Squire (Ed.), *The dynamics of language learning.* Urbana, IL: ERIC, 335-357.

Johnston, P. (1989). Constructive evaluation and the improvement of teaching and learning. *Teachers College Record*, 90, 4, 509-528.

Juliebo, M. & Elliott, J. (1987). The child fits the label. *Elements*, 19, 1, 19- 21.

Langness, L. & Levine, H. (1986). *Culture and retardation*. Boston: D. Reidel.

Lave, J., Murtaugh, M., & de la Rocha, O. (1984). The dialectic of arithmetic in grocery shopping. In B. Rogoff & J. Lave (Eds.), *Everyday cognition: its development in social context*. Cambridge: Harvard University, 67-94.

Lave, J. (1985). The social organization of knowledge and practice: a symposium. *Anthropology and Education Quarterly*, 16, 171-176.

Lieberman, L. (1984). *Preventing special education for those who don't need it*. Weston, MA: Nob Hill Press.

Lytle, S. & Cochran-Smith, M. (1992). Teacher research as a way of knowing. *Harvard Educational Review* 52(4):447-74.

Mandelbrot, B. (1977). *The fractal geometry of nature*. New York: W. H. Freeman.

Marston, C. H. (1992). A framework for the New Hampshire assessment plan executive summary. January 15.

Matthews, K. (1990). Responding to the call. In N. Atwell (Ed.), *Workshop 2: beyond the basal*. Portsmouth, NH: Heinemann Educational Books.

Meek, M. (1986). *Learning to read*. Portsmouth, NH: Heinemann Educational Books.

Mehan, H., Hertweck, A., & Meihls, J. (1986). *Handicapping the handicapped: decision making in students' educational careers*. Stanford: Stanford University Press.

Newkirk, T. (1989). *More than stories: the range of children's writing*. Portsmouth, NH: Heinemann Educational Books.

Newman, J. (Ed.). (1985). *Whole language: theory in use*. Portsmouth, NH: Heinemann Educational Books.

Opie, I. & Opie, P. (1959). *The lore and language of school children.* Oxford: Oxford University Press.

Oransu, J., McDermott, R., Boy kin, A.& the Laboratory of Comparative Human Cognition. (1977). A critique of test standardization. *Social Policy,* 8, 2, 61-67.

Polanyi, M. (1983). *The tacit dimension.* Gloucester, MA: Peter Smith.

Prigogine, I. & Stengers, I. (1984). *Order out of chaos: man's new dialogue with nature.* New York: Bantam Books.

Raloff, J. (1989). In-school breakfasts improve test scores. *Science News,* (October 14), 16, 247.

Resnick, L. (1987). Learning in school and out. *Educational Researcher,* 16(9), 13-20.

Rogoff, B. & Lave, J. (Eds.). (1984). *Everyday cognition: its development in social context.* Cambridge: Harvard University Press.

Rose, M. (1989). *Lives on the boundary: the struggles and achievements of America's underprepared.* New York: The Free Press.

Rothman, R. (1989). NAEP board is seeking a consensus on reading. *Education Week,* (September 27), 7.

Sacks, O. (1989). *Seeing voices: a journey into the world of the deaf.* Berkeley: University of California Press.

Schickedanz, J. (1986). More than the ABC's: the early stages of reading and writing. Washington, DC: National Association for the Education of Young Children.

Schrader, C. (1989). Written language use within the context of young children's symbolic play. *Early Childhood Research Quarterly,* 4(2), 225-244.

Schultz, J. (1989). Unit news, council on anthropology & education, the future. *Anthropology Newsletter,* 30(7), 10.

Scribner, S. (1984). Studying working intelligence. In B. Rogoff & J. Lave (Eds.), *Everyday Cognition* (pp. 9-40). Cambridge: Harvard University Press.

Scribner, S. (1986). Thinking in action: some characteristics of practical thought." In Steinberg, R.J. and Wagner, R.K., eds., *Practical intelligence: nature and origins of competence in the everyday world*. New York: Cambridge University Press.

Shannon, P. (1989). *Broken promises: reading instruction in twentieth-century America*. Granby, MA: Bergin & Garvey Publishers.

Shepard, L. (1989). Why we need better assessments. *Educational Leader*ship, 46(7), 4-9.

Sloan, D. (Ed.). (1984). *Toward the recovery of wholeness: knowledge, education, and human values*. New York: Teachers College Press.

Sternberg, R. & Wagner, R. (1986). *Practical intelligence: nature and origins of competence in the everyday world*. Cambridge: Cambridge University Press.

Taylor, D. (1983). *Family literacy: young children learning to read and write*. Portsmouth, NH: Heinemann Educational Books.

Taylor, D. (1988). Ethnographic educational evaluation for children, families, and school. *Theory Into Practice*, 27(1), 67-76.

Taylor, D. (1989). Toward a unified theory of literacy learning and instructional practices: A Critical Response to Chall and Carbo. *Phi Delta Kappan*, 71(3), 184-193.

Taylor, D. (1991a.). From the child's point of view: alternate approaches to assessment. In J. Roderick & J. Green (Eds.), *Developing context-responsive approaches to assessment*, NCRE. Urbana, IL: NCTE.

Taylor, D. (1991b). Family literacy: text as context. In James Flood et al., eds., *Handbook of Research on Teaching the English Language Arts*. New York: MacMillan.

Taylor, D. & Dorsey-Gaines, C. (1988). *Growing Up literate: learning from inner city families*. Portsmouth, NH: Heinemann Educational Books.

Taylor, D. & Strickland, D. (1989). Learning from families: implications for educators and policy makers. In J. Allen & J. Mason (Eds.), *Reducing the risks for young learners*, Portsmouth, NH: Heinemann Educational Books.

Teale, W. & Sulzby. E. (1986). *Emergent literacy: writing and reading*. Norwood, NJ: Ablex Publishing Corporation.

(1988). *Testing of young children: concerns and cautions*. Washington, DC: National Association for the Education of Young Children.

Turner, R. (December 1989). The 'great' debate- can both Carbo and Chall be right? *Phi Delta Kappan*, 276-283.

Vygotsky, L. (1978). *Mind in society*. Cambridge: Harvard University Press.

Wolf, D. (1989). Portfolio assessment: sampling student work. *Educational Leadership*, 35-39.

A VISIT WITH DENNY TAYLOR

"It starts at five in the morning," Denny Taylor, founder and CEO of Garn Press, described on my visit to her New York City apartment that serves as the central hub for the press. Surrounded by books and notebooks filled with years and years of ethnographic notes, Denny tells me about the Garn Press books, "We love these books. It is a labor of love and no one here has a *job*. I mean this is a life force that's taking place and, when we are working on one of these books, it's almost like a living, breathing thing."

"I think that's why the script exhausted me. I went back into every book and when you go back into every book, you are there with the author," Denny said of preparing the reader's theatre script for the upcoming Garn Press Author Celebration that was held in August 2016 in the Rare Books Room at the Strand Book Store in lower Manhattan.

"So, I think it's pretty cool to have gotten this far, I think the books that we are publishing are remarkable."

Garn Press and the mission behind the press occupies much of Denny's time since she retired from Hofstra University's Literacy Studies Department as Professor Emeritus. Denny has had an illustrious career as a researcher and academic. Denny was inducted in the International Literacy Association's Reading Hall of Fame in 2004, nominated for a Pulitzer Prize, and received an award from the Modern Language Association in1988. Denny earned her doctorate from Columbia University and her dissertation was published as a book *Family Literacy: Young Children Learning to Read and Write* in 1983, which created an entire new field of literacy study.

"I sat the 11+ when I was 10 years old and failed the test," Denny recalled of her educational experiences. Failing the test was a defining moment for her. "It was the moment when I fully understood that life in the U.K. is rigged in favor of the upper classes," she said. "I realized even as a young child that I was institutionally separated because I was working class and not supposed to be academically bright enough to go to a grammar school, but I thought that was stupid and I refused to accept it."

"I never for one moment questioned my intelligence and I have never wavered in my determination not to allow those who consider themselves bestowed with privilege to define me."

It is with this determination, resilience, and resoluteness that Denny has advocated for children throughout her career, which transcends four decades of research and writing. The *Biographic Literacy Profiles Project* described in *Teaching Without Testing* was but one of many projects conducted in the 1990s and included 120 teachers.

"We really didn't think of it as a study as much as we were doing this work," Denny reflected. "The teachers would try different ways of capturing information about every child, documenting ethnographic observations of every child during the period of a week. They were doing it in a regular classroom and they came up with their own systems of making sure that they observed every child. We would get together and one of the teachers would say, 'Well, I tried this,' and she would show everyone some system that she had come up with. Then the next time the same teacher would come and would say, 'Now I am using this.'

"They kept experimenting and trying new ways, but the object was always to try to observe every child in a disciplined and systematic way on a weekly basis," Denny explained of the purpose of the *Biographic Literacy Profiles Project*

Garn Press is the culmination of Denny's life work. "Garn is kind of where my grandmother's village is. The coal mining trade union started in the Whistle Inn. At the beginning of the 20th century, coal miners began to pushback. So Garn comes from the idea of the social justice model of society," Denny described. "And I think about that a lot. I think about what we have done with Garn and how extraordinary it would have been if it had been in a university setting, where it could have grown in different ways. So, you spend your entire life doing certain kinds of work that you want to take further, and so I told my granddaughter and also my daughter, 'When obstacles are put in your way, you have to flow around them.'"

Garn Press publishes a range of books, including picture books, novels, poetry, and academic books, and boasts award-winning authors. Nancy Rankie Shelton's heartfelt book *5-13: A Memoir of Love, Loss and Survival* was awarded the 2016 USA Best Book Awards. Anthony Cody's compelling book *The Educator and The Oligarch: A Teacher Challenges the Gates Foundation* was the recipient of the National Council of Teachers of English's 2015 George Orwell Award. Denny notes that Garn Press provides a critical, progressive social milieu for authors to push the boundaries of mainstream ideas, "I think that's what our books do. They create spaces for people to do things that they might not have thought about doing otherwise. Who would have thought of all this?"

My interactions with Denny date back to the summer of 2001, when I was a graduate student at Hofstra University, studying for my Masters in Literacy Studies. It was during my class with Denny that I began looking at and thinking about young children's writing as less than a mechanical skill and more of an art form, in which they express themselves in multiple modalities to understand who they are in a world filled with writing.

Then in the fall of 2001, New York City and its surrounding areas, including Long Island, experienced one the greatest tragedies in recent history: September 11th, the attacks on the World Trade Center. Teachers taking graduate classes with me talked about securing their students in their classrooms during the attacks. Several cried as they found out that they had children in their classes who had a parent who was killed in the attacks. How were they to teach? What did the New York State tests matter to students who watched and felt the pain of others?

Remembering that day, Denny mentored the teachers in her graduate classes by encouraging them to put the curriculum to the side to consider a humanizing pedagogy. "There was a huge difference the day after 9/11. All the work that we did, the observations that we made, the work teachers did in schools to support children because they took the *Family Literacy* course. We met the day after 9/11. And all the initiatives that were taken, the creative work that was done that semester to support children, to reach out to families, to do things within their schools that hadn't been done before was unbelievable."

"And then suddenly, ten to twelve years later none of that work can be done because of the set curricula. The work that teachers did (in 2001) did not fit with the various protocols in the school 12 years later. Teachers couldn't do work in the community and were not allowed to do the kind of outreach from schools. There was such a profound difference between the amount of creative first responder work that was possible in 2001 and then in 2012."

Denny's dedication to teachers as first responders led her to conduct ethnographic work in New Orleans after Hurricane Katrina in 2005. "The amount of extraordinary work that was going on (after Hurricane Katrina). It is interesting because I just had an email from Cindy Elliot saying that the situation in some of the schools and parishes that I was working in after Katrina is worse with the flooding that just happened. This particular flood (the Louisiana Flood of 2016) is worse, and there are whole areas that they had to go and evacuate."

Denny does not take these shifting and drastic weather changes lightly. Climate change is a serious concern that dominates much of Denny's current writings and research. "The thing that disturbs me the most is that corporations are systematically denying climate change. The ones who make money from the petrochemical industry and all of those industries are also the ones pushing for corporate reforms in school."

"So it is the capitalist corporate world. They need students to support their industries, but their industries are industries that are destroying the planet. The idea that we would shift our focus and change the ways that kids are taught in school so that schools become these creative dynamic places is critical. We need our students *to think* because they are going to *have to*. We don't know what they are going to have to do in 10-15, maybe even five years. And they are not going to have those skills because we are not preparing them for that kind of thinking."

In an article *Don't Scare the Kids*, Denny provides advice for talking with children about climate change. "I think we have a problem in talking to children about climate change. There is this set of arguments to tell kids how bad the climate is. I think the most important part is not to focus on the temperature risings, floods, and pestilence, the scary stuff. We need our children to be creative, imaginative problem solvers. This is Chomsky's question, 'How come a mosquito can fly in the rain?' So, kids need be exploring questions that have to do with society, but also with ecological issues. How come mosquitoes can fly in the rain? It is the asking of questions or creating of environments, and reforms movements have created an environment where there is no room for that kind of creative work in schools."

"If our kids are going to survive, they need to be able to think through what's happening in places like Louisiana, when an entire parish is so deep under water that everyone has to be evacuated. How do we create communities that are self-sustaining, that are acting in ways that not only sustain the community, but also impact the larger society? And that work is not going on. None of that work is going on," Denny explained of the current corporate-led reform movements that place the standardization of assessment and curricular models as a priority over a humanizing pedagogy.

Denny's ethnographic study of Louisiana after Hurricane Katrina became the inspiration for her most recent book *Split Second Solution*, a novel that eerily reflects the current state of political affairs. "The book starts with Louisiana, and I have created this terrible storm in 2008 in the book. The whole idea that time is an artificial construct is part of the book as well. Also, I am playing with gender and racial identity."

As our afternoon visit filled with coffee, laughter, and some tears, came to a close, Denny asked one of the most provocative questions that left me wondering as I made my way back from Midtown Manhattan, "In 20 years, will there be public schools? Will there be anything left except the remnants? Will a new layer have taken over?"

Like climate change, the state of our relationships with countries around the world and the stability of the economy, I ponder the future of education, and of meaningful ways to bring about educational reform that addresses the oppressed and the hidden inequalities built into public policies that disadvantage children of differing races, genders, and socio-economic statuses. I stood on the platform waiting for the 1 train. As I stared down the dark, gloomy tunnel looking for any sign of lights, I wondered if instead of a train, the Sick-Reapers from Denny book's *Split Second Solution* would appear out of the dark tunnel like in Denny's book. If they did, we would have to be ready.

BOOK TWO

NEGOTIATING A PERMEABLE CURRICULUM: ON LITERACY, DIVERSITY, AND THE INTERPLAY OF CHILDREN'S AND TEACHERS' WORLDS

INTRODUCTION

BOBBIE KABUTO

Curriculum is the heart and soul of educational systems, and it is in jeopardy of a coup d'état by corporate and political forces. It has not always been this way. As a teacher in the mid 1990s, I knew a time when money was invested in the professional development of teachers rather in high-stakes testing. States possessed state curricular standards, and teachers were directly invested in collaborative planning. Curriculum development and mapping were the major foci of the regular professional development workshops in which I participated. Our first priority was not teaching to national standards or for our students to pass state tests, it was about developmentally and culturally appropriate teaching. It was about knowing our students and looking at them as social beings who bring varied levels of understanding and background knowledge to the curriculum. Teaching was about creating a dynamic, dialogic curricular model in which students were engaged and worked at their individual levels of understanding.

It is not all that surprising that the research in the 1990s in language and literacy, focused on a humanistic pedagogy, made an influential impact on me as a teacher and, later, an as educational researcher and scholar. It is, therefore, with great pleasure that I introduce Anne Haas Dyson, who will be the focus of this volume as part of the Garn Press Women Scholars Series. Dyson's seminal work and prolific writings on childhood writers began in the early 1980s and continues to this day.

Originally published in 1993 in the National Council of Teachers of English (NCTE) Concept Paper Series, *Negotiating a Permeable Curriculum: On Literacy, Diversity, and the Interplay of Children's and Teachers' Worlds* revisits Dyson's powerful concept of a permeable curriculum. According to Dyson, a permeable curriculum is more than a set of content standards and objectives, it is a socially constructed learning space created by teachers and children. Dyson (1993a) writes of a permeable curriculum, "Such a shared world is essential for the growth of both oral and written language, and it is essential as well if teachers and children are to feel connected to, not alienated from, each other" (p. 200).

Thus, through the creation of a shared space, the curriculum is no longer identified as a set of skills and ideas that needs to be transmitted from the more knowledgeable teacher to the inexperienced student. Instead, children are positioned as social negotiators as "they explore and exploit the power of symbolic tools as social mediators" (Dyson, 1993a, p. 202). Curriculum is negotiated between teacher and student. As Dyson (1993a) argues, "the worlds of the teachers and children come together in instructionally powerful ways" (p. 201).

Dyson's words stand in stark contrast to the current moves in education with the implementation of the Common Core State Standards (CCSS). Much has changed since I was a teacher in 1995. In 2010, the CCSS were released as a set of standards devised to create national benchmarks of student knowledge and skills in literacy and math. While not specifically mentioning curriculum, the CCSS explicitly outlines what should be taught from kindergarten to grade 12, and they have in fact had a major impact in establishing a national curriculum and assessment system led by private, corporate companies.

Researchers and grassroots movements from parents, students, and community leaders have tirelessly challenged the motivation, necessity, and reliability of the CCSS in creating college- and career-ready students, as well as questioning the privatization of education. Opponents of the CCSS call for more local autonomy in establishing curricular standards in their schools and school districts. These recent political, corporate, and grassroots changes in education make the revisiting of Dyson's permeable curriculum timely and necessary.

In what follows, I will introduce the reader to three tenets that build a foundation for *Negotiating a Permeable Curriculum*. I will do so through the voice and world of a child writer, my son Ricky, who I observed learning to write from the time he picked up a plastic eggroll from his kitchen set at 2 years old thinking that he could use it to mark on a piece of paper, to the present time when writing is now about finding evidence in the passage to support the main idea of his paragraph. So here I return to Ricky's second-grade year to examine the social worlds of the child composer and the official world of school, as well as the impact that the curriculum had in positioning Ricky as a struggling learner.

Composing Through Form and Function

Writing is a symbolic tool that children learn to employ in order to navigate through their social worlds before they learn to fully control the tool itself. The early research on beginning writing – by researchers such as Denny Taylor (1983) in *Family Literacy*, Jerome Harste, V. Woodward, and Carolyn Burke (1984) in *Language Stories & Literacy Lessons*, and Marcia Baghban (1984) in *Our Daughter Learns to Read and Write* – focused on close observations of young children learning to write. This body of early research contributed to our understandings of two aspects of writing – learning conventional written language forms and employing written language for complex social functions.

"Conventional written language forms" refers to the written forms that compose a writing system. For instance, the English language uses the Roman alphabet as its written language form, while Chinese uses Chinese *kanji* (Chinese characters) as its written form. While learning how to form letters that make up the Roman alphabet is one entry point in learning to write, children also learn a variety of social conventions that guide how they use the written forms. Children learn to use a capital letter to begin a sentence and to capitalize the first letter of a proper noun, like in a name. The term, "social convention," connects to the idea that written language forms are given meaning by social and cultural guidelines, or conventions. Therefore, when children begin to make marks on a piece of paper or write a letter on a page, they are learning how to participate in a larger social and cultural structure that gives meaning to the marks that they make.

This notion is particularly important when we think about social and cultural diversity, and how more experienced writers, like teachers, interpret the writing of novice writers. For instance, both the English and Spanish languages use the Roman alphabet for their written language form. While this may be the case, each language is comprised of a different system of sounds. Speakers of English apply the English sound system, or phonology, to the Roman alphabet, while Spanish speakers apply the Spanish sound system. A bilingual English- and Spanish-speaking child, who has a range of linguistic resources, applies a range of sound systems based on the English and Spanish phonology to the Roman alphabet when spelling and writing.

To provide an example, a teacher who was in my graduate class was quite perplexed as to why a bilingual child wrote the following sentence, "My brother is 10 years old," as "Mai prasr ev 10 ya ot." The teacher felt that the bilingual child was "confused" because his Spanish interfered with his English writing, and wondered if there was a possible learning disability. This, in fact, was not the case, and there are linguistic reasons to explain the child's writing behaviors. This bilingual speaker applied his knowledge of the Spanish and English phonology to the Roman alphabet when spelling words.

I refer to these types of linguistic behaviors as part of translanguaging, which denotes the dynamic nature of language and counters the additive approach to bilingualism and biliteracy (Garcia & Wei, 2014). Translanguaging does not position Languages (I use the capital *L* to denote language in its formalized sense) as separate autonomous systems (i.e. a Spanish Language or an English Language), as language can transcend traditional bounded forms. The writing of this bilingual student was aimed at communicating a message and, in order to communicate that message, he needed to break down traditional language boundaries.

While this may be the case, the teacher interpreted the child's bilingual writing behavior through a deficit-oriented perspective. Her concern was about the surface features of the writing, in particular his spelling, and spelling is not synonymous with writing. Without realizing it, this teacher was in the process of socially constructing an identity for this bilingual writer that positioned him as "at-risk" and "confused." Dyson (1993a) describes the challenges that teachers like this one face:

> Indeed, research in schools serving children from diverse sociocultural backgrounds suggests that teachers and children often do feel disconnected, a feeling exacerbated by differences in race and class. (p. 200)

Teachers who enact a permeable curriculum reject that idea that students like this bilingual student need to fit into neat categories, and follow a predicted line of developmental learning when learning the range of surface features of writing, which includes spelling, grammar, and handwriting.

Becoming a writer, however, is not only about learning written language forms and social conventions that guide the use of those forms. It is also about social enactments, or functions. The research and writings of Dyson have made a major impact in understanding how writing is about "taking action, of entering into a social dialogue" into which the youngest of writers can engage (Dyson, 1993a, p.205).

Dyson (1993a) argues, "As teachers, then, we must attend to much more than children's invented words on a page, for writing is not just a specialized way of marking (although it's that, too)" (p. 205). While children do need to learn the conventional forms of written language and social conventions, learning to write is about learning about the world – the people, places, and things that make up the world – and being someone who engages in it.

To illustrate this point, I go back in time to when Ricky was 7 years old and in the second grade. Ricky, who was an avid *Mario Cart* player, liked to challenge his uncle in an occasional, friendly game. During a visit to his aunt and uncle's house, the friendly game became a little competitive, and when $10 was on the line for winning, Ricky decided to draw up a contract (see Figure 1).

Ricky wrote, "If Ricky wins, then ___ (his uncle initialed) has to give me $20 (which Ricky crossed out because his uncle would not agree and wrote $10) $10 bucks. But if ___ (his uncle initialed) wins Ricky has (to) give me $30 (which Ricky crossed out because I would not agree and wrote $20) $20 bucks." There are several stipulations listed in the contract, which Ricky's aunt added. They are (1) no quitting, (2) no starting over, (3) the car has to be an automatic one, and (4) the course and distance. Both Ricky and his uncle initialed and signed to recognize the stipulations.

This example illustrates how writing was the result of "joint constructions" by the participating members of Ricky's social circle as it served the goal of creating a "social cohesion" (Dyson, 1993b, p. 59). There is evidence in this piece of writing of Ricky learning how to control the social conventions of written language, such as spelling, but Ricky was not constrained by writing "correctly" and, thus, was able to use written language to communicate a socially meaningful message.

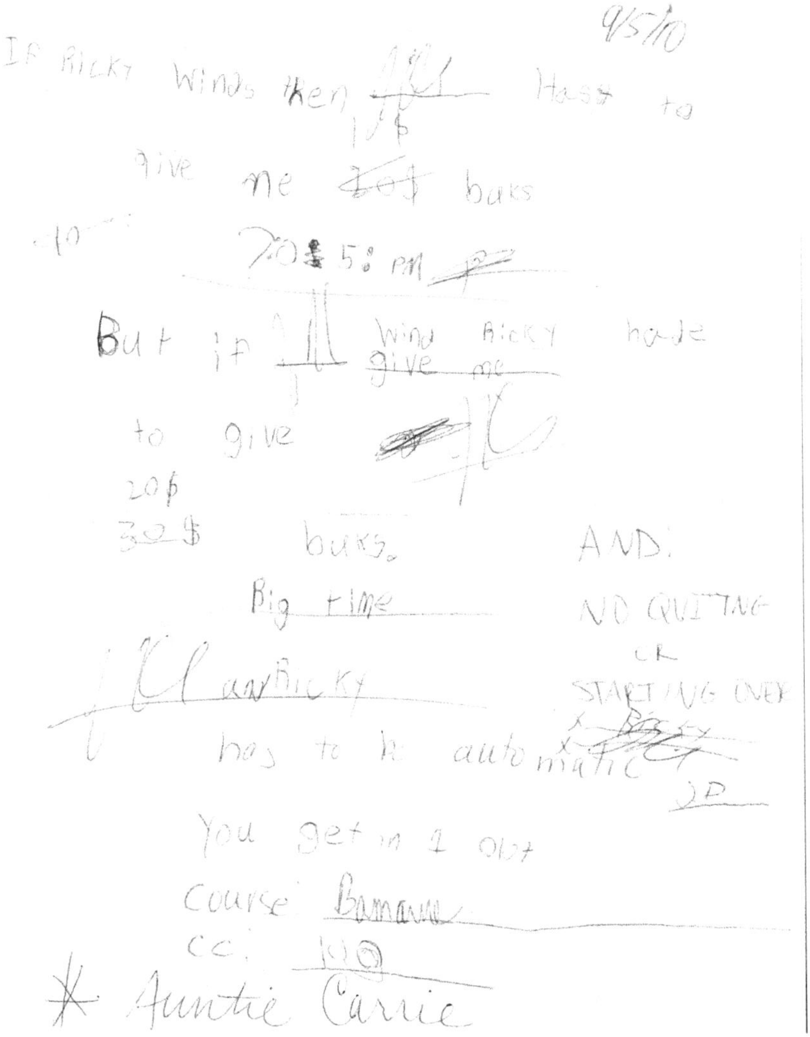
9/5/10

If Ricky winds then ___ Hass to give me ~~20$~~ buks

20$ 5: PM

But if ___ wind Ricky hade ~~give me~~ to give

20$

30$ buks.

Big time

AND!

NO QUITING OR STARTING OVER

has to be automatic

You get in 1 out

course Banana

cc: 100

Auntie Carrie

Figure 1: Ricky's Mario Cart Contract

In *Social Worlds of Children Learning to Write*, Dyson (1993b) writes, "Writing, like all language use, is always a situated response, an addressing of another in a particular time and place, a motivated making of words for some end" (p. 217). Through the creation of the contract, Ricky could exercise control and agency within the space – his contract was a situated response to meet some end. The relationships through and around the written language were authentic, not generic, and they were permeable, as the individuals involved had invested interests in the outcome of the writing.

Dyson (1993a) cautions about creating a generic nature to pedagogy when she writes, "Moreover, making use of children's social intelligence entails rethinking the generic nature of writing pedagogy for young children" (p. 226). She continues, "Considering children as social actors thus suggests that 'audience,' 'editor,' and 'response' are situated, not generic, terms that can be explicitly discussed and planned for with children" (p. 227). Within Ricky's *Mario Cart* contract all participants acted as audience, editor, and responder, and they actively constructed an authentic space that gave meaning to the contract and their relationships with each other.

The Official and Unofficial Worlds of Child Writers

Ricky constructed the *Mario Cart* contract within the natural context of the family, or in a space within the "home world" (Dyson, 1993b, p. 54). Researchers (e.g. Maderazo, 2014) have documented how writing within the home can differ from the types of writing activities produced in school, potentially positioning children as having learning difficulties. While the home environment supports everyday contextualized writing, writing in school is often decontextualized – pulled apart so that children are forced to work with written language forms and social conventions in a meaningless manner.

Describing writing pedagogy, Dyson (1993a) argues that "pedagogical writing about child literacy often assumes that the developmental goal is 'decontextualized' written language, that is, language in which ideas are made explicit in tightly constructed prose, rather than implicitly understood by familiar interlocutors" (p. 227). And yet children like Ricky find ways to work outside of the official worlds of school when writing.

Figure 2: Ricky's The Apple Book

Another example of Ricky's writing that occurred in the home during his second grade year is his authored book *The Apple, Book 1* (see Figure 2, Ricky wrote four books in his *The Apple* series). On separate sheets of paper, Ricky wrote the text and drew the pictures page by page. The book reads as follows:

Page 1: The apple. It was small. I eat apples.

Page 2: But here comes the wind. The apple could fall off.

Page 3: The wind was so fast it made the apple fell

Page 4: Poor apple. It's all alone.

Page 5: But someone is coming. He could eat the apple.

Page 6: It is a he. He was getting the apple.

Page 7: He eat the apple. It was so delicious. Now his apple was his favorite.

Page 8: He eat the fall apple. The End.

Paying close attention to how illustrations also tell a story, Ricky drew his illustrations to match his written text. For instance, when Ricky wrote about the wind, he drew short horizontal, blue lines across the page, and when the wind blew the apple, he drew the apple in the air falling from the tree. After Ricky finished with the text and illustrations, he cut the pages so he could make a small book. What Ricky enjoyed the most, however, was reading the book to me. His book was not just a book because he tried to make it look like one. It was a book because he could share it with me and other people. Ricky went on to write three more books in the series, and other books like his nonfiction book, *What is a Plane?*, and his fictional stories, *The Gingerbread Guy* and *The Little Candy Cane*.

He wrote the last two books in his third-grade year, starting each book at home to bring to school, crossing the boundaries of home and school. Once Ricky brought the book to school, it entered into what Dyson (1993b) terms as the unofficial world of the classroom. Ricky's classroom friends became characters in the book, took on different characteristics, and engaged in dramatic events. For instance, Ricky's friend Tommy became Tom Gingerbread who was the "sneakiest guy at Gingerbread World."

In collaborating in the creation of the books, Ricky's friends jointly created an imaginative world where each person could take on alternative identities, or as Dyson would describe, the joint construction of *The Gingerbread Guy* developed a social cohesion within Ricky's peer world. Ricky and his friends worked on his book between official classroom routines, especially over the indoor recess time when they spent time in the classroom because of the cold New York winters. As Dyson (1993b) explains, while teachers organize the official classroom routines, children organize the unofficial worlds, which are "formed in response to adult-governed worlds, but they were collaboratively enacted within the life space of the children" (p. 52).

Similar to what Dyson (1993b) found, the unofficial spaces that Ricky created with his books were "socially dramatic places, where children worked hard to proclaim their own uniqueness in ways that would gain the respect of others" (p. 66). For Ricky, these spaces did not always fit into the official world of school nor were they always accepted by his teachers. Often, Ricky's books did not count towards assessing and evaluating Ricky's reading and writing performances, because the books were not considered part of the school's official space and were either forgotten or simply ignored.

Rigidity and Permeability

Ricky's second-grade year was a particularly challenging one for Ricky. Examining the social worlds and the unofficial spaces within which Ricky participated highlights the ways in which he used writing as a tool to navigate his social worlds as well as the people and actions embedded within them. Ricky's difficulty was not necessarily with his underlying ability to read and write, it was the ways in which the rigidity of the curriculum, and how his teachers interpreted the curriculum, positioned him as a struggling learner.

The official world of school was about the forms and conventions of written language. Children who mastered those two pieces of written language were deemed as better readers and writers than children who did not. In the second grade, Ricky's primary work around reading and writing was through the school reading specialist rather than through his classroom teacher. While I never saw or received an in-depth report from Ricky's classroom teacher for reading and writing, I received one from the reading specialist at my request. The reading specialist provided me with the following conclusions from Ricky's January, 2010 assessment:

- Ricky reflected limited understanding of the text he read. He mentioned a few facts or ideas but did not express the important information or ideas.
- Ricky's decoding is on grade level.
- Ricky's comprehension is weak using the GRADE (assessment) and Running Record.
- Ricky's word knowledge score was weak using the Gates-MacGinitie assessment.

Based on this assessment report, Ricky's reading specialist recommended him to the Intervention Services Team (IST) who would determine if Ricky needed further school interventions. After their initial meeting, of which I was not notified, the school speech and language specialist contacted me for permission for speech and language testing. At this point, my intervention was the turning point in Ricky's second grade year, and I called for an immediate halt of further testing or even talk of further testing.

When I received Ricky's assessment results in April of his second-grade year, however, there was the same discourse by the reading specialist as she noted the following:

- Ricky reflected a limited understanding of the text he read. He mentioned a few facts or ideas but did not express the important information or ideas.
- Ricky's comprehension remains a concern.
- Ricky reflected no understanding of the text when he was asked to write about the story.

For the last point, Ricky was asked to read a story and write from the point of view of one of the characters. Ricky was asked to write three behaviors that the character found annoying and to compare those behaviors to another character. Ricky wrote verbatim:

They both like swimming.

They are both messy.

They like to away's like to go outside.

I do not deny that Ricky's responses to the written questions did not fully address the questions and, most likely, did not demonstrate his understanding of the story. Ricky's performances on these tasks, however, are in stark contrast to his performances when creating the *Mario Cart Contract* and *The Apple, Book 1*, and later *The Gingerbread Guy* in his third-grade year. The rigidity of the curriculum in Ricky's classroom during his second-grade year was more reflective of the work of Taylor (1991), who documented how the official world of school constructed the disability of a student.

The perspective of the official world also contrasts with that of Dyson's work, which readers will encounter in this volume. Dyson (1993a) shows us both hope and the possibilities of a permeable curriculum where "teachers with such curiosity talk with (not simply about) parents and community members, seeking insight into children's lives beyond the school walls and into the language use that pervades those lives" (p. 230).

Ricky's teachers played crucial roles in reproducing and perpetuating a perceived learning difficulty by a rigid interpretation of what should be taught, what students should learn, and how they should perform in school. Ricky's teachers did not look "beyond the school walls" to see the complex social and intellectual work that he could do in his growth as a writer and a learner.

The tasks built into the official spaces of school favored the disembodied uses of language. They were generic tasks, particularly the writing tasks, which did not possess a motivated construction of meaning to meet some socially important and oriented goal. What Ricky learned to do well in his home world did not translate to the school world because the world of school presented a different type of writing.

Exploring Ricky's experiences as a learner through the concepts put forth in *Negotiating a Permeable Curriculum* raises the critical question: "When does a learning difficulty become a problem with the curriculum rather than a problem with the child?" In other words, how does a curriculum socially construct the identities and abilities of children like Ricky? I am left wondering what would have happened if the permeability of the curriculum had created a space where Ricky's unofficial world could have entered into the official world of the school? How could the worlds of Ricky's teachers and Ricky come together in "instructionally powerful ways" so that a new space could be created – a transgenerational space where learning transcended the borders of time and space and of teacher-student generations?

Final Thoughts

Applying *Negotiating a Permeable Curriculum* to Ricky's experiences in school 22 years after its original publication date shows that *Negotiating a Permeable Curriculum* is a timeless piece that offers readers a renewed look into what a critical, dialogic pedagogy can look like if enacted in classrooms. The concept of the permeable curriculum has much to offer in thinking about schooling and pedagogy. For me, it provided a lens to think about how curriculum can be a space which can be constructed by teachers and students, and how a non-permeable curriculum can be used to position students and construct sometimes false labels through its rigidity.

Others build on the concept in different ways. Salazar (2013) uses the concept of a permeable curriculum to describe a "humanizing pedagogy" that allows for the "inclusion of students' linguistic, cultural, and social resources" (p. 139).

Salazar further explains:

> Educators orienting toward a humanizing pedagogy foster permeability when they accept code switching in student discourse, support heritage-language use as a means of fostering student comprehension, facilitate student input into the curriculum, provide opportunities for students to make personal connections to content, and include topics that reflect the diversity of students' lives. (p. 139)

Other researchers expand on the relationships between a permeable curriculum and linguistic, social, and cultural diversity. Rex (2006) discusses issues of race in classroom interactions, using the concept to better understand how "social identity is enacted and received in the social world and for observing what the intersection of culture, structure, and human agency produces" (p. 315).

Kuby, Rucker, and Kirchhofer (2015) bring forth a discussion of writing within an official curricular space. Similar to Dyson's work, these researchers question students' intentions when participating in Writer's Workshop in a second-grade classroom. They argue:

> Dominant discourses in schools, published writing curricula materials and educational standards privilege alphabetic writing. We noticed that children did not always have an end goal in mind when constructing during Writing Workshop. On many occasions, writing was an exploration of bodies, modes and materials in social interactions. (p. 3)

Focusing on the role of the teacher, the authors contend that teachers are critical in how children "intra-act" with materials and space when writing in the classroom.

In the conclusion of *Negotiating a Permeable Curriculum*, Dyson talks about pushing back the "curricular curtain" to wonder about the complex social and intellectual work in which children engage when they *become* writers. The emphasis on *becoming* focuses on how learning to write is always a dynamic state, as children learn about themselves while they learn about written language.

When I moved the curricular curtain aside in Ricky's second-grade year, I observed how he saw writing as a tool of the imagination and a way to enact his freedom and control in the complex cartographies that defined his social worlds. As readers enter into *Negotiating a Permeable Curriculum*, I encourage them to push back the curricular curtain that has begun to cloud our senses on what teachers should teach and what students should learn. This is the first step in generating a permeable curriculum where the social and intellectual energy of our students can penetrate into the official classroom worlds.

REFERENCES

Baghban, M. (1984). *Our daughter learns to read and write: A case study from birth to three*. Newark, DE: International Reading Association.

Dyson, A. H. (1993b). *Social worlds of children learning to write in an urban primary school*. New York, NY: Teachers College Press.

Dyson, A. H. (1993a). Negotiating a permeable curriculum: On literacy, diversity, and the interplay between teachers and children's worlds. Concept Paper. Urbana, IL: NCTE, 1993.

Garcia, O. & Wei, L. (2014). *Translanguaging: Language, bilingualism, and education*. New York, NY: Palgrave MacMillan.

Harste, J. C., Woodward, V. A., & Burke, C. L. (1984). *Language Stories & Literacy Lessons*. Portsmouth, N.H.: Heinemann.

Kuby, C., Rucker, T.G., & Kirchhofer, J. (2015). 'Go be a writer': Intra-activity with materials, time and space in literacy learning. *Journal of Early Childhood Literacy*, 15(3), 1–26.

Maderazo, C. (2014). The struggle for literacy: Leo's story. In B. Kabuto & P. Martens (Eds.). *Linking families, learning, and schooling: Parent-researcher perspectives* (pp.51-65). New York, NY: Routledge.

Rex, L. (2006). Acting "Cool" and "Appropriate": Toward a framework for considering literacy classroom interactions when race is a factor. *Journal of Literacy Research*, 38(3), 275–325.

Salazar, M.C. (2013). A humanizing pedagogy: Reinventing the principles and practice of education as a journey toward liberation. *Review of Research in Education*, (37), 121-148.

Taylor, D. (1991). *Learning denied*. Portsmouth, NH: Heinemann.

Taylor, D. (1983). *Family literacy: Young children learning to read and write*. Portsmouth, NH: Heinemann.

NEGOTIATING A PERMEABLE CURRICULUM ON LITERACY, DIVERSITY, AND THE INTERPLAY OF CHILDREN'S AND TEACHERS' WORLDS

ANNE HAAS DYSON

Imagine that it is the end of a long teaching day. You are thumbing through your students' work and come across second grader Eugenie's text (see Figure 1). You sigh and take a closer look at Eugenie's "follow-up" writing to your lesson on the Civil War and Abraham Lincoln. The assignment had been to fold a paper into eight boxes, number each box, and then draw and write in each something important about Lincoln. You hadn't, so far as you can recall, discussed Lincoln's personal life. But here, in Eugenie's paper, is an unidentified woman declaring her love (for Lincoln?) and what you assume to be a marriage scene, "Do you? Yes I do" being a common script among your children for wedding vows. You start to wonder, as teachers often do, if you and Eugenie had participated in the same lesson; if, indeed, you were in the same world.

Figure 1: Eugenie's important facts about Lincoln

This feeling of separation from and puzzling about the lives of children is basic to the topic of this essay: how teachers construct a shared world with their students, or, to rephrase, how they might enact a "permeable" curriculum that allows for interplay between teachers' and children's language and experiences. Such a shared world is essential for the growth of both oral and written language, and it is essential as well if teachers and children are to feel connected to, not alienated from, each other. Indeed, research in schools serving children from diverse sociocultural backgrounds suggests that teachers and children often do feel disconnected, a feeling exacerbated by differences in race and class (Committee on Policy for Racial Justice, 1989; Rothman, 1992).

To counter such alienation, many educators turn to the language arts. For example, we as teachers engage children in literature that reflects the diversity of children's lives and the commonalities of the human spirit, and we encourage children themselves to craft their own experiences, real and imagined, on paper. And yet, whatever curricular materials and activities educators offer, deep in children's own lived worlds, these activities are renegotiated, influenced by social goals which educators might not anticipate and infused with cultural material – thematic content and literacy genres – which they may not value.

Thus, building on what children do – the longstanding truism of both developmentally and culturally appropriate teaching – is not so easy, because doing so involves granting legitimacy and visibility to social purposes and cultural materials that educators may view as trivial, irrelevant, and even distasteful. The permeable curriculum is an idea, like democracy and social justice, that is easy to embrace – until one is faced with the diversity of human values and behaviors, with, for example, a second grader's cryptic text about love, marriage, and Lincoln.

In this essay, I explore the concept of a permeable curriculum, aiming to provide concrete examples of the social and cultural challenges it entails. I draw on a recent study in Eugenie's urban school to illustrate the diverse kinds of social goals that energize young children's language use, particularly their composing, the diverse kinds of cultural material they draw upon, and, most important, the ways in which teachers may work to enact a permeable curriculum, in which the worlds of teachers and children come together in instructionally powerful ways.

Undergirding this essay is a perspective on children and on literacy that differs in emphasis from those most dominant in current pedagogical discussions of the language arts. Informed by the psycholinguistic insights of the seventies and, particularly, by studies of child language development (e.g., Brown, 1973; Read, 1975), pedagogical texts stress that young children are inventors; assisted by others, they figure out how written language works.[1] By engaging in the processes of composing and response, children move beyond egocentric play with writing to true communication.

In contrast, influenced by recent social theories about child language (e.g., Bruner & Haste, 1987; Rogoff, 1990; Stern, 1985), the emphasis herein is on children as social negotiators; addressing others, they explore and exploit the power of symbolic tools as social mediators. The pedagogic goal is not to socialize egocentric child writers but to make varied ways with written language sensible to socially sensitive children, children who live in an increasingly culturally and politically complex society. I introduce this perspective in the following section and then, after two sections featuring the curricular negotiations of Eugenie, her peers, and her teachers, I elaborate on the theoretical substance of the permeable curriculum in the paper's final section.

Dialogue and Development: Children as Social Negotiators

From a sociocultural perspective, the development of language, oral or written, is couched in dialogue. Indeed, words "can only arise in interindividual territory" (Volosinov & Bakhtin, 1973, p. 12), that is, between people who are members of a social unit. Thus, within the interactional rhythms and daily routines of their family lives, young children begin to use language to interpret their experiences. They take words learned from others and use them to give voice to their own feelings and thoughts (Bakhtin, 1986). As Stern (1985) explains:

> Meaning results from interpersonal negotiations involving what can be agreed upon as shared. And such mutually negotiated meanings (the relation of thought to word) grow, change, develop, and are strug-

gled over by two people and thus ultimately owned by us. (p. 170)

Language, therefore, both contributes to and is acquired within common interpretive worlds, in which adults and children share intersubjectivity or "mutually created meanings" about experiences.

On a broader plane, negotiating meanings is also negotiating culture, or the meaning structures shared by people who belong to a particular group (Geertz, 1973). As children grow up in families and communities, they learn ways of interpreting and acting on the world through language. Those culturally patterned ways of using language are evident in stories, jokes, prayers, arguments, and other genres through which people construct their social lives together. The development of language, then, occurs as children learn to participate in ever more effective ways in culturally valued activities mediated through the tool of speech. Children enter into their culture as they tell stories, tease, argue, pray, and, in other ways, interact with others through publicly shared words or other signs (e.g., songs, dramatic actions).

In homes and classrooms, children begin to use written language also as a cultural tool for constructing symbolic worlds and for engaging with others. Young children's written texts are often multimedia affairs, interweavings of written words, spoken ones, and pictures; and yet their graphics, too, can be used as tools within their own worlds, as Eugenie and her peers will illustrate (see also Dyson, 1989; McLane & McNamee, 1990; Newkirk, 1989).

This notion of children entering, through language use, into social and cultural dialogues is complicated in our schools, though, because schools are not homogeneous worlds. Although the teacher governs the official school world, in which children must be students, the children are also members of an unofficial peer world, formed in response to the constraints and regulations of the official world, and they are members as well of their sociocultural communities, which may reform in the classroom amidst networks of peers (D'Amato, 1987; Erickson, 1987; Roberts, 1970). (See Figure 2.)

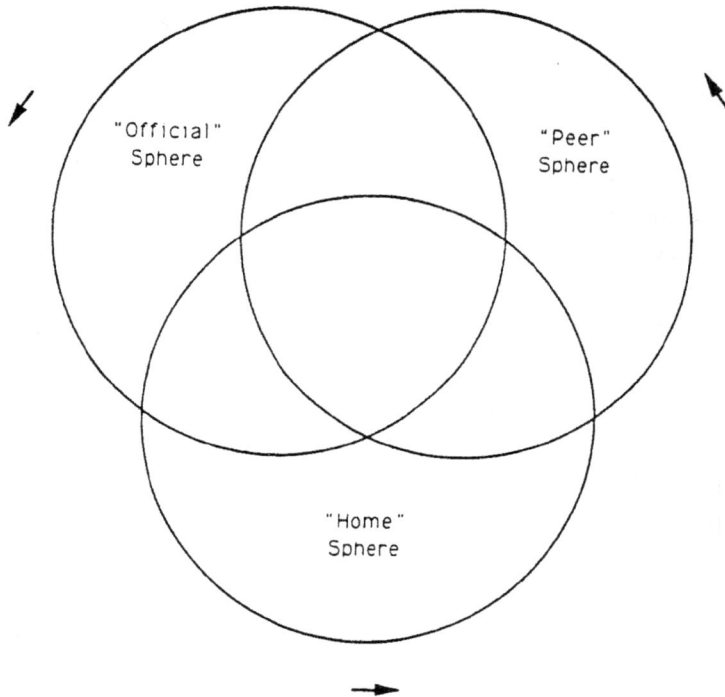

Figure 2: The multiple social worlds of the classroom (Note: In classrooms, children are at once members of diverse reference spheres. The intention here is not to pull apart that essential dynamic but simply to provide a graphic metaphor of the existence of these spheres. There are no neat boundaries between "home" and "school," nor between the official [teacher-controlled] sphere and that of peers.)

Within each world, children have different kinds of relationships to each other and to their teacher, and, moreover, they enact those relationships through intersecting but nonetheless distinctive ways of using language; that is, each world may have differing notions of effective language use, of appropriate discourse themes, structures, and styles (Hymes, 1980). Thus, teachers offer what they hope will be relevant and intellectually engaging activities, but, within the children's worlds, those activities are interpreted in new ways, infused with unexpected social and cultural meanings.

As teachers, then, we must attend to much more than children's invented words on a page, for writing is not just a specialized way of marking (although it's that, too). Moreover, we cannot assume that our notions of authentic social purposes for writing and response are shared with our young students. Rather, we must attend to children's worlds, for literacy is a way of taking action, of entering into a social dialogue (Bakhtin, 1986; Scribner & Cole, 1981). On the one hand, we must allow – indeed, support – the embedding of written language in children's social worlds, so that they find it a useful symbolic tool (a suggestion made by educators as separated in time and space as Ashton-Warner, Freire, and Vygotsky). But, on the other hand, we must also help children expand and negotiate among the sociocultural worlds – the dialogues – in which they participate.[2] In the words of Rosen and Rosen (1973), a classroom should be

> [a] meeting place of...the children and the adult. The open [permeable] classroom not only welcomes the children and their own ways of thinking and feeling, but it also creates a life of its own...a delicate web of relationships...which is as complicated as that in any home. As complicated but different, for it creates new possibilities, new speculations, new styles. (pp. 31-32)

To illustrate the interplay possible between the worlds of young children and of teachers, I turn to the social and intellectual work done by children and teacher in Eugenie's kindergarten/first-grade classroom, particularly during the daily composing period; the composing period was rich in such interplay, since it was a relatively unstructured time when children were, in fact, supposed to "express themselves" and the teacher was supposed to "respond." Then, to clarify this concept of permeability, I offer an interpretive vision of Eugenie's "Abraham Lincoln" event in a first- and second-grade classroom, an event in which the curriculum was much more impervious to child intrusion.

The Evolution of a Permeable Curriculum

Eugenie's kindergarten/first-grade classroom was in an urban primary (K-3) school in the East San Francisco Bay Area. The school served both an African American community of low-income and working-class households on the southwest side of its attendance area, and an ethnically diverse but primarily European American community of working- to middle-class households on its northeast side. For two years, I observed in this school, guided by six "key" children, kindergartners through third graders, all African American, who allowed me access to their peers and neighborhood friends. While I focused on children from one sociocultural group in one school, my research concern was not behaviors specific to any one group of children but, rather, the dynamics of, or the interplay between, children's official (teacher-governed) and unofficial (child-governed) classroom worlds and how that interplay figured into children's language use, particularly their composing.[3]

Eugenie's teacher Louise was European American and in her forties; she was an experienced and highly skilled teacher, knowledgeable about recent pedagogical innovations and sensitive to the social issues important to her children. Each day she structured a daily composing period, in which all twenty-seven children drew, wrote, talked, and dictated. After they finished their work, the children gathered on the rug to present their own texts to the classroom audience.

In response to her children, Louise commented on the individual messages and broader genre qualities of their work (i.e., the themes, structures, and styles), and she stressed child reflection and decision making about their texts, as in the following example:

It's early in October. The children are joining Louise on the rug after a composing period. Louise first notes that Edward J. is making his writing book all about sports. Today he has drawn a boxer and written a backwards "3." The three, Edward then explains, is because "it's the third round."

Other children, comments Louise, have decided to "label" their pictures. For example, Monique has drawn a tepee and written, "This is me and my TP." Louise comments that hers "could be a picture book."

"A picture book for a little kid," adds a child.

Austin has a twist on the picture book idea. He says that he has made a "guess-what's-happening book." Louise points out that, on the back of each of his pictures, there's a "description of what's happening."

Calvin's is a "wordless picture," featuring a tree, a man, and a hat.

"What do you think Calvin was thinking of?" Louise asks.

"Caps for Sale," sings the child chorus.

"He doesn't have a mouth," comments a child.

"Does he need a mouth?" Louise asks Calvin.

"No," says Calvin.

"No," says Louise.

As the year progressed, Louise not only used the genre labels of books (e.g., "picture books"); she and the children noted connections of topic, character, plot, and language style (e.g., the use of a rhyming pattern). In this way, she helped children "grow into the intellectual life of those around them" (Vygotsky, 1978, p. 88). Informed by workshops on writing-process pedagogy, she expected that, as the year progressed, the children's desire to communicate and to understand others' texts would lead to their assuming increased responsibility for offering advice to each other as writers (see, for example, Graves, 1983).

But a permeable curriculum – a negotiated classroom culture – cannot emerge from a unidirectional curricular vision. Teachers as well as children must be open, curious, and willing to imagine worlds beyond their own. Louise was such a teacher. In her classroom, the daily meeting time did not progress quite as she had planned. She had, after all, invited the children in as individual decision makers and social actors. And, in time, the children brought their own social goals and, as a result, unanticipated language resources to the daily sharing time.

Their own offerings, and Louise's willingness to respond to those offerings, led to the evolution of what Bruner might call a "cultural forum" (1986, p. 127), in which children's social work and cultural resources and those officially introduced by Louise were connected and expanded in new ways. It was this forum that yielded a dialogic interplay between teachers' and children's worlds and, thus, a permeable curriculum. Before I return to Louise's daily meeting, then, I turn to the children's worlds, where diverse social dialogues occurred as the children took control of the interactional space Louise offered.

Dialogues at Sea: The Social Work of Child Composing

All of the children engaged in a variety of kinds of social work; that is, they established and maintained diverse sorts of relationships with others. Moreover, like adult language-users, they drew upon different genres and different discourse traditions, including those of popular culture and of their sociocultural community. Herein, I aim only to highlight dominant kinds of social work, illustrating children's typical (but not mutually exclusive) ways of making social use of the daily composing time. The categorization or naming of these kinds of social work provides a helpful heuristic for discussing the children's actions, but it is only a heuristic. Children can accomplish varied kinds of social action simultaneously, and they can change social stances quite quickly (as can, of course, adults).

To illustrate their social work and cultural materials, I focus on three child products made during a study unit about oceans, in which Louise and the children talked and read about varied ocean creatures and visited a local aquarium. Fish became a popular topic during this time, as is evidenced by Lamar's "I am a swimmer" piece, Jameel's word-producing fish, and Eugenie's "Callm [clam] lives in here." (See Figures 3, 4, and 5.)

The children, then, had common official curricular experiences to draw upon, and they also were participants in a common official writing "workshop": they were to compose and then share their products, serving as a responsive, helpful audience for each other. And yet, the children enacted very different social dramas as they each took to the sea. Imagine, then, moving to different corners of Louise's classroom as I bring Lamar, Jameel, and Eugenie in focus one by one.

Establishing Social Cohesion: Lamar and Trouble at Sea

Kindergartner Lamar's "I am a swimmer" piece was not energized by an anticipation of rug-time sharing but by composing-time collaborative play. That is, his evolving text was a tool for carrying on a dominant kind of social work in children's as well as adults' worlds – not simply communicating messages but establishing social cohesion, constructing a common world (see Table 1).

Sample Text	Dominant Purpose	Text Sense	Addressee Role	Sample Addressee Response
Lamar's sea text	Social cohesion	Shared	Involved collaborators or confirmers	"Oh yeah!" "I know"
Jameel's song	Entertaining performance	Humorous/ Artful	Appreciative audience	"That's funny!"
Eugenie's clam text	Communication of information	Explicit/ Informative	Needy student	"Thank you"

Table 1: Samples of Children's Social Work during Composing Time
Note: This chart is not intended to be comprehensive. It is intended only to illustrate that words like *audience* and *sense* do not have generic meaning.

To establish cohesive relationships through oral stories, many children drew on material from popular culture – stories about superheroes, verses by rap stars, or scenes from horror movies. Such material was apt to elicit an "Oh yeah, I saw that too" from a child addressee, or a "Me too, I like that too." Sometimes the children jointly recounted the "best parts" of stories from the popular media. "'Member when?" the children would say one after another as episodes were recalled. Sometimes too they engaged in rounds of storytelling, in which they recounted similar (if exaggerated) experiences, as each child outdid the other in the daringness (or silliness) of their actions.

Such responsive interaction was evident in Lamar's early forays into written composing as well, just as it was in his "I am a swimmer" event. In this event, Lamar's collaboration with his good friend James was filtered through each child's separate paper, as it were; but it was collaboration nonetheless, as the following excerpt illustrates. (Note that the ellipses between quotes are indicative of deleted text, and colons within quotes are indicative of elongated pronunciation of the preceding syllable.)

Lamar and James are drawing ocean scenes, in which they will confront the admired and dreaded shark, sometimes referred to by the boys as "Jaws," after a popular movie featuring a shark. Both boys tell and, sometimes, perform a story as they draw.

James:	(chants) I'm swimming in the lake, I'm swimming in the lake. I won't come in and eat my cake. This gonna be the waves. (drawing waves) This gonna be the waves
	…
Lamar:	Do you know what these lines are? (pointing to his own drawing [see Figure 3]) They're the waves. They're pushing me this way.
James:	Look at these waves (pointing to his own drawing).
Lamar:	And then the water gets higher (drawing his waves higher). (Note that "and then" links Lamar's turn with his own previous turn, not with James's.)
James:	Mine's gonna get higher, too. My water's higher than you. (Note the use of pronouns ["Mine's"] and repetition ["gonna get higher, too."], both indices of story collaboration [Eder, 1988; Goodwin, 1990])
Lamar:	Shoot. Mine is higher than yours
	…
	Mine is over my head. Told you mine's higher than yours. Mine got deeper. Deeper.
	…
	(to Tyler) Ain't this deep – ain't this deeper than James's?
Tyler:	(nods) It's pretty deep.

| James: | Look at me diving in the water. Lamar, look at me diving in the water. Look at me diving in the water, Anthony. |

...

| Lamar: | And then a shark was coming. Then a shark was coming. (The "and then" links back to Lamar's previous storylines.) |

...

| James: | If they had a shark in the water, we'd get ready to get out of the water. |
| Lamar: | I'm getting ready to get out of the water 'cause the shark. (Lamar takes James's idea and incorporates it into his own story.) |

...

| | (chanting) I'm deep in the water. The shark's gonna kill me. |
| James: | But oh ! There's a shark in the water. (Now James incorporates Lamar's idea into his own story. The "But oh !" refers to a development in James's own piece.) |

...

| Lamar: | I'm gonna make the blood coming out 'cause the shark bit the octopus. I'm gonna make the blood in the water. (adds red by octopus) |

Later, with the help of Mrs. Johnson, a teaching assistant, both boys write "I am a swimmer."

The social meaning of Lamar's multimedia story (woven from talking, drawing, and writing) was linked to that of James's.

The children declared themselves as vulnerable but brave – or "braver than you" – boys in a world of monsters. Each text was motivated by, and contributed to, the boys' relationship as best friends.

Figure 3: Lamar's adventure at sea

Taking the Spotlight: Jameel and the Singing Fish.

Although Lamar's efforts were energized by his ongoing play with James, first grader Jameel's crafting of his fish text was fueled by the anticipation of rug-time sharing. But he did not eagerly await communication with helpful peers; he anticipated an artful performance for an appreciative, admiring audience (see Table 1). He brooked no advice from others when his moment in the spotlight finally arrived.

Although Jameel was the most consistent performer in his class, all of the observed children engaged in performances. In doing so, they often drew on their oral folk resources (i.e., the features of verbal art, which highlight the musical and image-creating properties of language [Bauman, 1986; Smitherman, 1986; Tannen, 1989]), and they also tended to explicitly manipulate their texts; for example, they tried to make words rhyme, phrases rhythmic, dialogue fast-paced, and images funny. The aim was not a confirming "me, too" but a pleased and perhaps surprised "Oh!" or even laughter.

To compose his singing fish, Jameel combined his interest in rhythmic, poetic, humorous prose with an interest in scientific exposition, and he brought together his enjoyment of popular cartoons with his fascination with the ocean study unit.

Jameel: [I wrote it] 'cause I love singing. Then I started loving animals. And then I thought, "I'll make 'em singing a song. A singing fish."

As seen in Figure 4, on the top of his paper, Jameel had drawn a fish with four large bubbles coming out of its mouth. These are both comic-like and air bubbles – a visual pun. In each bubble is a "tune," that is, the words being sung by the fish. (The words of the song had, in fact, come from comic-like and surreptitious operatic singing ["me me me" and "my my my"] many children, including Jameel, had been doing during morning singing.)

The bottom half of the page is an exposition of the fish, written in a performative style, with paired, contrastive variants of a sentence.

The voice on the bottom text is an "announcer," as Jameel explained. Moreover, Jameel had made a stapled pocket on the bottom of his song. This, he said, was for the money donations that would surely follow when he took his singing fish to the streets.

Jameel: [People will] pay money for it, the fish. But it's gonna be me [taking the money]. And I'm only give the fish a itsy bitsy piece of candy. And I'm gonna keep the money.

However, the streets of most immediate concern were those of his classroom neighborhood. As he worked, Jameel did not want to sing his song to any of his neighbors, so to speak; they would have to wait for the appropriate time, that is, for show time on the rug.

Figure 4: Jameel's singing fish: "That fish isn't any ordinary fish. It's a singing fish."

Helping a Needy Colleague: Eugenie and the Clam in the Shell

Lamar's and Jameel's peer Eugenie, a first grader, displayed two different kinds of social work as she composed her ocean piece. One sort of work is similar to that displayed by Lamar, since it involves social cohesion. But it does not necessarily involve collaboratively producing a text. Rather, it involves collegially acknowledging peers as people in the same boat, as it were. That is, the children commiserated about the trials and tribulations of learning to write, including spelling and spacing, doing it over and trying to read it. Listen, for example, to Eugenie's reaction to Shawnda's lament (colons in text are indicative of an elongated sound or syllable):

"Shucks," said Shawnda. "I erased that whole row [of writing] and I'm doing it over. (Eugenie giggles.) I don't care if it is recess time. I'm gonna do it over and I might do it over 10,000 times. I mean that."

"O::, I know how you feel, gir::l!" responded Eugenie with great conviction. "I KNOW, HOW, YOU, FEEL!"

The children valued informal, mutual helping. Colleagues help each other and do not expose each other's weaknesses in public places. Still, when the opportunity presented itself, Eugenie, like all the observed children, took the opportunity to teach a needy other, often using, at least in part, Louise's straightforward style and professional vocabulary. To accomplish this other kind of social work (see Table 1), Eugenie, as teacher, required a student, preferably a grateful one, and she found Vera a willing learner in the "clam" event. In the following excerpt, note how Eugenie presents a collegial "we" to Mrs. Johnson, despite her adoption of a leadership role with Vera. (Figure 5 presents Eugenie's completed text.)

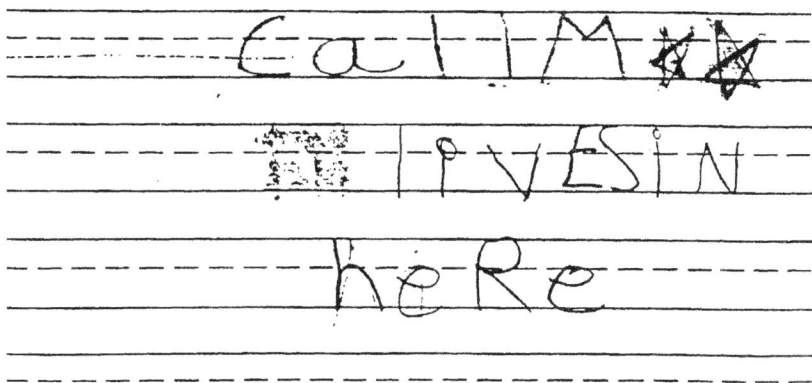

Figure 5: Eugenie's hypothesized clam shell.

Eugenie and Vera have taken a shell from a large basket in the classroom. They are each going to write about what might have lived in that shell.

Vera: Now what does live in this shell?
            …

Eugenie: This is not fact. This is fiction. (Note the use of the school terms "fact" and "fiction.")
            …
            Do you think a clam might be living in here? See, like a clam might be living in here. But he left his color of this spot to let us know. It might be a little clam. (Note how Eugenie puts forth a hypothetical statement and links that statement to a previous observation [that the shell had a brown spot].)

Vera: That's true
            ….

Eugenie: Mrs. Johnson, come here. Me and Vera made a decision. We thought that a clam might live in the shell. (Note the explicit reference to making "a decision"; such reference was common in Louise's talk to children but not common in the children's unofficial talk.)

Performers, colleagues, collaborators, teachers, and students – Lamar, Jameel, and Eugenie were complex social actors in classroom worlds, and these ends influenced their ways of enacting, participating in, classroom literacy events. They drew upon diverse sorts of cultural materials as they worked toward varied ends.

A Cultural Forum in Action

The children, with their diverse social roles and resources, did not fit neatly into the social order Louise originally had imagined. She had, for example, suggested an opening ten minutes of "quiet writing time," but her children talked. Moreover, Louise had anticipated children corning to the rug to communicate to a peer "audience" which would offer comments and suggestions. But the desire to communicate per se was not necessarily the children's dominant goal – indeed, sometimes the major goal was achieved before they arrived at the rug (as with Lamar's collaborative work with James). Further, the children objected to an advice-giving audience, a role, after all, that differs substantively from that of editor or formal critic in our common culture (for elaboration of this point, see Dyson, 1992, 1993).

Nor was it so easy for Louise to figure out what advice she should give about content. Most pedagogical suggestions for young children assume making a better, more sensible text has to do with making ideas more explicit (i.e., writing less "egocentrically"). But the crafting of the singing fish text, for example, did not have to do with explicitness but with rhythm.

The children were exploring the ways in which they might act on and in their worlds through the written medium. In response, Louise, first, allowed continued space for what the children were doing; after all, colleagues must be free to consult and commiserate, to admire and admonish – and to find a space apart for private shaping and reflection. Similarly, collaborators require partners, performers need an audience, and "teachers" must have "students," or they cannot enact their roles, display their skills, or accomplish the ends that make their lives satisfying. Louise sometimes explicitly and officially acknowledged that social work. For example, she talked with her children about their preferred ways of composing, making explicit the variation and offering choices. Did they wish to write alone? With a partner? In a quiet corner? On a table with other composers?

Second, Louise took advantage of the diversity of cultural material the children brought to the rug. In the presented examples, the genres included horror stories and pop songs, but they could have been cartoons or raps, "true stories" filled with hyperbole, or expressive "love stories".[4] In response to the children's inclusiveness, Louise worked to help children name their efforts, to place their work in the social landscape of discourse.

To do this, Louise provided children's texts with the dignity of a name (e.g., fiction, nonfiction, descriptions, songs, games, poems, jokes), a practice the children gradually engaged in as well. And she worked to establish connections between their efforts and that of the wider world of discourse. For example, when Lamar brought his "shark" piece to the meeting on the rug, he explained to the class about the shark, the octopus, and his own precarious presence in the water; in turn, Louise helped his piece become part of general class reflection on fish stories that were mainly factual and those that were mainly fictional. (Louise herself introduced the term "whale of a tale.") Eugenie's piece fed into the cultural forum in similar ways, although, unlike Lamar, Eugenie made sure the class knew that she and Vera had worked on the same shell (a point made in part to irritate Vera's friend Shawnda, with whom Eugenie herself had a rather tenuous relationship).

Jameel's piece fed into the class forum in a particularly dramatic way, and therefore the interplay between Jameel's social intentions and Louise's response is particularly revealing. Jameel had come to the rug specifically to entertain the class – and he did so. Sitting on the rug during sharing time, Jameel sang his song for his classmates in a crooning voice, like Bing Crosby or Nat King Cole. His singing is presented in phrase groups, with hyphens indicative of a careful pronunciation of the letter itself. (Note that colons are indicative of elongated pronunciation of the preceding syllable.)

Jameel: M-Y-M-Y: (sings each letter in a smooth, rising
            tune, elongating the last Y; he has written periods
            after each letter [e.g.,
            M.Y.M.Y.] to indicate that each is to be sung sepa-
            rately.)
            M-Y-M-Y: (sings similarly)
            M:-M: (continues on the high pitch with
            elongated Ms)
            me me me: (even pitch)
            you you you: (even but higher pitch)
            my my my: (even but higher pitch)
            M-Y-M-Y: (as before)
            I: lo::ve (elongated and with a rhythmic drop and
            then rise in pitch)
            you, to, boop boo bee do (syncopated)
            M-Y-M-Y: (as before)
            That fish isn't any ordinary fish. It's a singing fish.
            (reads in an announcer's voice; note the repetition
            and variation in sentence structure)

Jameel's song received much applause and laughter. It was, in short, a hit. In the afternoon following his morning perfor-mance, many of his classmates decided to write songs them-selves.

Louise responded to the songs by incorporating them and their participation framework (i.e., the performer and audience roles) into the official classroom world. As was Louise's strat-egy, she used professional language to establish links between the children's songs and those of the wider world and, just as importantly, to provide tools for reflection. She explained the necessity of taping their tunes; without special writing skills, taping would be the only way that those tunes could be remembered. She brainstormed with the children about other books they had read that contained tunes whose graphic features they could study, and she consulted with the school music teacher, who talked to the children about how music was written. Perhaps this respectful and serious response (filled, as it was, with good fun) contributed to Jameel's increased reflectiveness about his songwriting (e.g., purposefully checking his songs before performances, adjusting lines that didn't "work," that is, sound right to his ear).

Louise's response to Jameel's songs is indicative of the larger interplay among cultural material in her classroom. The children studied the local symphony and local rappers; they read folktales of varied peoples and children's books written in diverse vernaculars. Each child's own composed text thus entered into an intertextual universe – a school culture – that was not some kind of anemic world, where words are disembedded from social contexts (cf. Donaldson, 1978); it was one where words reverberated with the diverse rhythms and sounds of human voices. And, of course, one to which the children contributed. Thus, the enacted curriculum in Louise's classroom included a diversity of texts, of kinds of sense, and of possible dialogic responses to children's oral and written words.

From Permeable Curricular Main Roads to Limiting Side Roads

To clarify this concept of the permeable curriculum – this interplay between children's and adults' worlds – I consider events of one year later. Eugenie was then in the second grade and in another classroom, one in which interactive space and academic demands were more clearly specified, as, in fact, is a typical change in classrooms as children move through school (Goodlad, 1984).

The "follow-up activity" to the Lincoln lesson was illustrative – the children were to fold their paper into eight boxes, unfold them, and then draw and write a fact about Lincoln in each box. In many similar activities, sample sentences were put on the board. While the children did not orally present their work, it was regularly "published;" that is, the work was bound in class-made books or displayed on bulletin boards.

The activities in which Eugenie and her peers engaged were commonplace. Her teacher was hardworking and caring, not an out-of-touch educator who passed out dittos and basal readers. But the very typical nature of the activities – and the ways in which they were enacted within the children's social worlds – made the classroom an invaluable setting for applying and, thereby clarifying, the concept of permeability.

To reiterate, the aim herein is not to make generalizations about particular teachers or teaching practices but, through examining such particulars, to illuminate an idea – permeability – that might help educators in other situations "ferret out the unapparent import of things" (Geertz, 1973, p. 126), things like a child's text about Lincoln and love.

Historical Facts or Fiction: Eugenie and Mr. Lincoln

As Eugenie set to work on the Lincoln piece, she looked up from time to time at her two friends in the second grade, Vanessa and LaToya. (The friends' desks were strategically separated by her teacher.)

Eugenie began by drawing Lincoln wearing a tall hat, but her drawing was interrupted by a loud whisper from Vanessa, who was holding up her picture. Vanessa was hard to hear, but she clearly had drawn Abraham Lincoln getting shot at a theater. Eugenie quickly wrote "He was nice" under her first picture and began work on her own theater picture. She drew a girl with long blond hair – Lincoln's child, she said, or maybe "a friend of his." (She wasn't sure if Lincoln had any kids or not.) Nonetheless, Eugenie had a dramatic scene in mind, one centered on what might have happened before that fateful trip to the theater:

Figure 6. Vanessa's important facts about Lincoln.

Eugenie: (presenting her work to me) She's [the drawn girl] saying, "I love you." Because before he got ready to go to the theater, she said, "Even if you get killed, I still love you." (said with great feeling)

Eugenie wrote "I Love You" in a bubble coming out of the girl's mouth. Then, with a glance at her teacher (in the corner with a child), she moved over to Vanessa's desk. LaToya soon followed. Vanessa presented her completed paper to her two friends (see Figure 6).

She had not focused on Lincoln's political life, the emphasis of the lesson, but on his personal life. While lacking in precise details, she had drawn Lincoln as a little boy by a house, Lincoln as a man by yet another house, Lincoln's girlfriend, Lincoln getting married (complete with wedding vows), and the house where Lincoln and his wife lived. Interspersed with Vanessa's presentation of her work, the children discussed their own views on boyfriends (they currently did not have them), growing up (much anticipated), and babies (they all wanted them).

Mrs. Walker, the classroom teaching assistant, who had just entered the room from another classroom, sent the girls back to their seats. Back in her own place again, Eugenie drew Lincoln's house, his wife, and his wedding day (complete with vows). (See Figure 1; final three pictures completed at another time.)

Eventually, Vanessa and LaToya came to Eugenie's desk. Eugenie now presented her work to her friends, dramatically reading the line "I love you" and explaining its import. LaToya then motioned her friends into the classroom library; she had a dance step to show them. Her teacher saw the dancing and sent them back to their seats.

During this event, Eugenie's stance was primarily a collegial, at times collaborative, one. She discussed her decisions and textual content with her friends. Moreover, Eugenie's written voice was influenced by the social work she engaged in with her friends; her piece on Lincoln reflected the themes and dramatic style of the girls' talk among themselves. Eugenie had, in effect, composed an official school text by drawing on unofficial worlds. But that text did not function as a kind of crossroad among worlds.

There was no public forum for Eugenie to present her work in the official world, to bring out her performative language, the dramatized event she had imagined, the family life she had constructed when drawing. Without a forum, there was also no way to socially analyze the work (for example, the decision to imagine details), to compare it to other classmates' decisions, or to connect it with varied kinds of genres in the larger world (e.g., historical fiction, melodramas or child "love stories"). Her unofficial social and language work could not become part of the official classroom culture. Her text would be checked for completion according to the required assignment – paper folded into eight boxes, eight pictures and eight sentences about Lincoln's life, all nongenre-related criteria. In the official world, her "I do's" and "I love you" became textual equivalents to dancing in the library, behaviors clearly off the curricular main road.

Thus, Eugenie's social and language resources did not enter into the larger classroom community, nor, for that matter, did the language of the larger community enter in a substantive way into Eugenie's collegial talk and composing. Eugenie was not making decisions about potential kinds of literacy dialogues ("This is not fact. This is fiction."). She had composed along a curricular side road, one with limited possibility of connecting up with the main road.

Reflections on the Permeable Curriculum: Theoretical Themes

This essay began with an image of a teacher puzzling over Eugenie's piece about Mr. Lincoln. The teacher felt unconnected to the life world of her student, at a loss in her efforts to understand where Eugenie was coming from. This image is reflective of the feelings of many teachers about their students – and of the feelings of many students about their teachers (Rothman, 1992). Indeed, by the middle school years, the life worlds of school and those of peers and communities are often rigidly separated in the minds of students (Sleeter & Grant, 1991).

The intention herein is not to devalue the social and cultural materials of the official curriculum. But it is to suggest that those materials are of no use unless they engage children with the social and cultural worlds they know best and, moreover, to suggest that both child worlds and school worlds would be considerably enriched by the interplay made possible in a permeable curriculum. Such a curriculum seeks to acknowledge and respect the complexity of children's social worlds and cultural materials. And it attempts, not only to create bridges between worlds, but to support children's own naming and manipulating of the dynamic relationships among worlds. That is, it aims to help children understand and negotiate among multiple social worlds by means of diverse ways with words (Hymes, 1980). In complex modern societies, it is negotiating among – "managing" (Hymes, 1980, p. 45) – diverse ways with words that is the essential discourse challenge.

By highlighting the experiences of the children in Eugenie's school, I hoped to provide concrete examples of such permeability, of what respect for children's social worlds, and for their cultural materials, might look like, and of how a cultural forum might help both children's and teachers' worlds expand. Just as important, I hoped to illustrate the theoretical ideas about literacy, particularly composing, about cultural diversity, and about teaching that undergird such an evolving curriculum. Next, I highlight three key ideas and their implications for the permeable curriculum.

Composing as Social Dialogue

From the perspective of this essay, composing is always a situated response, an addressing of another in a particular time and place, a motivated making of words for some end. That is, written words are only mediators and, for young children especially, only partial mediators of social action. Approaching children's texts as social action, then, requires sensitivity to the logic of children's own social worlds. And those worlds, in turn, require interactive space in our classrooms. In the intimate worlds children construct together, they use a range of cultural resources to enact roles as colleagues and collaborators, performers and audience members, teachers and, of course, students.

Moreover, making use of children's social intelligence entails rethinking the generic nature of writing pedagogy for young children. Teachers are encouraged to arrange social situations in which child composers receive "responses" to their texts from "authentic" audiences of peers. But a teacher's quiet writing time might be a child's collaborative work period; a teacher's "whole-group writing" conference might be a child's show-time stage; and a teacher's occasion for peer editing might be viewed by the children as an occasion for collegiality. Considering children as social actors thus suggests that "audience," "editor," and "response" are situated, not generic, terms that can be explicitly discussed and planned for with children. And it suggests as well the importance of diverse situations for composing – and diverse text types.

To elaborate, pedagogical writing about child literacy often assumes that the developmental goal is "decontextualized" written language (e.g., Olson, 1984), that is, language in which ideas are made explicit in tightly constructed prose, rather than implicitly understood by familiar interlocutors. But, given that written language always exists within a kind of social relationship, so-called "decontextualized" language also exists only in certain situational and text contexts, that is, in certain genres. Moreover, children can begin writing by producing a diversity of genres – and any one child may control diverse sorts of texts. Official recognition of diverse types or genres, though, necessitates a dialogic perspective, not simply toward literacy, but toward cultural traditions themselves.

A Dialogic Perspective on Cultural Traditions

As social actors, young children draw on a diversity of cultural materials. The easy ways in which they move among cultural traditions, creating stories that blend folk, popular, and written traditions, reflect, in fact, the complex, dialogic relationships that link traditions. For example, the daily rhythms of music and talk that arise from the regional and ethnic cultures of our society – from the "folk" – have transformed both "popular" and "high" culture (Gates, 1989). In addition, popular cultural forms can express an oppositional attitude – a distancing, a playfulness – to the "high," the serious, the "towering" (Bakhtin, 1981), which may account for their appeal to the young.

However, most discussions of young children as literacy users draw firm lines between the literacy experiences of children who have had extended preschool exposure to children's literature and, particularly, storybooks, and of those who have not had such experiences. Through reading and talking about books, parents introduce children to the explicit or "decontextualized" prose valued in school. And yet, children's literature draws on a diversity of cultural genres, including jazz tunes and folk songs, cartoons and oral lore, as well as the wealth of spoken English vernaculars (Kushkin, 1980). Moreover, cultural labels are themselves quite fuzzy; for example, in nineteenth-century America, "popular culture" – the cultural art forms meaningful to diverse regional, class, and ethnic groups – included Shakespeare, opera, and classical music, along with juggling, parodies, and songs (Levine, 1988).

Recently, scholars working with older students have emphasized how the rhetorical features of peer and folk ways with words (e.g., oral stories and language plays, metaphors and insult games) are potentially powerful learning and language tools across the curriculum. And they have written about their efforts to help students make deliberate use of their range of discourse strategies in both literary and academic writing (Ball, 1992; Redd, 1992; Scott, 1990; Smitherman, 1986, 1994). We who work in early childhood and elementary education can contribute to such efforts by broadening our vision of the kinds of cultural resources that support literacy growth.

Perhaps there is a fear of acknowledging and building upon diverse discourse themes, genre structures, and styles, because of our human propensity toward dichotomous thinking. As educators, we have categorized children as "at-risk" or not, "mainstream" or "nonmainstream," and we have associated certain categories – and the possibility of school success – exclusively with certain ways of using language. More broadly, as a society, we have used speech styles and art forms as ways of gauging intellectual and aesthetic superiority and inferiority, of reinforcing boundaries of class, ethnicity, and culture (Hymes, 1980; Levine, 1988).

But language in use is inherently diverse – changing with situation, role, and activity – and humans are remarkably flexible language users; given a reason (and opportunities for practice), we are code-switchers, register collectors, and players with speech (Garvey, 1990; Gilyard, 1991; Labov, 1969). There is no reason to assume that a child who writes pop songs for a singing fish cannot deliver a lecture on the nature of ocean creatures – certainly Jameel could (particularly when given an opportunity to teach; for examples, see Dyson, 1992, 1993). Nor, of course, is there a reason to think that an effective lecture can be given in only one style (Farr, 1993). To repeat, the essential language skill is not mastery of any one genre or style – it is the capacity to negotiate among contexts, to be socially and politically astute in discourse use.

Further, while there is ample reason for adult concern about the sometimes sexist, racist, and violent images of the popular media, children's literature is not immune from such charges (Gilbert, 1989; Sims, 1982). Moreover, lack of acknowledgement of many young students' deep fascination with the popular media does not help them develop a critical perspective.

The acknowledgement of human and language complexity seems to be a critical first step in respectful relationships between teachers and students and in the building of a shared life, which leads to the final idea that undergirds the permeable curriculum, that of a cultural forum.

Curiosity, Respect, and the Cultural Forum

Like us all, children negotiate membership in overlapping, sometimes contradictory, worlds governed by "imaginative universes" – cultures, as it were, or shared ways of infusing objects and actions with meaning (Geertz, 1973). But, as teachers, we only have access to parts of children's selves. Respect for the diversity of children's worlds and for the partiality of our own visions keeps us from putting children into neat "sociological categories of race, social class, ethnicity and family structure [which then] become the primary factors of differentiating among children" (Lightfoot, 1978, p. 211). Respect also fuels our interest in children's lives, our desire as teachers to understand the factors that contribute to a child's wholeness, to their individuality.

Teachers with such curiosity talk with (not simply about) parents and community members, seeking insight into children's lives beyond the school walls and into the language use that pervades those lives (for suggestions about such talk, see Barr et al., 1988). Moreover, they invite children themselves to share responsibility for negotiating the language life – the valued texts – of classroom life (Genishi, 1992). In this way the negotiated culture of the classroom is enriched, as diverse genres, diverse cultural traditions, mingle on the classroom stage, giving rise to "new possibilities, new speculations, new styles" (Rosen & Rosen, 1973, p. 32).

Critical to such negotiation is an ongoing cultural forum. I am not referring to a "whole-class conference," the main purpose of which is to support the development of individual children's writing. Rather, I am suggesting a forum, within which children might explain about Lincoln and imagined loves, about Jaws in the deep and decisions about clams, and within which we as educators connect their efforts with the world beyond. And, at the same time, it is a forum in which our own world view is enriched by those of the children.

In Closing: Behind the Curricular Curtain

In *The Woman Warrior*, Maxine Hong Kingston (1977) writes about the puzzlement and alarm her elementary school teachers expressed about her school paintings.

"I painted layers of black over houses and flowers and suns," she wrote, "and when I drew on the blackboard, I put a layer of chalk on top" (p. 192). Her teachers consulted with her parents rather than with the silent Maxine, but her parents did not speak English. What no one, parents or teachers, knew was that Maxine "was making a stage curtain, and it was the moment before the curtain parted or rose." When her parents took her pictures home, Maxine "spread them out (so black and full of possibilities) and pretended the curtains were swinging open, flying up, one after another, sunlight underneath, mighty operas."

In a similar way, dramas unfold behind the curtain of the official curriculum. Those dramas, like the ones of Hong Kingston's imagination, are the stuff of children's lives (indeed, they are the stuff of our own memories of childhood) – dramas of friends and fights, of imagined melodramas and high adventures, and, in fact, of the thrill of being behind the curtain, protected in some way from the judgments and orders of the adult world. Still, if we are to teach the children, we have to tap into these child worlds, and we have to offer them tools – ways of thinking and talking – that will help them negotiate their way into a future of possibilities.

In a troubled world of poverty and violence, of racism and sometimes breathtaking indifference, we cannot pave children's way. But, as teachers, we can help. Within our classrooms, children compose texts that declare their existence in the world, but that existence is acknowledged, momentarily completed, only by the response of the other (Bakhtin, 1986). In our own responses to the children, we help shape their understanding of what it means to be an educated person in our society. If our classrooms are not places for a diversity of social action and a wealth of cultural materials, we risk sending messages of alienation, messages that say that educated people are not rooted in their own histories, in strong relationships with people that matter.

Moreover, we deny them, and ourselves, the scholarly benefit – and the good fun – possible when language and experiences are shared. For, in answering the children, we are also composing ourselves. In their plurality, in their diversity, our children offer us the opportunity to open wider the curtains framing our own world view, so that we might see aspects of experience that otherwise would remain invisible to us, so that we might better understand ourselves as situated in a complex world of multiple perspectives (Greene, 1988).

Eugenie's piece on Lincoln and love, for example, set me wondering about the story of the Civil War and about history itself as it was taught to me, that is, as a series of wars. I wondered what a little girl like Eugenie (or like the once-me), so attuned to relationships, could identify with in such a story – what would tap her experiences and feelings, what would feed into her social talk with friends. I thought about why she and her friends had snuck around behind the curricular curtain, situating Lincoln in the themes of their own play. And I wondered about how the children's fascination with Lincoln and his loves connected with the political stories of relationships (sanctioned and not) that pervade our political campaigns. I reflected on how history (including war) becomes a dehumanized topic, on how humanized history attracts so many of us (as did the PBS special on the Civil War).

I wondered and wandered far from Eugenie, Lincoln, and the second grade, and then returned again to underscore, as I do now, the complexity of social work and intellectual thought that are revealed when we push back the curricular curtains. Children's texts are sites for negotiation among multiple social worlds, worlds energized by dreams and fears, friendships and kinships. In working to create a permeable curriculum, we bring at least some of the energy of these worlds into the official classroom world and, in so doing, we enrich the cultural conversations of us all.

NOTES

1. Temple, Nathan, Temple, and Burris (1993) is a thorough text (now in its third edition) that, in emphasis, represents well dominant perspectives. The first chapter begins with an example of invented spelling. Although the importance of adult modeling is emphasized, the child is characterized as egocentric, with reference to Piaget, and learning to write is presented primarily as an act of discovery.
2. For an illuminating autobiographical portrayal of a child's negotiation among worlds, see Gilyard, 1991.
3. To elaborate, I was interested in the contextual specifics of children's discourse use. I wondered how children used varied kinds of language art forms and cultural traditions (e.g., those of their ethnic communities, of popular culture, of shared classroom literature) as they interacted with teachers and peers throughout the school day, that is, as they engaged in social work through oral and written language. (For discussions of the ethnography of communication, the traditions of which guided this work, see Gumperz & Hymes, 1986; for details of data collection and analysis, see Dyson, 1993.)
4. "True stories" was a term used by the children. It

referred to exaggerated stories with elements of truth in them (for discussions of the role of such stories in African American culture, see Smitherman, 1986, and Heath, 1983, who uses the same emic term). "Love stories" was also a child term, introduced by Jameel, to refer to texts composed of questions and statements about classmates' special friends.

REFERENCES

Bakhtin, M. (1981). Discourse in the novel. In C. Emerson & M. Holquist (Eds.), *The dialogic imagination: Four essays by M. Bakhtin* (pp.259-422). Austin, TX: University of Texas Press.

Bakhtin, M. (1986). *Speech genres and other late essays.* Austin, TX: University of Texas Press.

Ball, A. (1992). Cultural preference and the expository writing of African-American adolescents. *Written Communication*, 9, 501-532.

Barr, M., Ellis, S., Hester, H., & Thomas, A. (1988). *The primary language record.* Portsmouth, NH: Heinemann.

Bauman, R. (1986). *Story, performance, and event: Contextual studies of oral narrative.* Cambridge, NY: Cambridge University Press.

Brown, R. (1973). *A first language: The early stages.* Cambridge, MA: Harvard University Press.

Bruner, J. (1986). *Actual minds, possible worlds.* Cambridge, MA: Harvard University Press.

Bruner, J., & Haste, H. (Eds.). (1987). *Making sense: The child's construction of the world.* New York, NY: Methuen.

Committee on Policy for Racial Justice. (1989). *Visions of a better way: A Black appraisal of public schooling.* Washington, DC: Joint Center for Political Studies Press.

D'Amato, J. D. (1987). The belly of the beast: On cultural difference, castelike status, and the politics of school. *Anthropology & Education Quarterly, 18,* 357-360.

Donaldson, M. (1978). *Children's minds.* New York, NY: Norton.

Dyson, A. H. (1989). *Multiple worlds of child writers: Friends learning to write.* New York, NY: Teachers College Press.

Dyson, A. H. (1992). The case of the singing scientist: A performance perspective on the "stages" of school literacy. *Written Communication, 9,* 3-47.

Dyson, A.H. (1993). *The social worlds of children learning to write in an urban primary school.* New York, NY: Teachers College Press.

Eder, D. (1988). Building cohesion through collaborative narration. *Social Problems Quarterly, 51,* 225-235.

Erickson, F. (1987). Transformation and school success: The politics and culture of educational achievement. *Anthropology & Education Quarterly, 18,* 335-356.

Farr, M. (1993). Essayist literacy and other verbal performances. *Written Communication, 10,* 4-38.

Garvey, C. (1990). *Play* (enlarged edition). Cambridge, MA: Harvard University Press.

Gates, H. L., Jr. (1989). Canon-formation, literary history, and the Afro-American tradition: From the seen to the told. In H. A. Baker, Jr. & P. Redmond (Eds.), *Afro-American literary study in the 1990s* (pp. 14-38). Chicago: The University of Chicago Press.

Geertz, C. (1973). *The interpretation of cultures: Selected essays.* New York, NY: Basic Books.

Genishi, C. (Ed.). (1992). *Ways of assessing children and curriculum: Stories of early childhood practice.* New York, NY: Teachers College Press.

Gilbert, P. (1989). *Gender, literacy, and the classroom.* Carlton

South, Victoria: Australian Reading Association.

Gilyard, K. (1991). *Voices of the self: A study of language competence*. Detroit, MI: Wayne State University Press.

Goodlad, J. (1984). *A place called school: Prospects for the future*. New York, NY: McGraw-Hill.

Goodwin, M. (1990). *He-said-she-said: Talk as social organization among black children*. Bloomington, IN: Indiana University Press.

Graves, D. H. (1983). *Writing: Teachers and children at work*. Portsmouth, NH: Heinemann Educational Books.

Greene, M. (1988). *The dialectic of freedom*. New York, NY: Teachers College Press.

Gumperz, J., & Hymes, D. (Eds.). (1986). *Directions in sociolinguistics: The ethnography of communication* (2nd ed.). New York, NY: Basil Blackwell.

Hymes, D. (1980). *Language in education*. Washington, DC: Center for Applied Linguistics.

Kingston, M. H. (1977). *The woman warrior*. New York, NY: Random House.

Kushkin, K. (1980). The language of children's literature. In L. Michaels & C. Ricks (Eds.), *The state of the language* (pp. 213-225). Berkeley, CA: University of California Press.

Labov, W. (1969). The logic of nonstandard English. In J. E. Alatis (Ed.), *Report of the twentieth annual roundtable meeting on linguistics and language study* (pp. 1-44). Washington, DC: Georgetown University Press.

Levine, L. (1988). *Highbrow/lowbrow: The emergence of cultural hierarchy in America*. Cambridge, MA: Harvard University Press.

Lightfoot, S. (1978). *Worlds apart: Relationships between families and schools*. New York, NY: Basic Books.

McLane, J. & McNamee, G. (1990). *Early literacy.* Cambridge, MA: Harvard University Press.

Newkirk, T. (1989). *More than stories: The range of children's writing.* Portsmouth, NH: Heinemann.

Olson, D. (1984). "See! Jumping!" Some oral antecedents of literacy. In H. Goelman, A. Oberg, & F. Smith (Eds.), *Awakening to literacy* (pp. 185-192). Portsmouth, NH: Heinemann.

Read, C. (1975). *Children's categorization of speech sounds in English.* Urbana, IL: National Council of Teachers of English.

Redd, T. (1992). "Styling" in black students' writing for black audiences. Paper presented at the meeting of the American Educational Research Association, San Francisco, CA.

Roberts, J. (1970). *Scene of the battle: Group behavior in urban classrooms.* Garden City, NY: Doubleday.

Rogoff, B. (1990). *Apprenticeship in thinking: Cognitive development in social context.* New York, NY: Oxford University Press.

Rosen, C., & Rosen, H. (1973). *The language of primary school children.* Harmondsworth, Middlesex, England: Penguin.

Rothman, R. (1992, December). Study from "inside" finds a deeper set of school problems. *Education Week,* 12 (13), pp. 1, 9.

Scott, J. C. (1990). The silent sounds of language variation in the classroom. In S. Hynds & D. Rubin (Eds.), *Perspectives on talk and learning* (pp. 285-298). Urbana, IL: National Council of Teachers of English.

Scribner, S., & Cole, M. (1981). *The psychology of literacy.* Cambridge, MA: Harvard University Press.

Sims, R. (1982). *Substance and shadow: Afro-American experience in contemporary children's literature.* Urbana, IL: National Council of Teachers of English.

Sleeter, C., & Grant, C. (1991). Mapping terrains of power: Student cultural knowledge versus classroom knowledge. In C. Sleeter (Ed.), *Empowerment through multi-cultural education* (pp. 49-68). Albany: State University of New York Press.

Smitherman, G. (1986). *Talkin and testifyin: The language of Black America.* Detroit: Wayne State University Press.

Smitherman, G. (1994). "The blacker the berry, the sweeter the juice": African American student writers and the national assessment of educational progress. In A. H. Dyson & C. Genishi (Eds.), *The need for story: Cultural diversity in classroom and community.* Urbana, IL: National Council of Teachers of English.

Stern, D. (1985). *The interpersonal world of the infant: A view from psychoanalysis and developmental psychology.* New York, NY: Basic Books.

Tannen, D. (1989). *Talking voices: Repetition, dialogue, and imagery in conversational discourse.* Cambridge, NY: Cambridge University Press.

Temple, C., Nathan, R., Temple, F., & Burris, N. (1993). *The beginnings of writing.* Needham Heights, MA: Allyn & Bacon.

Volosinov, V. N., & Bakhtin, M. (1973). *Marxism and the philosophy of language* (L. Matejka & I. R. Titunik, Trans.). New York, NY: Seminar Press.

Vygotsky, L. (1978). *Mind in society.* Cambridge, MA: Harvard University Press.

AN INTERVIEW WITH ANNE HAAS DYSON

BOBBIE:

You have been researching and writing about children's writing since 1981when you published your first article in *Language Arts* titled *Oral language: The rooting system for learning to write*. You are a prolific writer! Since that first article, you have published 12 books and over 100 journal articles and book chapters all regarding children's writing, or what you have learned from observing and researching children's writing. Can you talk a little about how you became interested in children's writing?

ANNE:

I became incredibly interested in children's writing when I started teaching in El Paso in the early seventies. When I gave my 6- to 8-year olds a piece of paper and a request that they write, I was amazed at the differences in how the children responded. My children, all without economic advantages but with the gift of bilingualism, responded in all sorts of ways.

One little one made quick work of the task, filling line after line with letter-like marks and then asking me to read what he had written (as would be the title of Marie Clay's 1975 book, *What Did I Write?*). Others drew, some copied whatever words they could find in no particular order, and then there were those who sought out words to write a bit of a message. It was if I had stepped into another world – what was happening here?

In time, as I learned to set up daily writing and sharing routines and to respond to a diversity of child approaches to writing, I started to notice all the talk accompanying writing and, then, how wrapped up in children's worlds writing could become. To understand these latter phenomena, I would need to sit and watch, but not from the teacher perspective but from – best I could – the child perspective.

I wasn't sure how to do this but, at the University of Texas at Austin, I took an anthropology and education class with Doug Foley and learned about an ethnographic stance and a critical frame as well – working toward a more just world; then I took an applied sociolinguistic class with Celia Genishi (my good friend was in her first years of a professorship then, to my great luck), and I learned how language could reveal children's worlds, including children whose voices were ignored in the literature (e.g., children who spoke a disrespected vernacular). And I was on my way.

I have never stopped being curious about writing, which I think of now as a mediator of children's relationships, and the relationships that matter in school most definitely include those among peers.

BOBBIE:

Who were the early influences in your academic career that pushed your thinking about children's writing?

ANNE:

I would say the first academic influences (aside from the two people mentioned above) were not about children's writing but about language as a social tool – Dell Hymes especially and what was then the new field of sociolinguistics (and, of course, his colleague at the time, John Gumperz).

Then there were the folks following little children around with tape recorders, respecting their language – Roger Brown, Susan Ervin Tripp, and Courtney Cazden, a one-time early childhood teacher too who has contributed so very much to our respect for classroom language. And certainly I read lots about (and knew from listening) the deficit language ideology applied to "other" children – Labov and Smitherman are two who influenced me in the seventies. Finally I have to mention Bill Corsaro, whom I met when I first went to Berkeley and who helped illuminate children's cultures.

As for writing, I was mesmerized by Marie Clay's books in the mid-seventies. She paid such careful attention to young children's production of text. I am of a different generation, so I am interested in how those text production decisions mediate children's social lives, but I learned to appreciate children's exploring of written text from Marie Clay. I knew from teaching that drawing was also important and there were scholars who located writing in children's use of other symbolic modes (an old but favorite is by Helen Eng).

And here I must mention Lev Vygotsky – *Mind in Society* was barely out but I read it when I was doing my dissertation and from Vygotsky I learned that, to understand writing, one had to see it within children's symbolic repertoire for representing and reconstructing and communicating about their worlds.

On a more practical side, I was inspired by Connie and Harold Rosen's book *The Language of Primary School Children*, whose chapter on children's writing I read and reread and read again. It was so practical and so child respectful –all about listening to a child and helping the child find a way into text and also about respecting children's playful interpretations of new kinds of writing tasks across the disciplines.

Perhaps because of my own humble roots – and my becoming a teacher in the late sixties early seventies, a time of great idealism among many of my generation – I have always been interested in children's resources that are not respected by the dominant ideology of school literacy (back to Labov, Smitherman, and Cazden too).

When I was organizing my dissertation, I kept reading about children speaking vernacular Englishes (especially African American kids) and emerging bilingualism. At this time, Graves was starting his studies of children's writing processes. I loved the respectful observation but still, I was finding my way out of the notion of a child author as an individual interacting with a paper into one of a child player, peer, and learner learning writing as a means of engaging with, and playing in, the world. So I was looking in another way. Sometimes realizing that one's path is different from another's is very useful – it pushes one to articulate and clarify one's path.

Later on, well into the eighties, I discovered Bakhtin on a table in a Berkeley bookstore and I felt my ways of looking at children expand. Voices answering voices, words echoing past conversations, people talking from somewhere addressing someone on their horizon – all of this helped me talk more confidently not only about writing as interaction but also about societal discourse of race, class, and gender – children were positioned in a world of differences but they were not stagnant representatives of some social group. We all move in space, finding different aspects of ourselves as we reach out to diverse others. The complexity of children of and in the experienced world became more manageable.

BOBBIE:

One of my favorite aspects of your writing is how you bring children to life. When I read your writing, I feel like I am in the classroom sitting next to you watching the scene unfold. I can feel the very unique and individual personalities of the different children. Do you have any particularly memorable experiences of the children?

ANNE:

Oh, I have lots of kids I remember like I knew them yesterday. I can measure out my adult life by the children I knew at one time and then the next. I get so close from that sitting and observing; I don't choose as focal children those who overly attend to me as opposed to their peers.

But still, I am not invisible. I am there "doing my job," as 6-year-old Jameel once said, and my job was "not to tell [him] what to do," as he explained to a peer he was annoying. Indeed, among the most memorable children was Jameel. He was a homeless child in the East Bay, initially kind of on edge, sensitive to being bumped or otherwise disregarded. But once he relaxed, this amazing child emerged; he used every bit of textual resource he had to imaginatively make a world on paper – cartoons from the TV, and commercials too (he had the used car salesman language down pat), soul songs, school books, and he could sometimes talk with the performative intensity of a preacher. When he was performative on paper, of course he didn't like his audience talking back. He called into question some taken-for-granted pedagogical practices – like the daily sharing time being conceived of as an editorial feedback time. Not for a performer.

I was fascinated by Jameel's playfulness with language, and he took to my interest in him. One day he was super excited because he was going to a pizza party for children who had had an especially great week in school. He told me this and then stopped, looked at me ever so sympathetically and said with great kindness "I don't think you're invited." (He is in *Social Worlds of Children Learning to Write*….) Jameel did SO well in his first grade with his fabulous teacher but then he was taken from his mother and put in foster care; given this regulation and that one, it was impossible to find out where he was.

Years later, I asked a former student who was working for the district central office to try to find Jameel in the system. He found out that Jameel was attending an alternative high school for children who were having troubles in school. Such a smart child should not have been having troubles in school, but there it was. I have had that experience more than once, of having young children with fabulous starts to schooling somehow defeated, not so much by academics, but by the experience of schooling amid life and its troubles. I dislike the rhetoric that if children somehow learn their letters and sounds at younger and younger ages, oh they'll progress through school with no troubles at all. Ridiculous.

BOBBIE:

The life that you bring to the children on paper often begins with your titles. You often quote them or use their words in the titles. Just to name a few titles:

"N spell my grandmama"

"Oh ppbbt!"

"I'm gonna express myself"

Donkey Kong in Little Bear Country

The stolen lipstick of overheard song

The case of the singing scientist

How do you come up with fantastic titles that capture the heart and soul of the piece that you are writing?

ANNE:

Oh thanks so much for the compliment. I don't have any particular strategies. A child will say something that keeps reverberating in my head as I think about the project (Jameel referring to himself as a "singing scientist") or an image will appear that can be translated into words (Noah's drawing of Donkey Kong in Little Bear Country). Book publishers seem to like straight forward titles for educational books. Not so much space for play.

BOBBIE:

I was a classroom teacher in the late 1990s and now I am a teacher educator. It's interesting to see how so many things have remained the same when it comes to writing in school, especially in the lower elementary grades. My two children brought home workbooks pages that I could have given to my students when I was a classroom teacher.

And my undergraduate and graduate students want to give their students similar types of workbooks pages. In working with pre-service and in-service teachers, I find that they want to teach in a way that is 'safe' for them or teach 'what they know or what they experienced' instead of trying to push the boundaries of their own comfort level.

What advice do you have for teachers and teacher educators that can help them move away from traditional workbook-style teaching to seeing writing as part of a permeable curriculum?

ANNE:

Well, there are three ideas that are important for me and perhaps may be helpful to others:

First, writing is an intention-driven symbolic tool, through which we participate in particular kinds of social events.

What drives writing – what makes working to orchestrate this complex system worth it – is an intention. So this means, skills are just skills, writing is communication. So, from the beginning this matters. The little ones often chat with each other as they write, sometimes developing complex kinds of play within which the writing and drawing play a role. (There are lots of examples of this in *ReWRITING the Basics*; my favorite example is two little kindergarteners who are "playing sisters, on paper" – one adds the other to her drawn family and then writes [with mock writing combined with the other child's exactly written name] about how she loves her "best sister.")

If we do not let the children talk when they write, we may get no writing; the intentional context may be destroyed, along with the help and feedback children offer each other. If we have a daily sharing time, children may anticipate that sharing time and whether or not others will laugh or otherwise like their work.

Second, as Jimmy Britton said, we as teachers can't teach children we don't know. This makes teacher observation basic to teaching writing.

We can learn of children's interests and their chosen companions or what language they use to comfortably discuss their writing or even collaborate during writing in some way. We learn about the social arrangements that prevail when they are most participatory – small groups? of which children?; pairs? of which children? We may learn too about their chosen symbolic tools for representing. (how might writing be incorporated in multimodal productions – comics? digital stories? murals or collages? picture books?)

Obvious in what has been said, I do not think we should look at children only in terms of some checklist of competencies. We have to know our children as human beings with interests, dispositions, friends and avoided peers, symbolic preferences (drawing, singing, dancing, sculpting), and particular sensitivities, based, perhaps, on their sociopolitical position in society or particular complexities of home life. If we know our children, then we can figure out possible social arrangements (kids can collaborate, for example), possible genres, including multimodal ones, particular inquiry projects that children may find compelling for the daily writing period or for writing across the curriculum.

Finally, teaching means, within one's goals, responding to and building on what children are trying to do.

Whatever our plans, if the bulk of children's writing time does not include intentional writing – intentional being defined from children's view point – supported by their teacher and their collegial peers, then, in the end, we are not teaching writing at all.

BOBBIE:

You began your teaching career in 1972 and then received your Ph.D. in 1981. How has the research on children's writing evolved since that time?

ANNE:

I do want to begin by saying that I think researchers interested in children's writing – and contributing to our collective knowledge – should, in my view, do two things:

1. know the literature in the area and, also, the particular theoretical and conceptual tools that particular research literature has used; and
2. locate the studied children in the complexities of how the children are situated in society.

The latter has definitely evolved dramatically in the research area on children's writing. I remember when I ventured into doctoral work, there were articles being published with titles like "the six-year-old writer" and some such. Not only is there no one path into writing, and no one "six-year-old writer," our children, like children the world over, are specific individuals located in particular sociocultural and geographic locales and carrying particular cultural resources (chief among them, their languages but also their experiences with varied sorts of texts, whatever their medium); too, their teachers are under varied pressures to teach and demand particular kinds of academic performances.

When we read research, we want to know, how are these children located in the sociocultural and linguistic world? And since their knowledge of school writing will be formed through particular educational activities, what is the teacher's curriculum like and what pressures is she under (e.g., to have children pick out from a selection the correctly punctuated sentence – since that will be on a test). I think our expectations as readers of research are more sophisticated now. We need all this information, since any generalizations to be made will depend on comparison of children engaging in writing activities across settings.

Another change, I think, has been a widening interest in children's engagement with and use of popular culture. I can go back to the early studies I did in grad school in the late seventies – they are full of popular culture, but it never occurred to me to ask questions about what children's participation in popular culture meant to the children themselves, as well as to their teachers. This was most certainly to change (e.g., *Writing Superheroes*).

There is now a recognition that contemporary childhoods tend to be infused with the popular media (although that media will vary across geographic and sociocultural sites; for example, in my current global project on children learning to write, children in a Kenyan village did not have access to television, but they did listen to the radio; that radio was the source of their popular songs; few U.S. studies would highlight the radio as a central media source for child affiliation and pleasure [although it certainly was among the children in *The Brothers and Sisters Learn to Write*].)

Related to this has been the interest in issues of young children's use of digital media –the media itself or the experience of engagement with the media – in their ventures into writing. These studies in the U.S. have not usually been located in low income communities, where I think access to particular media may be limited by economics. Still, I think studies that plan projects to engage children with composing tools via computer and tablets are interesting – they may demonstrate new possibilities, particularly for multimodal composing.

Finally, I want to comment on the changing role of drawing and, more broadly, multimodality. When I first began my studies, drawing was seen as a temporary form of "writing," to be replaced by written text. This no longer makes sense. I think (tied to the comments above) now there is an interest in how children differentiate their symbolic repertoire, so that they understand the particular strengths and limits of varied symbolic tools.

BOBBIE:

What do you think about the state of education today?

ANNE:

I think it should be a time of excitement – when child agency is realized across the curriculum through inquiry projects, even as the arts play a huge role as playful children are guided into new forms of expression and learning. But it is not. I think, spurred on initially by No Child Left Behind, the push toward accountability through standardized tests narrowed the educational curriculum and contributed to the intensity of the push-down in isolated academic content.

Children are greeted into kindergarten with tests of letter names and sounds and, from the get go, may be judged as "bright" or "not" on the results of narrow testing before anybody's tried to get to know the children as human beings, players, friends, and learners, indeed, before anyone's tried to teach whatever it is judged as critical for young children to know and to learn. And play, that mainstay of child learning, may be absent from the kindergarten.

Narrow curricula that provide little space for children to negotiate their ways into school activities and that provide a crimped view of who children are and what they know may eliminate children from powerful learning from the get go. I know there are teachers and programs that are full of lively, engaged children. But too often, there is a mandated "pedagogy of poverty" (to borrow Martin Haberman's phrase), of low level teaching of aspects of literacy that allow no agency for children to figure out what literacy is about and how it works and how it can work for them as children.

I just returned from a trip to South Africa; in the township schools, children were being taught through a rote recitation method the conventions of English literacy; in the more affluent city school that I visited, there was lively engagement of children in all manner of activity – and there was play. Some children are being taught superficial facts and to follow orders; others are being socialized as agents of inquiry and public expression. This has been true in may own lifetime when I read as a teacher-to-be the appalling book by Bereiter and Engelmann *Teaching Disadvantaged Children in the Preschool*, with its breathtaking ignorance of language, literacy, and sociocultural difference.

We all still have work to do.

I take inspiration from the educational reformer Deborah Meier, who, in her book *The Power of Their Ideas*, talked about how the kindergarten – the old fashioned kindergarten – was a model for all of education. Attention to imaginative play and to making friends is the beginning of empathetic concern for the world and the capacity to imagine it differently.

"As we eliminate from our schools and from children's after-school lives the time and space for exercising their creative imagination and building personal ties, we've cheated our children and our society in a far more critical way than we're inclined to understand" (Meier, 1995, p. 63).

BOBBIE:

For those who are interested in researching and studying children's writing, what advice would you give them?

ANNE:

There is room for all kinds of work on children's writing. I think, though, that what is key is understanding that the heart of the story is not on the page but in the world being mediated by the page. Observational skills matter. And the observer cannot attend only to one child writing but to the larger social happening in which the child is (or is not) participating by means of that writing.

If writing is situationally merely a task or a set of rote skills, then the researcher may have no access to children's intentions, agency, and social lives, nor, in fact, to composing at all. Of course, in the cracks of the curriculum, children may be found composing as part of their unofficial worlds – love letters (and their opposite), birthday party invites, funny stories …

BOBBIE:

What areas of further research would you like to see in the area of children's writing?

ANNE:

I think all the trends mentioned above are good ones. As for me, I have just finished a project (I believe I already mentioned it) in which children's early entry into school and school writing was described as it unfolded in 8 very different sites around the globe.

I think the notions of how children move into writing are too narrow, given that ideologies of childhoods, schooling, and writing itself are different across the globe, as are children's textual resources. Finding common themes and different articulations of child writing is to the benefit of us all; narrow notions of how children begin, of useful resources, of "best" home supports leave some children's entry into composing outside the realm of curricular imagination.

Most of all, I would like to see researchers approach children's writing as embedded in their lives as friends, players, and scholars across the curriculum. The questions then open up, limited only by the researchers' curiosity and imagination.

BOOK THREE

TIME IN EDUCATION: INTERTWINED DIMENSIONS AND THEORETICAL POSSIBILITIES

INTRODUCTION

BOBBIE KABUTO

From the first day of kindergarten to the day that their children graduate high school, families organize their lives around school-based timeframes down to the year, month, day, and even minute. Children have to be in school by a certain time, and sometimes families have to struggle around work schedules to make sure their children are cared for before and after school. Some families have a time for starting homework, and others plan vacations around the school calendar. Families whose children are in school live within chronological timelines organized by different types of calendars like the Roman calendar or the Lunar calendar, while simultaneously living within school-based timelines, such as the change in a grade or a school year.

Despite the complex cartography of time that consolidates, arranges, structures, and categories the experiences of families, educational structures attempt to provide a uniform way of systemizing concepts like *development*, *ability*, and *learning* around reading and writing. Benchmarking and content standards, such as those represented by the Common Core State

Standards, are broken down to grade levels so that by the end of each grade level students are expected to meet a benchmark or standard for performing at grade level expectations.

Within educational systems, psychological processes are assumed to be measured within a socially constructed system of time such as grade level, that may have little to do with other timeframes, such as biological, physical, or historical. As Sorokin (1943) would argue, time organized within school-based frames – such as grade level, vacation breaks, and changes in school years – has a social and cultural nature that gives a rhythm to our social lives.

This edition of the Women Scholars Series will further explore the intersection of literacy and the construct of time within education through the work of Catherine Compton-Lilly. Originally published in *Time and Society*, *Time in Education: Intertwined Dimensions and Theoretical Possibilities* highlights the complexity of studying the concept of *learning* and how and what people learn over time within school-based structures. These structures were designed to not only organize educational experiences, but they also have built in power structures that define who we are as learners, privileging certain type of learners and marginalizing others (Ball, 2016).

At the same time, Compton-Lilly presents a theoretical kaleidoscope of studying learning and literacy over time, and she illustrates how our perspective of a learner can change as we rotate different theoretical lenses. The question that arises is how do we reconcile, or do we need to reconcile, these sometimes complementary or contradictory framings of learners? This is a dilemma that I have faced within my own research in working with families to better understand how and why parents support or challenge school-based definitions of their children as learners.

Families and Schooling

In 2003, Compton-Lilly introduced the educational community to her first book, *Reading Families: The Literate Lives of Urban Children*. Through the study of discourse, Compton-Lilly expanded the field of family literacy and the works of Heath (1983), Taylor (1983), and Taylor and Dorsey-Gaines (1988). *Reading Families* is based on Compton-Lilly's experiences as a first-grade teacher that led her to study families in urban settings. In this current volume, Compton-Lilly reflected on her past research for *Reading Families*:

> While the neighborhood around my school struggled economically and media reports about the community focused on drugs arrests and shootings, I continued to be impressed by the resilience and commitment to children exhibited by family members despite the lack of resources. (p.282)

As a teacher-researcher, Compton-Lilly interviewed, visited the homes of, and collected school documents for ten of her first grade African American students. The culmination of this work illustrated not only the literacy practices of nine students, it also inserted issues of equity and marginalization into researching and studying families of color.

The field of family literacy has highlighted the mismatches between home and school. The grounding break ethnographic work of Heath (1983) provided deep insights into the border conflicts at the mismatch of home and school literacy practices. This research lead other researchers to consider how "success" and "failure" had more to do with mirroring school-based practices and ideologies than it did with any sanitized notion of educational ability.

Taylor and Dorsey-Gaines (1988) were among the first researchers to study families living in urban, inner-city areas. They effectively illustrated the diverse literate practices of the inner-city families and how they supported their children's educational experiences as they navigated home and school literacy practices. In spite of their abilities, Taylor and Dorsey Gaines (1988) argued for the children, "Their daily lives and their complex social and cognitive communicative abilities were not relevant to the definitions of school learning, which were limited by the exercises that were given and the tests that were set" (p. 209).

Like Taylor and Dorsey-Gaines, Compton-Lilly put issues of identity, race, poverty, agency, and power at the heart of her discussion in *Reading Families*. In describing the purpose of the book, Compton-Lilly (2003) wrote:

> This book explores how generally accepted discourses concerning the use of literacy and the possibilities created through literacy learning operate within a community in which many families have been denied access to mainstream ways of life that many people take for granted (safe communities, homes that meet safety codes, jobs that provide a living way, health diets, adequate educational experiences). (pp. 5-6)

Compton-Lilly (2003) suggested that families living in urban communities were stereotypically portrayed as being at odds with schooling. She explained:

> In contrast to the stereotypes of urban parents that portray them as unconcerned about their children's academic progress, the parents I interviewed taught me otherwise. Parents consistently expressed their strong beliefs about the importance of reading in their children's lives, and no parent ever questioned the value and importance of reading; parents felt that reading was among the things children needed for "survival." (pp. 4-5)

Compton-Lilly's findings uncovered many assumptions around urban families. She argued that assumptions such as "urban families of color are lacking in education and resources" or "are uninterested in schooling," were:

> ... generally based on media depictions and an urban mythology that attempts to explain the academic difficulties of urban schools by blaming parents or offering simplistic notions of teacher incompetence (poor pedagogy, lazy and uncaring teachers). (p. 10)

Compton-Lilly (2007b) further explained how children's actual abilities in school can be overshadowed by other types of capital forms, such as behavior, the ability to speak English, and economics.

Four years after her initial study, Compton-Lilly returned to the families to provide a longitudinal examination, presented in the book *Re-Reading Families: The Literate Lives of Urban Children, Four Years Later* (Compton-Lilly, 2007a). As a sequel to *Reading Families*, *Re-Reading Families* presented a "re-reading of the children and their families" in order to "revisit and re-examine their literacy learning over time" (Compton-Lilly, 2015, p. 62). It was within this context that Compton-Lilly took an interest in time and temporality. As Compton-Lilly wrote in *Re-Reading Families*:

> Time haunts me as a researcher. I contemplate the trajectories that awaited my former students and the severe consequences of attending underfunded schools in a high poverty community. I recall my amazing six-year-old students and the potential they brought to my classroom. I consider the parents' unwavering hope for their children's futures. I lament the opportunities they did not find in school, the stifling instruction that they reported, and the failed tests, low report card grades, and stringent behavioral policies that they recalled.

Five years after *Re-Reading Families* was published, Compton-Lilly again returned to the same families. In her book,

Reading Time: The Literate Lives of Urban Secondary Students and Their Families (Compton-Lilly, 2012), she revisited the children as middle school students. While the research continued to focus on literacy, the accounts of students and their parents extended to school policies and practices as well as peers and popular culture. As she spoke with students and their parents, again, time proved to be salient. She explained:

> Students and parents revisited experiences from their past, compared the past to the present, spoke of the pace of instruction, described progress in school, and their hopes for the future. Based on these accounts, I argue that humans are temporal beings, and time plays a significant role in literacy learning, identity construction, and schooling. (p. 1)

In 2017, Compton-Lilly published the final book in this series, *Reading Students' Lives: Literacy Learning Across Time*, which followed the children into high school. While spaces of hope and possibility continued to be evident across the cases, it was clear that the challenges that accompanied attending an underfunded school in an underfunded community had taken its toll on the students and their families. Some students were retained in school multiple times, while others experienced altercations with the law. Most left school. Some continued to aspire towards college.

Compton-Lilly turned her attention to equity, arguing that "this longitudinal study contributes to understandings about how the achievement debt continues to operate in innocuous and devastating ways across time" (p. 119). She highlighted the importance of research that attends to temporality, arguing that:

> … longitudinal conversations must recognize the long-term trajectories of *becoming* as students move through school. People's social histories, both individually lived and historically imposed matter and

these histories continuously converge in the lives of individuals. (p.121)

Thus, revisiting these families revealed the confluence of students' trajectories, families' histories, and larger social histories that defined both schools and American society – including the inequities that continue to operate.

Referencing the concept of revisiting, Sefton-Green (2015) suggested that returning to previous research sites and participants allows researchers to study how participants contend with changes in their experiences over time, or how they 're-experience,' particularly as they attempt to reconcile past and present experiences to see future trajectories and goals.

In my own research, I discuss this mobilization of meaning through re-experiencing over time as transgenerational within families. Within a transgenerational perspective of family literacy, I reconsider how *family* does not necessarily mean the immediate family at any given time. Rather, a transgenerational perspective forefronts the historicity of the family and understanding how past experiences relate to decisions in the present.

For instance, parents may draw upon their own educational histories to make sense of, not just experiences on longer timescales like their children's performance from grade to grade, but also of situated experiences on shorter time scales, like reading a sentence. Consequently, families carry and construct models and beliefs about learning that are solidified through activities and relationships that families have with other people and institutions such as schools.

These models and beliefs emerge out the stories that families tell, and as Compton-Lilly (2011) argued, parents "repeatedly returned to some stories while neglecting and forgetting others or framed some stories as examples of larger patterns" (p. 248).

Time in Educational Research

In this Women Scholar Series, Compton-Lilly explores the concept of *time as context* to challenge learning as static or linearly progressive. In an enlightening discussion of the plurality of time across the social and physical sciences, Sorokin (1943) outlines different conceptions of time. More importantly, Sorokin effectively illustrates how these different conceptions of time can be confused and conflated within sociocultural contexts, particularly in the discourses that individuals employ to make sense of their lived experiences.

Some of the conceptualization of time include physico-mathematical time, biological time and psychological time, all of which have been of interest to the fields of education. For instance, researchers in early writing have painstakingly documented the development of writing through inventive spellings (Kamii & Manning, 2002; Masterson & Apel, 2010) and name writing (Both-de Vries & Bus, 2008). Other researchers have documented the development of writing and drawing forms and name writing (Clay, 1975; Puranik & Lonigan, 2011). This body of research has led to the idea of predictability and orderable stages in writing development. When children do not progress across stages in an anticipated fashion, then families or teachers become concerned and talk about children as "working below age- and grade- level expectations". These discussions can cause families to search out educational professionals for testing and evaluation.

What is talked little about is how, as researchers and educators, we have used these time concepts to construct ideas and beliefs around learners' abilities. As Sorokin (1943) argued, "Observation shows that persons equally old according to the physical clock are physiologically at quite different stages of development" (p. 163). Yet there are areas in educational research that attempt to normalize development, create age- and grade- level expectations, and require students to make adequate yearly progress. We treat words like *age, grade*, and *year* as static, neutral numbers that measure consistent and continuous phenomena when they are, in fact, words with socially constructed and evolving meanings. To provide an illustration of how families use discourses around time to talk about, frame, and make sense of their children as readers and literate individuals, I will describe how the concept of *year* indexed a variety of meanings within families' lived experiences, was defined through sociocultural meanings, and acted a discourse connector and time-bridge to the past as families constructed their understandings of the present.

A Year in Time

In the study *Revaluing Readers and Families* (Kabuto, 2015), I have examined the ways in which school-based structures intersect and reconstruct family structures. Studying seven families, I had a particular interest in how families understood themselves in relation to a myriad of school-based concepts such as "learning disabled," "language disorder," "Attention Deficit Disorder," and "dual-language learner." Through the 90 hours of audiotaped data, which included interviews and parents and their children orally reading and reflecting with each other, the families in the study exemplified how they understood their experiences around school-based concepts through the *context of time* (Compton-Lilly, this volume). In other words, school-based timeframes not only synchronized familial routines, they also provided a point of reference in or entry into understanding and discussing their children's learning and progress in school. These points of reference epitomize the time-bending nature of discourse, or how discourse is a means to "recursively revisit some experiences" and make sense of "the tensions that accompany school trajectories, and the long-term embodiment of ways of being – including ways of being literate" (Compton-Lilly, this volume).

Within the 90 hours of audiotaped discourse, the families used the concept of year to organize their experiences around schooling. Consider the following examples from the parents when they discussed their children's progress in school:

Terry: I wish you could meet her [my daughter's] classroom teacher. They saw a little something going on. They were going to test her [and] we said we're not waiting until next **year**. We're going to go ahead and test her. It's not likely [but] it's a possibility [because] the other two have trouble.

Donna: This is the last **year's** book and it wasn't hard enough so I asked the teacher for the activities.

Nancy: For a **year** and a half, I kept asking what they [the teachers] are doing and they could never tell me what they were doing.

Maria: Which ever book is more exciting she will like better. I don't like Jenny's teacher because she is not as attentive as her teacher from last **year**. Hopefully next **year** she'll have a better teacher.

Francis: This **year** it has so far has been challenging. I have been less strict this **year** and her grades have dropped. This has been very strange for me.

Carole: She works with a special ed [education] teacher who throws them all together and throws Wilson [Reading Program] at them because that's what comes up for reading purposes based on the initial evaluation. So it's nothing. At least, though, she's been a very good girl and participating in the group reading in the classroom last **year** and the beginning of this **year**.

In each of these examples, the mothers use the term *year* to measure a grade-level rather than a calendar year, and using the concept of year as a school-based structure allowed the mothers to index some point in time in their children's experiences in school. These points in time may have described a performance measure, such as in Francis' comment. Being concerned about her daughter Sophie's progress in the fourth grade, Francis further explained her concerns by stating, "This **year** Sophie brings home 70's and 60's while last **year** she brought home A's."

The process of classification and declassification were also events that the mothers tracked throughout grade-level constructs. This point is exemplified in Terry's comment about her youngest daughter's progress in school. Her two older children were classified in school from the first grade. Because her youngest daughter was in kindergarten, she felt that she should wait until the first grade to start the process for classification.

Year as a school-based structure also referenced programs and curricular materials for the families. Donna's, Nancy's, and Carole's comments illustrate this point. Donna expressed frustration that the school did not academically challenge her daughter, who was diagnosed with a pervasive developmental disorder not otherwise specified (PDD-NOS), as well as a speech and language impairment. She often approached the teachers to ask for work that she could take home to do with Nina. Donna's comment above refers to an unchallenging book that Nina, who was in the fourth grade, read when she was in the third grade.

Nancy expressed a similar frustration. Since Becky was in the first grade when she was classified with a learning disability, Nancy often inquired about the types of reading instruction that the teachers provided Becky, or asked about strategies that she could use with Becky at home. Nancy expressed frustrations about the Committee for Special Education (CSE) meetings and the lack of concern they exhibited to her comments and questions. Similarly, Carole, with dismay, discussed how the school used the Wilson Program for her daughter. While

Carole could not attest to the effectiveness of the program, she noted that Christie had participated in the program beginning in the second grade.

Mothers spoke about their daughters' experiences in terms of years. The concept of "year," however, held sociocultural meanings and social references to time, rather than representing a continuous, measureable, and mechanical span of time. How the mothers' used discourses related to time were coordinated by the school-based culture and milieu within which these families lived. Furthermore, the concept of year as a school-based structure illustrates how time is an extension of memory and synchronization of past and present activities – or provides a context to make sense of the experiences of their children's successes and struggles in school, as illustrated in the discourses above.

Carole and her daughter Christie's case study provide a powerful example of the contextual nature of time. Out of the seven families, I followed two of them over time, engaging in the process of revisiting as described earlier in this introduction. I first met the family when Christie was in kindergarten. They began participation in the study when Christie was in first grade (Phase 1), and I revisited them when Christie was in third grade (Phase 2). My last revisit was when Christie was in the eleventh grade (Phase 3). Christie was classified with a speech and language disability when she entered kindergarten. I have written extensively about various parts of my research with Carole and Christie, and I have now begun to look across my research encounters with them to understand how Christie has understood herself as a literate individual working within the special education system.

To examine how time provides a context to understanding one's experiences, I examined how Carole and Christie used the concept of year in relation to past, present, and future experiences. There were two notable findings I gleaned from the data. First, the term *year* increased per session over each phase of the study. For instance, the concept of year appeared three times in session 1 of the first-grade data (one example was presented above), nine times in the session 1 of the third-grade data, and sixteen times in session 1 of the eleventh-grade data. Furthermore, when the concept of a year occurred in each of the phases of the study, it indexed events on a longer timescale.

For instance, over the phases of the study, Carole regularly returned to her frustration at the type of reading instruction that Christie received in school. As noted above, Carole described how Christie participated in the Wilson Program. When Christie was in third grade, Carole advocated for Christie to work with a reading specialist. Carole described, "I met her [the reading specialist] at the evaluation. They finally gave it to us after all this asking... at the end of the **year**. It'll be the last six weeks of school." Not only did Carole use the concept of a year as a school-based structure to discuss the services her daughter had received, she also used the concept as a way to monitor her daughter's growth and maturity as a reader. During our first session in Phase 2 of the study, Christie read *Little Blue and Little Yellow* (Lionni, 1969), and Carole asked about the difficulty level of the book. In order to make sense of Christie's oral reading performance, she compared it to how she thought Christie had read the previous year. Carole said, "You did awesome. You know a **year** ago you would not have been able to read the story with her [Christie]. There's a certain maturity about her that she did not have one **year** ago."

As these examples illustrate, Carole used the concept of a year as a school-based structure to contextualize and make sense of what she was observing. This theme occurred across data from the seven families. When the families used a year as a school-based structure, they used the term as a time-bridge to connect past experiences with present ones. This was particularly true in the case of Christie as she attempted to make sense of her mounting experiences in special education that would eventually cause her to graduate high school at 19 or 20 years of age.

Christie was more vocal when I revisited her in eleventh-grade, and her use of "year" began to extend over longer time-frames. Christie explained:

> Yeah. And I'm bad in math now – it's like I'm in Algebra. But math will take me a while to practice, because I've been in basic math and also the life skills. So that's going to be 10 times worse, because middle school destroyed me. Like the whole **year** in middle school, because I have to be in life skills.

In this example, Christie explained how math had become a difficult subject for her by returning to her experiences in middle school, when the CSE tried to place her on the life skills path which incorporated 'basic math.' Christie's use of year connected back to her middle school experiences as she explained not only how she was resistant to being placed on a life-skills path in school, but also how she started attending her CSE meetings in order to vocalize her objections. Christie felt that being placed in life skills had had a negative impact on her learning, and that being in basic math had held her back from being successful in math in eleventh-grade. Consequently, the word "year" was not a mathematical connector in time, rather it was a sociocultural connector so that her past experiences assisted her in making sense of more current ones. Similar to Marvin (Compton-Lilly, this volume), Christie had to negotiate "a school system filled with expectations and tracked instructional experiences". As Compton-Lilly further explained, "The instructional experiences he [Marvin] experienced – heavy-handed discipline, low expectations, special education placement, retention, and racism – informed his sense of self and the dispositions that he brought forward."

These discourse samples illustrate how making sense of and interpreting one's learning experiences are as much about as one's historicity as they are about experiencing events in the present. Occurrences in the present are not decontextualized activities, instead they often reflect a re-experiencing of connected or related activities. Each time activities are re-experienced, they are given new and renewed meanings.

Researching Time

In the next section of this book, Compton-Lilly provides an in-depth perspective of "time as context" by presenting three different and interrelated perspectives for framing time in educational research. After re-introducing Marvin from *Reading Families*, Compton-Lilly takes the reader through a kaleidoscope that repositions Marvin's experience in school, which "was often punctuated by altercations with other students and run-ins with teachers". With each slight turn in the kaleidoscope, readers have the opportunity to grasp how, as Compton-Lilly explains, time is "a significant contextual dimension that contributes to how people make sense of themselves, their experiences, and their worlds."

Building on the work of Bakhtin's (1981, 1986) concept of chronotopes, other researchers have argued for a more integrated discussion of time in educational research. For instance, Boylan (n.d.) proposed the idea of expansiveness in mathematics education based on expansive chronotopes. Boylan contrasts expansive chronotopes with regulated time in education, which mirrors an industrial timescale that "denies the historicity of the learner" as "the orientation is on the future and on outcomes" (p. 16). White and Pham (2017) further suggest how chronotopes can be used as a tool to understand how students author themselves as English language learners, and how to include discussions of agency and emotion into the idea of timescapes.

It is here that I invite readers into realms of time to consider how discourses around time, the ways that we use time to organize our lives, and how time as context are used for making sense of our students' experiences. As Sorokin (1943) wrote:

> We have broken man's life into mathematically equal
> units of time and computed its duration in these units,
> as a result, man's life has slipped between our fingers.
> The meaningfulness, the essential states through
> which it passes, all the characteristics of these stages
> – in brief, almost the whole content of man's life –
> disappeared in our numbers. (p. 203)

Students like Marvin and Christie are more than numbers
that describe individuals who are incarcerated, graduate high
school after four years, or are in special education. Compton-
Lilly's work in this Women Scholars Series presents a powerful example of how "all [that] is left is a row of numbers, like
millions of other rows indicating the mean, the median, the
mode" when meaning is removed from those numbers (Sorokin,
1943, 203).

REFERENCES

Ball, S. (2016). *Foucault, power, and education*. New York, NY: Routledge.

Both-de Vries, A. C., & Bus, A. G. (2008). Name writing: A first step to phonetic writing? Does the name have a special role in understanding the symbolic function of writing? *Literacy, Teaching and Learning, 12*(2), 37.

Boylan, M. (n.d). Towards a mathematics education for ecological selves: Pedagogies for relational knowing and being. Retrieved from: http://socialsciences.exeter.ac.uk/education/research/centres/stem/publications/pmej/pome32/Boylan-submitted.docx

Clay, M. (1975). *What did I write?: Beginning writing behavior*. Portsmouth, NH: Heinemann.

Compton-Lilly, C. (2003). *Reading families: The literate lives of urban children*. New York, NY: Teachers College Press.

Compton-Lilly, C. (2007a). *Re-reading families: The literate lives of urban children, four years later*. New York, NY: Teachers College Press.

Compton-Lilly, C. (2007b). The complexities of reading in two Puerto Rican families. *Reading Research Quarterly, 42*(1), 72-98.

Compton-Lilly, C. (2011). Literacy and schooling in one family across time. *Research in the Teaching of English, 45*(3), 224-251.

Compton-Lilly, C. (2015). Revisiting children and families: Temporal discourse analysis and the longitudinal construction of meaning. In J. Sefton-Green & J. Rowsell (Eds.), *Learning and literacy over time: Longitudinal perspectives* (pp. 61-78). New York, NY: Routledge.

Heath, S. B. (1983). *Ways with words: Language, life, and work in communities and classrooms.* New York, NY: Cambridge.

Kabuto, B. (2015). Transgenerational learning within families. *Journal of Family Diversity in Education, 1*(4), 45-65

Kamii, C., & Manning, M. (2002). Phonemic awareness and beginning reading and writing. *Journal of Research in Childhood Education, 17*(1), 38-46.

Lionni, L. (1959). *Little blue and little yellow.* New York, NY: Harper Collins.

Masterson, J. J., & Apel, K. (2010). The Spelling Sensitivity Score: Noting developmental changes in spelling knowledge. *Assessment for Effective Intervention, 36*(1), 35-45.

Puranik, C. S., & Lonigan, C. J. (2011). From scribbles to scrabble: Preschool children's developing knowledge of written language. *Reading and Writing, 24*(5), 567-589.

Sefton-Green, J. (2015). Introduction: Making sense of longitudinal perspectives on literacy learning – A revisiting approach. In J. Sefton-Green & J. Rowsell (Eds.), *Learning and literacy over time: Longitudinal perspectives* (pp. 1-15). New York: Routledge.

Sorokin, P. (1943). *Sociocultural causality, space, time: A student of referential principles of sociology and social science.* Durham, NC: Duke University Press.

Taylor, D. (1983). *Family literacy: Young children learning to read and write.* Portsmouth: Heinemann.

Taylor, D., & Dorsey-Gaines, C. (1988). *Growing up literate: Learning from inner-city families.* Portsmouth, NH: Heinemann.

White, C., & Pham, C. (2017). Time in the experience of agency and emotion in English language learning in rural Vietnam. *Innovation in Language Learning and Teaching, 11*(3), 207-218.

TIME IN EDUCATION: INTERTWINED DIMENSIONS AND THEORETICAL POSSIBILITIES:

CATHERINE COMPTON-LILLY

Giddens (1991) argued that few things in life as are commonplace as time. Time constantly passes as people allocate hours of their days and organize their lives. However, time is generally treated as a backdrop to experience and rarely contemplated as a significant contextual dimension that contributes to how people make sense of themselves, their experiences, and their worlds. For the past several years, I have explored time as a constitutive dimension of people's experiences that significantly affects how people make sense of themselves and their worlds.

Recognizing *time as context* is paramount to understanding how children and families make sense of literacy and school experiences. However, literacy researchers have generally failed to recognize the temporal nature of people's experiences and the longitudinal construction of meaning. This neglect of time can be traced to methodologies that generally involve relatively short-term snapshots of children's lives – 6 months, 1 year, and 3 years.

Because little qualitative research tracks children, teachers, or literacy development over long periods of time the full impact of long-term situations – living in high poverty communities, attending poorly funded schools, and being subjected to often oppressive instruction – has not been recognized. Researchers generally fail to recognize and appreciate the ways in which students selectively and recursively revisit some experiences, the tensions that accompany school trajectories, and the long-term embodiment of ways of being – including ways of being literate.

In this examination of time in schooling, I explore time in my own trajectory as a literacy scholar. I consider my own journey as a researcher following students over time alongside my transition from being a first-grade teacher to being a university scholar. Next, I present empirical data from a ten-year longitudinal study to explore the affordances of temporal analyses in educational research. My goal is not to explore findings from the study; these are explored elsewhere (Compton-Lilly, 2003, 2007, 2012, 2016). My goal is to examine the affordances of three theoretical perspectives for enabling literacy researchers to attend to how students construct meaning over time as they move through school.

Drawing on scholarship that presents time as multidimensional and intersectional (Adam, 1989, 2000; Schatzki, 2006), I challenge the notion of time as a simple, singular, and linear contextual dimension of people's experiences. Instead, I explore time as entailing multiple and overlapping dimensions that significantly affect how people make sense of themselves and their worlds. Adam (1989, 2000) situates time and space within "timescapes" (2000, p. 125) in which phenomena are encountered, processes are enacted, and events are experienced. She challenges social science researchers to maintain the complexity of situations and experiences that complicate time as simply passing. As Adam notes, "A focus on time highlights multiple realities that all bear on social life simultaneously" (Adam, 1989, p. 458).

The construct of timescape acknowledges the "spatial and temporal features of a social situation as well as the importance of the wider context. Moreover, time is conceived as not one but multidimensional" (Adam, 2003b, p. 96). Many scholars have recognized the multidimensional nature of time (Bidart, 2012; Cipriani, 2013; Firth & Robinson, 2014; Keightley, 2013). For example, Facer, Joiner, Stanton, Reid, Hull, and Kirk (2004) explore how technology can be used to provide opportunities for students to physically enact and interact within scenarios that support embodied activity within time – moving, thinking, talking, acting, planning, and ultimately learning.

To explore the multidimensional nature of time, I present my own trajectory. I then apply the work of three highly influential theorists – Lemke (2000), Bakhtin (1981, 1986), and Bourdieu (1980/1990, 1991) – to examine various temporal dimensions of schooling and learning as experienced by Marvin, one of my former students who participated in my ten-year longitudinal study. Each theory reveals critical insights into the roles time plays in educational spaces. Specifically, I argue that Lemke's notion of timescales highlights the temporally layered experiences that people draw upon to make sense of their worlds (Lemke, 2000). Bakhtin's description of chronotope invites the exploration of cumulating motifs and tropes that accompany being a successful or unsuccessful student (Bakhtin, 1986).

Finally, Bourdieu's notion of habitus draws our attention to the embodied ways of being that children assume early in life and carry with them across time (Bourdieu, 1971, 1980/1990; Bourdieu & Passeron, 1977). While I do not begin to claim that any one of these theories presents a comprehensive understanding of time, I propose that each theory contributes to thinking about the multidimensional nature of time and complicates time as a significant dimension of experience. Prior to presenting Marvin's story, I first present my own longitudinal becoming.

My Trajectory as a Researcher

In 1996, I was a first-grade teacher and doctoral student. I had worked in the same school for the prior eight years. While the neighborhood around my school struggled economically and media reports about the community focused on drugs arrests and shootings, I continued to be impressed by the resilience and commitment to children exhibited by family members despite the lack of resources. Larger issues related to social justice operated in this community. At the time of my study, there was no grocery store within ten miles of my school despite it being located in the middle of a city. The local library was in the process of being closed and the children were not allowed to play on the school playground due to disrepair and safety issues.

I taught at Rosa Parks Elementary School, a large urban school where 97% of the students qualified for free or reduced-price lunch. The children and their families lived in the housing projects and apartments that surrounded my school. While the neighborhood was characterized as violent and drug infested by the local media, I was continually impressed by the dedicated and compassionate parents who brought or sent their children to our school each day. My school was an underfunded elementary school located in this high poverty community, and one of the first schools in the country to be placed on our State's list of failing schools. Marvin was one of the children in my first-grade classroom.

For my doctoral dissertation, I conducted a teacher research study that explored the literacy practices of ten of my African American and Puerto Rican students. To begin my doctoral dissertation and document the literacy practices of my students and their families, I contacted the parents in alphabetical order as I moved down my class list. They all agreed to participate. Eventually, the families participated in the study when my former students were in grades one, five, eight, and eleven. During grade one, I collected multiple classroom observations and student work samples. During each phase of the project, I interviewed children and parents. When the children were in high school, I was awarded a grant from the Spencer Foundation that enabled me to visit children at school and interview their teachers. The year I collected the data for my dissertation, we faced the threat of being closed by the State unless our reading and math test scores improved.

During each phase of the longitudinal study, I collected reading assessments (Ekwall & Shanker, 1993, Leslie & Caldwell, 2006) and writing samples. Throughout the study, children and parents were asked about their reading practices, their use of technology, and their satisfaction with school. Children and parents described their favorite books and their plans for the future. Over time, children and families increasingly discussed school expectations and the challenges they faced at school. Thus, the focus of the study expanded beyond literacy as identity negotiations, school policies, and peer relationships became increasingly salient.

Across the study, data analysis involved transcription followed by a grounded coding of interviews and field notes (Strauss & Corbin, 1990). I soon learned that longitudinal analysis is inherently temporal. At times, data collected during an early phase of the research gained significance when viewed in relation to data collected years later. These longitudinal patterns were not well served by my separate attempts to code data from each phase of the project.

Longitudinal analysis required an additional time-consuming process of reading, and rereading stacks of data as well as using the search function on my word processor as particular words and ideas reemerged across the data set. While my teacher research perspective and my field notes were informed by my proximity to the children and our shared experiences in the classroom, my researcher perspective benefited from the luxury of revisiting data across a decade and by the application of multiple analytic procedures and theoretical frames.

I am now an endowed professor at the University of South Carolina, Columbia. Obtaining tenure at a top-ranked university involved a complicated dance. I needed to establish a presence in the literacy world, publish in the "best" journals, adhere to established writing norms, and cite the right scholars. The Internal Review Board process, my relationships with senior scholars, and the politics of professional organizations influence what I study. I have avowedly enjoyed benefits from this transition from teacher to scholar. In short, I have retired from the demanding life of a classroom teacher allowing me the privilege of thinking and writing about students that I taught two decades ago.

Meanwhile, time has also passed for my former students and their families. When I was a teacher, I was in my late 30's. The children's parents were approximately my age. Since then many of us have become grandparents and some of my former students have children of their own. Some parents have retired and more than one parent has passed away.

Eventually, my dissertation became a book and I assumed a position at the University of Wisconsin, Madison. My research with my former students did not end with my move to the university. Instead, I stayed in touch with my former first grade students and their families as the students moved through high school. I have written extensively about these students over the past 20 years.

Time haunts me as a researcher. I contemplate the trajectories that awaited my former students and the severe consequences of attending underfunded schools in a high poverty community. I recall my amazing six-year-old students and the potential they brought to my classroom. I consider the parents' unwavering hope for their children's futures. I lament the opportunities they did not find in school, the stifling instruction that they reported, and the failed tests, low report card grades, and stringent behavioral policies that they recalled. This does not mean that they did not encounter wonderful and inspiring teachers. Every student in my sample described teachers that they loved and remembered with fondness.

As I worked with the children and their parents, I recognized that parents often interpreted children's schooling experiences differently than the children's teachers. Nespor (1997) identified a critical mismatch. Specifically, he highlighted what I believe is an important distinction between how parents and teachers make sense of children's school experiences. Nespor noted that "teachers' acquaintance with kids generally begins and ends within a single school year" and that the "histories of students in earlier grades are generally hidden from view" (p. 32). In contrast, he recognized that parents know children and live beside children across time.

In essence, parents witness children's long-term educational experiences as "kids matured and took their places in society" (pp. 31-32). Teachers know children for only short periods and often focus on children's academic skills and competencies. Each year, teachers face a new class of students that consumes their care and attention. Thus, parents' conceptions of time and schooling can collide with school conceptions of success and teachers' narrow conceptions of success can trump the embodied, multidimensional, and longitudinal knowledge of children brought by parents (Nespor, 1997).

My current role as a professor allows time for reflection that was rarely available to me as a classroom teacher. As a researcher, I regularly spend my mornings in a local coffee shop with my laptop computer and stacks of data – a luxury that was never part of my employment as a classroom teacher. Thus time – both in its passing and in terms of the amount of time available to reflect on the voices and experiences of children and their families – contributed how I now understanding children's school experiences.

Introducing Marvin

In preschool, Marvin and his older sister moved among his parents' home, foster care, and his grandparents' home. By the time Marvin arrived in my first-grade class, he had been retained once and had been living with his grandmother and his step-grandfather, Mr. Sherwood, who participated consistently in interviews across the ten-year project. Marvin's grandmother occasionally participated, interjecting comments and insights as she felt necessary.

The school served a low-socioeconomic community in the Northeastern United States. In the 1960's this community had been the site of race riots. Since then, the largely White immigrant population moved to the suburbs and housing projects were built for the remaining African American and Puerto Rican families.

Rosa Parks Elementary School served over 1200 children from the lowest socioeconomic community of what was then the eleventh poorest city in the United States; 97% of the children who attended my school qualified for free and reduced lunch. While this description may seem bleak, the community was also the home of thousands of families who worked diligently to feed, clothe, and educate their children.

Marvin's journey through school was often punctuated by altercations with other students and run-ins with teachers. While generally well-intended, he had a short temper and was often frustrated by academic demands. One summer during middle school, Marvin attended a summer reading camp that I hosted at a local college. He worked with a teacher candidate who had extensive experience working with adolescents who found school challenging. That summer he conducted a detailed investigation of banana slugs.

By high school, Marvin was increasingly attracted to vocational classes, especially those that involved woodwork. By the end of our time together, Marvin had been incarcerated for stealing a car and later for taking metal from a construction site. Apparently, he had moved out of his grandparents' apartment and moved in with mother who was struggling with addiction issues.

Temporal Dimensions of Three Theories

In order to explore the complex nature of being within time, I present three highly influential theoretical constructs that have informed our understandings and interpretations of actors in educational contexts; each references a dimension of time: timescales (Lemke, 2000), chronotope (Bakhtin, 1981, 1986), and habitus (Bourdieu, 1980/1990, 1991; Bourdieu & Passeron, 1977).

While I present the three theories separately, I recognize and will later examine the ways in which the experiences of time captured by these three theories overlap and intertwine for Marvin. Specifically, I explore the temporal affordances of each theory and highlight its potential to inform current understandings of how students craft possible selves and make sense of their worlds, including school.

Lemke's Timescales

To explain long-term fundamental processes, including literacy development and schooling, Lemke (2000) proposed an ecological model that locates people within multiple, continuous, and simultaneous timescales ranging from the quick-moving microscopic changes to macro shifts of the universe.

To Lemke, these timescales are dimensions of an ecological system in which the lower levels are constituent of the higher levels with the higher levels involving conceptualizations and interpretations of lower level processes. Human semiosis, meaning making based on experience, involves interpretations of meanings that have been constructed and revisited over time.

Long-term processes, such as literacy learning and school affiliation, involve "fundamental changes in attitude or habits of reasoning" (Lemke, 2000, p. 282) that cannot occur within short timescales. Lemke's notion of timescales challenges conventional models that conceptualize time as linear and cumulative, by arguing that people experience time in recursive and non-linear ways as they draw on lived events and various texts across multiple timescales to make sense of their worlds. Individual voices are fashioned out of available social resources from across time as people appropriate various discourses to serve their own purposes. As Lemke noted, "the language others speak to us, from childhood, shapes the attitudes and beliefs that ground how we use all our powers of action" (Lemke, 1995, p. 1).

In accordance with Lemke's theory, I argue that students draw upon multiple timescales to make sense of themselves and school. Specifically, Marvin draws upon familial timescales that reference the experiences of family members and his own past, alongside ongoing timescales that capture his lived experiences. Marvin and the people around him draw recursively and selectively on these multiple timescales. It is within this temporally charged context that Marvin understands the world and his role within that world. In the following analysis, Marvin drew upon discourses voiced over time to make sense of his experiences and to solve the challenges that he faced as a recently incarcerated youth.

The Library as an Icon of Possibility

When I spoke with Marvin at age 18, he had been released from incarceration four months earlier and was attending a vocational high school. Coming from an eighteen-year-old former high school dropout, his comments about the library were intriguing. Marvin explained, "Sometimes I might go to the library, me and a couple of my home buddies and a couple of my home girls." He continued, "Like the other day, we all went downtown because we had this big essay. . . and I looked up [information] on the computer" (Grade 10).

While a researcher conducting a short term study might interpret Marvin's enthusiasm for the library as a simple example of his renewed dedication to getting his life back on track, data from this longitudinal study locates the library as an icon of possibility extending back four generations. The accounts presented below draw upon multiple timescales and include memories of family members, accounts from Marvin's past, Marvin's ongoing experiences, and accounts that reference the future. Across Marvin's experiences, literacy, computers, the Internet, employment, and the future are all associated with the library.

At one of our early interviews when Marvin was in first grade, his grandfather, Mr. Sherwood, told a story that I originally interpreted as merely an account of the challenges he had faced in learning to read. Learning to read in elementary school had been difficult for Mr. Sherwood and his teachers were doing little to help. He later explained, "I was just mumbling through the whole thing [when I read in class] . . . that's when I told my mother about it. . . She said 'It's time for you to get a library card.' Every Saturday morning. . . we [Mr. Sherwood and his twin brother] had to go to the library and we stayed at the library until we picked up on our reading" (Grade 1).

Over the course of the ten-year project, the library was often referenced as a motif of possibilities:

Mr. Sherwood: "We go to the library now. . . as a matter of fact, he spelt his name on the Internet." (Grade 1)

Mr. Sherwood: I had to take her [Marvin's sister] to the library and he [Marvin] mentioned [that] his mind [was] really focused on the computers. . . Cause we was playing around on the [computers]. I just started learning on them about four years ago. I know how to do it. I went to the library and learned myself. (Grade 1)

Mr. Sherwood: I used to take him to the library all the time. All the time, they love the library. It's a great place. . . . He's learned a lot about the Internet. (Grade 5)

Mr. Sherwood: Me and [Marvin's Grandmother] been trying to get him started going to the library you know. He [be] on [his] own [in] the neighborhood and stuff like that they [other family members] don't want him to go. But I want him [to] be responsible for himself so he can go and go to the library and get something and come on back. (Grade 8)

Mr. Sherwood: You got to start writing [on the computer] and start picking out what's this and that. (Grade 8)

Mr. Sherwood: I used to take him to the library, you know, get on the computers and stuff like that, but he got one upstairs now. (Grade 10)

While these comments recognize the library as a resource for literacy learning, they were also marked by words suggesting engagement and agency (e.g., "really focused," "they love the library," "getting involved," "responsible for himself"). For Mr. Sherwood, the library was a site of literacy possibilities.

The library not only helped Mr. Sherwood learn to read and offered similar opportunities to Marvin and his sister, it also provided Marvin and Mr. Sherwood with access to computers and thus possibilities for Marvin's future:

Mr. Sherwood: A computer is awesome. It's right now. It's the space age. You can't get around it. You just got to look in the paper, they want a computer programmer all that you know.

(Grade 1)

> Mr. Sherwood: He's trying, he's learned a lot about the Internet. . . .but I want him to get involved with [it] mainly like learn it [the computer]. (Grade 5)

Mr. Sherwood described the computers as "awesome," "right now," and "space age." He highlighted the importance of learning about computers by repeating the phrase "got to" and emphasized the connection between employment and learning to use computers.

Thus, the library carried meanings – related to literacy, computers, the Internet, employment, and the future – that were uniquely intertwined with and drew upon experiences at multiple timescales. Mr. Sherwood drew on his past when he recounted his own childhood experiences at the library and his hopes for Marvin's future. For a young man with a record of incarceration, visiting the library with friends was an agential act grounded in the past while simultaneously evoking future possibilities related to reading, books, computers, high school graduation, employment, and new friends who shared these interests and dreams.

While timescale analysis reveals how meanings are grounded in past experiences of family members, personal pasts, ongoing experiences, and perceived futures, this is only one dimension of a lived experience of time (Schatzi, 2006). Time is also experienced against the backdrop of institutions, the enacted mores of society, and the historical contexts that privilege particular ways of being and acting, as well as the embodied ways of being that people assume as a result of positionings and expectations.

Bakhtin's Chronotope

Marvin also operated within institutions, including schools that imposed temporal expectations. Bakhtin (1981, 1986) drew from philosophy, literary analysis, and linguistics, to explain how meanings are understood within complex social fields involving dialogic negotiations and unequal power dynamics. Bakhtin applied the construct of *chronotope,* which literally means *timespace,* to refer to "the intrinsic connectedness of temporal and spatial relationships" (Bakhtin, 1981, p. 84). Bakhtin explained that when authors create worlds they are obliged to draw upon the organizing categories of the real world – specifically recognizable time/space relationships.

Bakhtin identified and described literary genres based on how characters operated in time and space. He argued that these genres, or chronotopes, were constituted by the chronotopic motifs, or narrative tropes, that authors use and readers understand. These tropes might involve characters traveling along roads or paths as they move through narratives, unexpected encounters that change the directions of the stories, and nature as a symbol of pastoral and simpler worlds. These chronotopic motifs are meaningful because of the past literate and life experiences that readers bring to novels. As Bakhtin explained, conceptualizing possible meanings from stories requires passing thorough the "gates of the chronotope" (Bakhtin, 1981, p. 258) and drawing on pre-existing meanings to make sense of new experiences.

Motifs in Literacy and Schooling	Associated Meanings
Not reading fluently	Not proficient in reading, assumed to have difficulty com-prehending text, unsuccessful reader; poor public display of reading
Reading grade level texts	Proficient in reading, on-track, normal, successful, not in need of intervention
Failing standards-based English Language Arts examination	Being left behind, below standard, inadequate progress, literacy problem

Taking honors English course	Advanced, college track, capable, literate
Meeting criteria on standardized writing rubric	Proficient writer, college-bound, literate
Promotion/Retention	Success/failure, ability, normalcy, abilities correspond to age
Graduation	Accomplishment, success, achievement, grade attainment
Meeting grade level standards	Abilities commensurate with grade level, proficiency, suc-cessful
Special education	Failure in regular programs, needs extra help and addition-al time, slower pace, diminished potential
Vocational education	Salvageable, potentially worthy, academ-ically challenged

Figure 1. A Sampling of Chronotopic Motifs in Literacy and Schooling

Chronotopic motifs also operate in schools, carry meaning, and have real life significance (see Figure 1). Promotion and retention carry meanings related to students' abilities. Being in third grade is embedded with the temporal expectations for being eight-years-old. Compensatory education and special education services suggest that some students require more time to learn (Heshusius, 1989; Hocutt, 1996).

In recent years, grade level standards, standardized testing at particular grade levels, and being able to read texts at particular levels have increasingly defined students relative to temporal expectations. Essentially, failure in school is not merely about what students can and cannot do; it is about what skills and strategies they display or do not display at particular points in time.

Just as chronotopes in literature shape the meanings of stories, chronotopes in school shape the meanings people construct about their lives and the lives of others. Failing to meet chronotopic expectations has real meanings and consequences for students in terms of their options such as honors classes, special education placement, or summer school, as well as their futures for college, employment, and income. Students are aware of the meanings associated with chronotopes of schooling and these meanings sediment, contributing to the ways in which students construct themselves and others as successful or unsuccessful.

However, chronotopes do not carry static and universal meanings. As Brown and Renshaw (2006) maintained, chronotopes continuously draw upon multiple available discourses and meanings and are experienced as hybrid syntheses that carry multiple meanings. Burton (1996) agreed; he presented chronotopes as interwoven, replacing one another, contradicting each other, and existing in complex interrelationships. Official chronotopes may suggest a particular reading of experience, however, other possible meanings grounded in marginalized perspectives exist in direct contention with dominant chronotopic readings (Burton, 1996).

In other words, while chronotopes of schooling, for example failing the fourth grade, have implicit meanings related to inability or immaturity that are generally recognized by school officials, chronotopes are always open to multiple interpretations and alternative readings – for example, failing fourth grade might be attributed to an incompetent teacher.

While Bakhtin's theoretical constructs of carnival and dialogism have been applied extensively to education (Ball & Freedman, 2004; Lensmire, 2000; Morris, 1994), the construct of chronotope has been used less frequently (for exceptions see Bloome et al., 2009; Brown & Renshaw, 2006; Mutnick, 2006). In the following section, I examine the construct of chronotope as a means to highlight time as context in schools. Marvin's failure to meet the expected chronotopes of schooling carried meanings that affected his school trajectory.

The Construction of Failure

When Marvin was five-years-old, he moved back and forth between his parents' and his grandparents' homes. Mr. Sherwood described this as a "negative experience. . . [Marvin] was going back and forth he didn't know where he was going" (Grade 1). Over the course of that year, he missed a lot of school and ended up repeating grade 1. Thus, when I met Marvin he was already a year behind in school.

Unlike most of the first graders, Marvin was already able to read when he entered my class. By June, he was well-prepared for second grade; however, Marvin again fell behind with reading. He failed both the 4th grade and the 8th grade State English Language Arts test. When in eighth grade, he read at the fifth grade level.

When Marvin was in fifth grade, he was identified as a behavior problem. Marvin was caught bringing a spray bottle of bleach to school. Marvin explained, "I brought the bleach to school to protect myself because he [another student] said he was going to get his brother and his other brother to jump me" (Grade 5). Marvin was suspended for several weeks. Later that same year, Marvin described a fight in which he broke a classmate's nose. Also in fifth grade, Marvin was diagnosed with ADHD and was placed on medication. While unconvinced that the medication would help, Marvin's grandmother was hopeful, "Cause he's a slow learner and he got this medication and that'll make him focus better" (Grade 5).

By eighth grade, Marvin was distraught and blamed his grandmother for allowing him to be placed in a special education class. Marvin noted that in special education classes the expectations were low, the pace of instruction was slow, and less work was assigned. His grandmother came to share Marvin's concerns. However, when she asked to have him placed back in the regular program, she was told that "he [would] have to work himself out" (Grade 8).

Ms. Sherwood viewed this situation as highly problematic and offered her own critique of the school's policy, "I've been reading up on it and they mostly put Black kids in them kind of classes and then they sunk them. And that's how you all [gesturing at Marvin who is sitting nearby] get behind" (Grade 8). While special education was presented as an opportunity for Marvin to catch up, Ms. Sherwood blamed special education for leaving Marvin behind.

When I returned to visit Marvin during high school, he had moved out of his grandparents' apartment and was living with his mother. Since I had visited him in eighth grade, he was arrested for stealing a car; later that year he was incarcerated for removing scrap metal from abandoned buildings. While I visited Marvin while he was incarcerated, data collection was suspended in accordance with IRB procedures until Marvin was released. Thus our final interview was held when Marvin was released and living with his grandparents. He was eighteen-years-old and entering the tenth grade.

However, despite this problematic school trajectory that resulted in Marvin being eighteen and faced with three more years of high school, Marvin and his grandfather rejected the official meanings that temporal disruption imposed on Marvin. While failing to meet the official chronotopic motifs associated with school success, these messages of failure were complicated by the discourses of goodness and possibility repeatedly voiced by Mr. Sherwood:

He on the ball. . . I mean he's sharp. (Grade 1)

He is a sweet boy. . . He wants to help people out. (Grade 5)

He's a very gullible person. . . Marvin ain't no bad person. (Grade 8)

There was so many good things he had going in here [motions to his heart]. (Grade 10)

Mr. Sherwood spoke to chronotopic meanings imposed by school that characterized Marvin as incapable, unintelligent, and bad. He described Marvin as "on the ball," "sharp," "sweet," wanting to "help people," not a "bad person," and having "good things" in his heart.

While the verbs Mr. Sherwood uses are inconsistent in terms of their fortitude (e.g., "I hope" versus "I know") and various contingencies are recognized (e.g., sending him back to his parents, "if we can get to him"), Mr. Sherwood's sense of agency is strong, and given the right circumstances he is confident in his abilities to help Marvin. Mr. Sherwood consistently extended this sense of agency to Marvin, noting his capacity to affect his own future:

> Mr. Sherwood: My main thing is "Marvin keep trying. Marvin, you do the best you can." (Grade 1)

> Mr. Sherwood: It's up to him. . . He's got to make that move. . . If he feel like he gonna do it. . . I *know* he can do it! (Grade 8)

> Mr. Sherwood: He had to make a difference hisself. And that's the secret. (Grade 10)

Bakhtin's construct of chronotope explains how people draw upon meanings that are embedded in meaningful motifs over time. Being retained in school, failing high stakes tests, falling behind with reading, being placed into special education, and incarceration are all temporal disruptions that defined Marvin as unsuccessful and resulted in his being three years behind at age 18.

While these disruptions were interpreted in particular ways and eventually coalesced to define Marvin's educational trajectory, Mr. and Ms. Sherwood challenged these meanings. They recognized alternative possibilities and potential. Not only were alternative accounts reiterated over time, but Mr. Sherwood also appealed to me, a researcher who had known Marvin for over ten years, saying "*you* know Marvin." While chronotopes carry meanings, those meanings are neither singular nor universal; they are open to interpretation and reflect people's beliefs and experiences.

Together timescales (Lemke, 2000) and chronotopes (Bakhtin, 1981, 1986) contribute to how we might understand the timescapes that accompany school. While timescale analysis (Lemke, 2000) highlights how meanings are constructed with and through the past, the present, and perceived possible futures and chronotopes, Bakhtin (1981, 1986) highlights the expectations that accompany those experiences, neither construct explains how ways of being are internalized and embodied over time which suggests yet another critical dimension of time.

Bourdieu's Habitus

Throughout his life, Bourdieu (1971, 1980/1990, 1986, 1991; Bourdieu & Passeron, 1977) attempted to explain complex interactions between culture, social structures, and individual agency. His work focused on how social systems of domination persist and recreate themselves across time (Swartz, 1997). Bourdieu identified the construct of "habitus":

> A system of lasting transposable dispositions which, integrating past experiences, functions at every moment as a *matrix of perceptions, apperceptions, and actions* and makes possible the achievement of infinitely diversified tasks. (italics in the original; Bourdieu, 1971, p. 83).

Habitus references how people's pasts are embodied in ways of being and knowing that accompany experience. Contrary to some interpretations of Bourdieu's work, people are not trapped in simple processes of social and economic reproduction (Albright, 2009).

Habitus is linked to the accumulation of cultural capital – ways of talking, acting, interacting and believing that privilege people in particular contexts. People who are able to accumulate large amounts of capital prior to seeking their place in the social/economic system have an advantage. Accumulation "depends on the length of time for which the family can provide him [the child] with free time, i.e., time free from economic necessity" (Bourdieu, 1986, p. 246). In addition, cultural capital is dependent "on the usable time (particularly in the form of mother's free time) available to it (by virtue of its economic capital, which enables it to purchase the time of others) to ensure the transmission of this capital" (Bourdieu, 1986, p. 253, parentheses in the original).

Bourdieu highlighted labor, patterns of consumption, and parent-child relations as conditions that inform habitus and in turn become the basis for the "perception and appreciation of all subsequent experiences" (Bourdieu, 1980/1990, p. 54). The factors that most significantly affect the development of habitus are subtle, involving non-verbal and unconscious ways of being, acting, and interacting including ways of looking, physical positioning, silences, and movements that are acquired unknowingly in the course of everyday activity (Bourdieu, 1991). While people can adapt their habitus to accommodate new situations, these changes are incorporated slowly and unconsciously as elaborations rather than drastic changes to existing dispositions (Bourdieu & Passeron, 1977).

While habitus is grounded in the past and involves limits and norms, it also acts "as an acquired system of generative schemes, the *habitus* makes possible the free production of all the thoughts, perceptions and actions inherent in the particular condition of its production" (Bourdieu, 1980/1990, p. 55). Habitus does not determine ways of being, acting, knowing, or believing, rather it evolves out of experiences and contributes to options made available within historical, social, and physical contexts. Habitus explains how individuals become whom they are – not through simple processes of reproduction – but through long-term participation in social structures and institutions that provide both affordances and limits for agency and identity.

Swartz drew on the work of Bourdieu to remind scholars that "not all social worlds are equally available to everyone" (Swartz, 1997, p. 107) and it is through habitus that prior life experiences teach people what may or may not be possible; agency is intertwined with past experiences. While researchers have readily applied Bourdieu's constructs of reproduction and capital to educational contexts (Dimitriadis & Kamberelis, 2006; Compton-Lilly, 2007; Lareau, 1989; Carrington & Luke, 1997), the construct of habitus, perhaps due to its longitudinal nature, has been less influential and rarely examined in-depth.

Possibilities of Being and Becoming

Habitus (Bourdieu, 1971) denotes the embodiment of dispositions across time; in the following account, we witness Marvin not only stating his desire to become a police officer, but also embodying ways of being that are consonant with this aspiration. For Marvin, being a police officer was grounded in a commitment to fighting injustice, interest in helping people, fascination with the job and the uniform, and his relationship with his grandfather. However, these dispositions were eventually challenged as Marvin negotiated multiple life experiences including interactions with police officers while incarcerated. Marvin's interest in becoming a police officer was reiterated across the study:

Mr. Sherwood: He want to be a policeman. (Grade 1)

Marvin: [To be a policeman, I need to] Go up in college and stuff [and read] the back of number cars [license plates] and when they have got crashed [and] the people get hurt and they [the police] try to figure out their names and stuff. (Grade 1)

Mr. Sherwood: I can speak for Marvin because I know what he want to do. . . He wants to help people. . . he always says he wants to be a police officer. He keeps on saying that all the time and stuff. I mean especially to help people. (Grade 5)

Mr. Sherwood: He wanted to protect and serve. (Grade 10)

Marvin's commitment to police work was not only consistently reflected in the words Mr. Sherwood used to describe Marvin's interest (e.g., "always," "keeps on saying") but it was also reflected in Marvin's actions. When Marvin was in first grade, Mr. Sherwood described Marvin's interest in watching "police stories" on TV:

He always [watches]. . . the highway patrol . . . He always talk about patrolmen. 'Cause I used to be a security guy he used to see me in my uniform and stuff like that so... his personality that's what he's gonna be. (Grade 1)

Marvin's developing habitus reflected a commitment to police work that was grounded in his interest in helping and protecting people, and serving his community. When Marvin was young, his grandfather reported that Marvin wanted to "arrest his daddy and mother because they was doing bad things" (Grade 10).

When Marvin returned to school following the bleach incident in fifth grade, the school principal tried to encourage Marvin by making him the school's "public safety" – a role that resonated with his interest in police work. Each morning Marvin opened the parking lot gate for the teachers when they arrived in the morning.

Marvin's interest in being a police officer was also grounded in his sense of injustice. In first grade, he listed things at school that bothered him, "fighting, big bullies, taking pencils away from people, pushing people in line, hit-slapping people in the back of the heads" (Grade 1). In middle school, Marvin described the "bad kids" at his school:

> They be cursing me. They be running around in the halls, fighting in the bathroom. And try to, pushing each other to get at the lockers. And with rubber bands they try to [Marvin snapped an invisible rubber band in my direction]. (Grade 8)

However, after being released from incarceration, Marvin was no longer sure that he wanted to be a policeman. Marvin explained, "I seen too many of them policemen." Despite his reservations about the police, he reported that law enforcement was "[still] kind of on my mind." At the time, he was applying for a job as a security guard, "If I get that security job, Grandpa, I'm telling you it's a wrap. . . I be having a flashlight. Yeahhhhh, yeah. I have a badge" (Grade 10). Ten years after Mr. Sherwood described Marvin as a six-year-old admiring his security guard uniform, Marvin ventriloquates those words referencing a badge and flashlight.

Following Marvin's incarceration, Mr. Sherwood was less confident about the possibility of police work. Mr. Sherwood reported, "He ain't got no plan now" (Grade 10). Marvin raised several possibilities including being a lawyer, nurse, or a carpenter.

Concerns about Marvin actually becoming a police officer first appeared when Marvin was in grade 8. This was the year Marvin was placed in special education; he continued to experience discipline problems at school. At the same time, Mr. Sherwood often commented on Marvin's ability to work with his hands:

> Mr. Sherwood: He's good with it [his hands] . . . he know how to fix a lot of bicycles. (Grade 8)

Mr. Sherwood: Vocational school I think would be best for him you know like an engineer or something like that. Cause he like to tear-up things and try to put them back together again. (Grade 8)

Mr. Sherwood: He liked to work on cars. . . he would tear stuff up, demolition, he loved it. (Grade 10)

Mr. Sherwood: He told me this morning, we was talking said he loves it [his vocational education classes]. (Grade 10)

While beginning in grade eight Mr. Sherwood highlighted Marvin's vocational abilities, Marvin was not convinced. While Marvin enjoyed his vocational education classes and was proud of his abilities, he struggled to retain his dreams of becoming a police officer. Simple and logical decisions, like becoming a carpenter, are not all that simple. They are caught up with the embodied selves constructed over long periods of time and contextualized within people's experiences.

Bourdieu (1986) maintained that a person's habitus is deeply rooted into a person's past and changed slowly over long periods of time. As evident in the accounts presented above, helping people and being a police officer reflected strong dispositions that were deeply rooted in Marvin's beliefs about himself and the world. While Marvin retained his dreams of becoming a police officer, these dreams were complicated by his arrest record.

Neither complete nor comprehensive, together timescales (Lemke, 2000), chronotope (Bakhtin, 1981, 1986), and habitus (Bourdieu, 1971, 1980/1990, 1986, 1991) illustrate the multiple dimensions of time. Time is not a simple linear sequence. It is not a just resource that can be invested and translated into learning. It is not simply a gauge against which student learning can be measured. As Adam (1989) explains, time's significance is multidimensional:

Time enters into every tiniest aspect of that moment.
It is implicit in waiting, in planning, in contemplat-
ing, and in guilt; just as it is central to memories, the
language structure, and to the speech as it was happening. (p. 468)

As Marvin's experiences illustrate, it involves ways of
making sense of the world, the expectations that accompany
our experiences, and ways of being that contribute to who we
are and who we become.

What do Theoretical Understandings about Time Offer Educators?

While I maintain that the multidimensional nature of
time has not been fully explored by educational researchers, educational researchers have not ignored time. Some
have treated time as a methodological variable. For example,
Roberts, Jurgens, and Burchinal (2005) examined the extent
to which home literacy practices of young children predicted
later language and literacy skills. In their study, which followed
children from age 18 months through their entry into kindergarten, they treated time as a methodological variable – the
length of the intervention. In an earlier study, conducted by
Leseman and de Jong (1998), children were tracked from ages
four to age seven to examine the relationship between home
literacy practices and educational outcomes. Assessments were
administered repeatedly at planned intervals of time to ascer-
tain the stability of established home literacy practices.

Other researchers have focused on development across
time. Classic studies in developmental psychology (e.g., Kohlberg, 1981; Piaget, 1953) identified stages that children progress through and/or benchmarks that children were expected to
meet at particular points in time. Developmental perspectives
focus on change over time and the degree to which individual

change reflects expected pattern of development. Thus time has historically been treated as a methodological variable that could be controlled and should be considered rather than as context in which people operate.

Still other researchers have acknowledged the significance of history, and recognized time within people's life stories. Critical race theorists (Dixson & Rousseau, 2006; Ladson-Billings & Tate, 1995) critique ahistorical accounts of schooling and arguing that current educational practices are deeply rooted in policies, practices, and attitudes of the past. Ladson-Billings (1994) situated her research with successful teachers of African American children within discussions about the historical segregation of African American and White students. She maintained that successful teachers challenged accepted beliefs, narratives, and instructional practices creating new possibilities for students.

Life story researchers, including McAdams (2001), argue that people's identities are conceived and expressed as stories that involve reconstructions of people's pasts alongside ongoing experiences and anticipated futures. Life stories are continuously constructed and reconstructed within social and cultural contexts. People's life stories are to a strong degree retrospective; individuals tell these stories to themselves and others to make sense of their worlds and themselves.

While life story researchers recognize the social nature of storytelling and the cultural contexts in which people live, they do not document how people exist and operate within time, the ways identities are constructed and reconstructed across time, or the ways time contextualizes people's lives.

In addition, time has been recognized as a consideration in discussions of educational practice. Time has historically been conceptualized as a resource that can be invested to increase learning. In the late 1800's, William T. Harris, then the U.S. Commissioner of Education, lamented the shortened length of school days and years (NECTL, 1994); he argued that that students would learn more if they spent more time in school.

Between 1910 and 1930 the efficiency movement attempted to make American businesses and schools more productive – producing more in less time (Callahan, 1962). Efficiency initiatives included the adoption of standardized achievement tests to monitor students' progress, rating systems for teachers, and policies that would ensure that time was not wasted, for example by minimizing transition time between classes and limiting the time students spent at the blackboard. These initiatives became the basis for contemporary schools that featured class periods and lecture-style classrooms.

Responding to arguments that unproblematically associate more time with increased learning, Slattery critiques what he calls the "exaggerated emphasis on manipulation of time" (Slattery, 1995, p. 612):

> time management, timed tests, wait time, time on task, quantifiable results over time, time schedules, time-out discipline centers, allocation of instructional days on annual school calendars, core academic time, Carnegie units, time between classes, year-round schooling, and the like. (Slattery, 1995, p. 612-613)

Time is not merely a resource that can be divided up, allocated, and manipulated. Time is not like money; it cannot be invested, accumulated, or saved (Adam, 2003b). Slattery proposed a vision of time as:

> . . . radically eclectic, determined in the context of internal relatedness, recursive in its complexity, autobiographically intuitive, aesthetically intersubjective, phenomenological, experiential, simultaneously quantum and cosmic, ironic in its kaleidoscopic sensibilities, and ultimately, a hermeneutic search for greater understanding that motivates and satisfies us on the journey. (p. 631)

Time encompasses everything that people have lived and

understood as well as the ways they make sense of themselves, their experiences, and their relationships. Slattery (1995) argued that educators must focus on "allowing the process of becoming, rather than the artificial demands of clocks and linear sequences, to dominate our personal and professional lives" (p. 616).

Neither researchers nor practitioners have attended to how people draw upon events at multiple timescales to make sense of their worlds, to negotiate the temporal expectations of schooling, or reference deep-seated dispositions that inform students' ways of being.

Above, I have presented three theoretical frameworks that explore various dimensions of time as context. Timescale analysis calls attention to events and the construction of meaning across multiple timescales as Marvin makes sense of himself and his experiences. This analysis revealed visiting the library as a recurring motif that was loaded with meanings grounded not only in Marvin's experiences, but also in experiences and stories that could be traced back to his step-great-grandmother.

These experiences related not only to literacy, but also to technology and possibilities for the future. Looking back across time and forward towards Marvin's future reveals negotiations among family members, peers, and school expectations that come together as Marvin chooses to visit the library. His actions are neither random nor arbitrary; they are selected from a range of possibilities offered by a particular present and a lived and interpreted past in the service of a possible future.

Chronotopic motifs related to literacy and schooling draw attention to how official definitions of school success reference time. Marvin's teachers interpreted temporal disjunctures as an indication that Marvin was slow, learning disabled, and a vocational student. Despite these positionings being repeatedly challenged by Marvin and his grandparents, over time, official disjunctures accumulated and limited Marvin's future educational options.

As Adam (2003a) argued, "embodied time is lived and experienced alongside, despite of, and in conflict with the culturally constituted social relations of time" (p. 61). The temporal expectations for children, grounded in rhetorics of standards, benchmarks, and No Child Left Behind (2001) are assumed to be universal – temporal expectations are not negotiable. While official meanings associated with chronotopes of schooling had real effects on Marvin's life, Marvin and his grandparents challenged these meanings and offered alternative readings of situations and events.

Finally, Bourdieu's construct of habitus highlights the process of becoming and the ways early experiences and beliefs are deeply engrained, embodied, and slow to change. Despite experiences in school and with the legal system that could be interpreted as evidence that police work was not a good fit, Marvin did not abandon his interests and the draw of the badge, helping people, and addressing injustice continued to inform his goal of becoming a security guard.

Challenging accounts that present children's future goals as arbitrary, habitus draws attention to the process of becoming as well as how goals and possibilities are deeply infused with self. Bourdieu's theories situate habitus within inequitable social fields (e.g., urban schools, high poverty communities) that privileged forms of capital that Marvin did not possess. Marvin's lack of economic capital (money), social capital (influential social networks), and institutional capital (a high school diploma) complicated the challenges he faced in realizing his goals.

While each of these theories highlights a particular dimension of time, together they provide an initial framework for understanding of how time operates in people's lives: timescales as layered experiences that people draw upon to make sense of their worlds; chronotopes as involving official temporal expectations; and habitus as embodied ways of being. These frameworks invite researchers to recognize the various manifestations of time and to recognize the role time plays in long-term processes such as literacy learning, identity construction, school trajectories, school achievement, and occupational aspirations.

Longitudinal qualitative research and temporal analyses offer important insights that explain the effects of long-term situations such as living in high poverty communities and attending poorly funded schools. Attention to time allows us to view students as eternally changing and growing. By attending to time, we recognize that the disillusioned teenager was once an enthusiastic first grade student. Rather than knowing a student at a certain time and place, attending to time allows us to view children across time in multiple situations and settings.

Finally, Marvin's story demonstrates the permanence of hope. While teachers and researchers may be inclined to dismiss particular children as incorrigible or uneducable, Marvin and his grandfather retained faith in his future. Despite repeated setbacks, temporal disruptures, and institutional policies that complicated Marvin's trajectory and limited his options, Marvin and his grandfather retained hope for the future, for example by visiting the library, taking vocational education classes, and returning to high school.

These enactments of hope and agency are grounded in the faith Marvin's grandparents had in Marvin and the faith Marvin retained in himself. Marvin is much more than an eighteen-year-old, African American, low income youth – he is the six-year-old who wanted to be a police officer, the little boy who loved storybooks, the child who brought bleach to school to protect himself from bullies, the middle school student who was fascinated by banana slugs, the special education student who was not challenged, and the talented vocational education student who was "good with his hands."

Attending to time allows us to view children as complex, nuanced and multifaceted people with rich histories and experiences. For Marvin, time as context reveals agency, lost opportunities, challenges, strengths, resilience, and hope.

While I present Marvin's experiences in relation to each of the three dimensions of time, these dimensions overlap and intersect. If we revisit Marvin and his dream to become a police offer, we witness an embedded habitus that supports this disposition. However, we also witness a school system filled with expectations and tracked instructional experiences that have been described as a school to prison pipeline (Wald & Losen, 2003; Winn, 2011).

Thus expectations related to school contributed to how Marvin came to define himself. The instructional experiences he experienced – heavy-handed discipline, low expectations, special education placement, retention, and racism – informed his sense of self and the dispositions that he brought forward. In addition, Marvin drew on past timescales (e.g., watching police shows with his grandfather, seeing his grandfather in his security uniform), and future possibilities suggested by the public library, as he made sense of himself – a recently incarcerated youth. Thus, the three dimensions of time identified in my analysis are intricately intertwined and reciprocally informative.

In order to recognize how students, educators, and researchers exist within time, we must move beyond simple equations that associate more time with increased learning. If we accept the premise that people make sense of their lives within and across time, we begin to acknowledge the importance of not just the here and now, but of considering children's longitudinal experiences in school in terms of educational policies, practices, and research. We recognize communities and families as bringing rich histories, sets of experiences, and understandings that are grounded in long term relationships with schools and literacy. We begin to understand that these experiences and the meanings that surround them exist within chains of events, experiences within institutions, and embodied ways of being.

What might a research agenda involve that recognizes time as critical to making sense of children's school experiences and literacy learning? Such an agenda has implications for theory, methodology, and educational practice. Theoretically, literacy researchers must:

1. Work to recognize and explain further manifestations of time in literacy learning;
2. Move toward a comprehensive understanding about the ways time operates in the lives of children, teachers, and in the evolution of schools, literacy instruction, and the field of education; and
3. Bring together scholars from various fields that share an interest in time including developmental studies, new literacy studies, sociology, historical educational studies, sociohistorical theory, and critical race theory to explore issues related to literacy learning.

Methodologically, we must:

1. Produce more longitudinal research, allowing more researchers opportunities to examine how time manifests itself in the experiences of students, educators, families, and in communities;
2. Develop and refine methodologies that access past and future experiences to understand how participants make sense of the present;
3. Explore methodologies that consider change and consistency, trajectories and disjunctures, setbacks and growth; and
4. Interrogate issues related to funding, tenure, and scholarship that work against researchers conducting long-term studies and thus attending to time.

Significantly, expanded notions of time invite educators and scholars to think about inequity "because time is largely taken for granted and therefore invisible, the social relations of time can continue to maintain existing inequalities and create new one in the globally constituted world" (Adam, 2003b, p. 119). As Lemke maintained, "We construct meaning of our lives . . . across multiple timescales of action and activity, from the blink of an eye to the work of a lifetime" (Lemke, 2005, 110). Our challenge as researchers and educators is to recognize and attend to temporal complexity to support teachers and their students across time and as they move through school.

Appreciation is extended to the Spencer Foundation for their support of the final phase of this research project

REFERENCES

Adam, B. (1989). Feminist social theory needs time. Reflections on the relation between feminist thought, social theory and time as an important parameter in social analysis. *The Sociological Review*, *37*(3), 458-473.

Adam, B. (2000). The temporal gaze: the challenge for social theory in the context of GM food. *The British Journal of Sociology*, *51*(1), 125-142.

Adam, B. (2003a). Reflexive modernization temporalized. *Theory, Culture, and Society, 20*(2), pp. 59-78.

Adam, B. (2003b). When time is money: Contested rationalities of time in the theory and practice of work. *Theoria: A Journal of Social and Political Theory*, 94-125.

Albright, J. (2009). Problematics and generative possibilities. In J. Albright & A. Luke (Eds.), *Pierre Bourdieu and Literacy Education*. Mahwah, NJ: Lawrence Erlbaum.

Bakhtin, M.M. (1981). *Four essays by M. M. Bakhtin* .C. Emerson C. & M. Holquist (Trans.). Austin, Texas: University of Texas Press.

Bakhtin, M.M. (1986). *Speech genres and other late essays*. M. Holquist & C. Emerson (Eds.). Austin, Texas: University of Texas Press.

Ball, A. & Freedman, S.W. (Eds.). (2004). Bakhtinian perspectives on language, literacy, and learning. Cambridge,

UK: Cambridge University Press.

Bidart, C. (2012). What does time imply? The contribution of longitudinal methods to the analysis of the life course. *Time and Society, 22*(2), 254-273.

Bloome, D., Beierle, M., Grigorenko, M. & Goldman, S. (2009). Learning over time: Uses of intercontextuality, collective memories, and classroom chronotopes in the construction of learning opportunities in a ninth-grade language arts classroom. *Language and Education, 23(4),* 313-334.

Bourdieu, P, (1971). Systems of education and systems of thought. In Young MFD (Ed.) *Knowledge and control* (pp. 189-207). Berkshire, UK: Open University Press.

Bourdieu, P. (1980/1990). *The logic of practice* (R. Nice trans). Stanford, CA: Stanford University Press.

Bourdieu, P. (1986). The forms of capital. In Richardson J.G. (ed.) *Handbook of theory and research for the sociology of education* (pp. 241-258). New York, NY: Greenwood Press.

Bourdieu, P. (1991). *Language and symbolic power* (G. Raymond & M. Adamson trans.). Cambridge, MA: Harvard University Press.

Bourdieu, P. & Passeron, J. (1977). *Reproduction in education, society, and culture.* London: Sage.

Brown, R. & Renshaw, P. (2006). Positioning students as actors and authors: A chronotopic analysis of collaborative learning activities. *Mind, Culture and Activity 13(3)*: 247-259.

Burton, S. (1996). Bakhtin, temporality, and modern narrative: Writing "the whole triumphant murderous unstoppable chute." *Comparative Literature 48(1):* 39-64.

Callahan, R.E. (1962). *Education and the cult of efficiency.* Chicago, IL: University of Chicago Press.

Carrington, V. & Luke, A. (1997). Literacy and Bourdieu's sociological theory: A reframing. *Language and Education, 11(2),* 96-112.

Cipriani, R. (2013). The many faces of social time: A sociological approach. *Time and Society, 22*(1), 5-30.

Compton-Lilly, C. (2003). *Reading Families: The Literate Lives of Urban Children.* New York, NY: Teachers College Press.

Compton-Lilly, C. (2007). *Re-Reading Families: The Literate Lives of Urban Children, Four Years Later.* New York, NY: Teachers College Press.

Compton-Lilly, C. (2012). *Reading Time: The literate lives of urban secondary students and their families.* New York, NY: Teachers College Press.

Compton-Lilly, C. (2016). *Reading students' lives: Literacy learning across time.* New York, NY: Routledge.

Dimitriadis, G. & Kamberelis, G. (2006). Pierre Bourdieu. In G. Dimitriadis & G. Kamberelis (Eds.), *Theory for Education,* (pp. 65-73). New York: Rutledge.

Dixson, A.D. & Rousseau, C.K. (2006). *Critical race theory in education: All God's children got a song.* New York: Rutledge.

Ekwall, E. E., & Shanker, J. L. (1993). *Ekwall/Shanker reading inventory* (3rd ed.). Boston, MA: Allyn & Bacon.

Facer, K., Joiner, R., Stanton, D., Reid, J., Hull, R., & Kirk, D. (2004). Savannah: mobile gaming and learning? *Journal of Computer Assisted Learning, 20*(6), 399-409.

Firth, R. & Robinson, A. (2014). For the past yet to come: Utopian conceptions of time and becoming. *Time and Society, 23*(3), 380-401.

Giddens, A. (1991). *Modernity and self-identity.* Cambridge, MA: Polity Press.

Heshusius, L. (1989). The Newtonian mechanistic paradigm, special education, and contours of alternatives: An overview. *Journal of Learning Disabilities, 7*, 403-415.

Hocutt, A.M. (1996). Effectiveness of special education: Is placement the critical factor? *The Future of Children, 6*(1),

77-102.

Keightley, E. (2013). From immediacy to intermediacy: The mediation of lived time. *Time and Society, 22*(1), 55-75.

Kohlberg, L. (1981). *Essays on Moral Development, Vol. I: The Philosophy of Moral Development.* San Francisco, CA: Harper & Row.

Ladson-Billings, G. (1994). *The dreamkeepers: Successful teachers of African American children.* San Francisco, CA: Jossey-Bass Publishers.

Ladson-Billings, G. & Tate, W.F. (1995). Toward a critical race theory of education. *Teachers College Record, 97(1),* 47-68.

Lareau, A. (1989). *Home advantage: Social class and parental intervention in elementary education.* London: Falmer.

Lemke, J. (1995). *Textual politics: Discourse and social dynamics.* New York, NY: Taylor and Francis.

Lemke, J. (2000). Across the scales of time: Artifacts, activities, and meanings in ecosocial systems. *Mind, Culture, and Activity, 7(4),* 273-290.

Lemke, J. (2005). Place, pace and meaning: Multimedia chronotopes. In Norris S. & Jones R. (Eds.), *Discourse in action: Introducing mediated discourse analysis* (pp. 110 – 122). New York, NY: Routledge.

Lensmire, T. (2000). *Powerful writing, responsible teaching.* New York: Teachers College Press.

Leseman, P. & DeJong (1998). Home literacy: Opportunity, instruction, cooperation, and socio-emotional quality predicting early reading achievement. *Reading Research Quarterly, 33(3),* 294-321.

Leslie, L., & Caldwell, J. (2006). *Qualitative reading inventory - 4.* Boston, MA: Pearson.

McAdams, D.P. (2001). The psychology of life stories. *Review of General Psychology, 5(2),*100-122.

Morris, P. (1994). *The Bakhtin reader: Selected writings of Bakhtin, Medvedev, Voloshinov.* London: Arnold.

Mutnick, D. (2006). Time and space in composition studies: "Through the gates of the chronotope." *Rhetoric Review,* 25(1), 41-57.

National Education Commission on Time and Learning [NECTL]. (1994/2005) Prisoners of time. Washington, DC: ED366115 [Available on-line at: http://www.ed.gov/pubs/ PrisonersOfTime/index.html]

Nespor, J. (1997). Tangled up in school: Politics, space, bodies, and signs in the educational process. London: Routledge.

No Child Left Behind Act [NCLB] (2001). Washington, DC: Retrieved July 8, 2009, http://www.ed.gov/nclb/landing.jhtml

Piaget, J. (1953). *The Origins of Intelligence in Children.* London: Rutledge & Kegan Paul.

Roberts, J., Jurgens, & Burchinal (2005). The role of home literacy practices in preschool children's language and emergent literacy skills. *Journal of Speech, Language and Hearing Research,* 48(2), 345-359.

Schatzki, T.R. (2006). The time of activity. *Continental Philosophy Review, 39,* pp. 155-182.

Slattery, P. (1995). A postmodern vision of time and learning: A response to the National Education Commission Report, Prisoners of Time. *Harvard Educational Review,* 65(4): 612-633.

Strauss, A. & Corbin, J. (1990). *The basics of qualitative research: Grounded theory procedures and techniques.* Newbury Park, CA: Sage Publications.

Swartz, D. (1997). *Culture and power: The sociology of Pierre Bourdieu.* Chicago, Illinois: Chicago University Press.

Wald, J., & Losen, D. J. (2003). Defining and redirecting a school-to-prison pipeline. *New directions for youth development, 2003*(99), 9-15.

Winn, M. T. (2011). *Girl time: Literacy, justice, and the school-to-prison pipeline. Teaching for Social Justice.* New York, NY: Teachers College Press.

AN INTERVIEW WITH CATHERINE COMPTON-LILLY

BOBBIE

Why did you become interested in studying time and literacy?

CATHERINE

In my original research, which became my doctoral dissertation, I was focused on 10 kids in my first-grade classroom. At first, I just wanted to document their home and school literacy practices. My theory was – and this was based on several years of teaching in the school – that even though they were from a very poor community they had very strong families. The families really did care about the kids, so I wanted to document the literacy practices in their homes. After I defended my dissertation, I became curious about the kids and went back to find them four years later, and then three years later, and then three years later.

So I ended up having this longitudinal data set. The more I considered the data set, the more I started thinking about what it means to "become" over time. How do people construct not only identities but also how do they interact with the world? What does the world mean to be a particular person in a particular space? I started asking these sorts of questions.

In sociocultural theories, we think a lot about context. When I think about scholarship in which people have discussed context, they often present context as either physical or social spaces. Context is often treated as the present in which things happen. I really try to complicate this idea of context by attending to time and how we make sense of the world as we operate across time.

For example, you are not just listening to me right now, and making sense of what I'm saying based on the words that are coming out my mouth. In your mind, you may be remembering something you read last week, or something that happened to you when you were six-years-old. You may be thinking ahead to what you're going to be doing later. So our minds are putting things together within longitudinal temporal contexts.

This idea of context has significance, particularly for children who have been historically underserved because they're living within a legacy that has created particular structures in schools and in society. So, I think about these children as being located within inequitable histories. In short, inequity doesn't happen in first grade or high school; inequity has been and continues to be constructed over time. There is a longitudinal trajectory in which some kids get access to resources and others don't.

BOBBIE

How does this work fit into the larger scope of family literacy, which has been the crux of your work?

CATHERINE

If you go back and look at what I consider the two quintessential volumes on family literacy, both of them have very strong longitudinal dimensions. In particular, I'm thinking of Denny Taylor's early work in her book *Family Literacy*. In that book, she spends a whole chapter on parents talking about their past experiences learning to read, and how those experiences inform what they do with their children. You get a generational form of prolepsis – a relationship between the parents' past and the child's present, alongside the parent's hopes for the child's future. So there is a rich temporal dimension of family literacy.

The other person whose work resonates with family literacy is Shirley Brice Heath. Her book, *Ways with Words*, was longitudinal, in that she worked in the communities described in her book for over seven years. In recent years, Shirley Brice Heath published a newer volume where she describes going back to find the families from *Ways with Words*, and revisits the families 40 years later. Thus, family literacy has temporal dimensions that we must recognize and honor.

Another slippery term for all of us to define and get our heads around is culture. We like to reduce culture to things, like food or festivals. I argue that the concepts of culture and family are similar in many ways. For example, there are powerful longitudinal dimensions of culture. What you bring forward and what gets passed on to the next generation is the "stuff" that transcends our particular time and space. Culture is always changing and it constantly hybridizes with other spaces and people.

BOBBIE

How do you differentiate between *longitudinal* and *ethnography* in the discussion of time? Within longitudinal research, researchers may say longitudinal is one year. Sometimes longitudinal is over three years, and sometimes longitudinal is a lifetime. Ethnographies look at social and cultural interactions within context over time.

CATHERINE

Good question, and I would throw in one additional term – revisiting.

I will try to talk through these terms. With ethnography, you immerse yourself in the community, cultural group, school, or classroom. You're living there and you are attempting to witness what it is like to be there. You might be studying what we call culture – the culture of the space, the classroom or community. You might be examining language or literacy practices in that space, but you're immersing yourself in that space. If you do that over a long period of time while attending attend to change over time, then I would say that your work is both ethnographic and longitudinal. However, you could occupy a particular space for years, but never attend to what is changing or emerging. Longitudinal research attends to time and change. Ethnography might not. That's how I distinguish between the two.

In contrast, I think the work that I did with the families from *Reading Families* is a revisiting study. I went back every three or five years. I didn't really follow the children. Instead, I captured snapshots every few years. I then tried to link the pieces of the puzzle together. For it to be longitudinal, I would have to follow those families and work with them much more often.

So I try not to use the term longitudinal to describe my own work. I argue that *Reading Families* and my other books related to these families are not truly longitudinal. In contrast, the newer study that we are doing with immigrant families is longitudinal. In that study we visit families two or three times each year.

BOBBIE

To go along with our discussion of time and change, how do you think the field of literacy has changed over time?

CATHERINE

Well, I've been working with Rebecca Rogers and Tisha Lewis Ellison on a meta-ethnography that asks that question. A few years ago, we conducted a review of family literacy research, which was published in the *Reading Research Quarterly*. In that review, we examined how diversity has been treated in family literacy scholarship. But that wasn't the piece we intended to write. We wanted to do a meta-ethnography. George Noblit and

Dwight Hare created meta-ethnography as a methodology for looking across qualitative studies.

For quantitative meta-analysis, you often examine effect sizes. For meta-ethnography, you analyze the metaphors that people use to describe and present their research. What metaphors are used to explain findings? What metaphors are used to explain the data? What metaphors are used by participants? Here's an example: "funds of knowledge" is a metaphor. Funds of knowledge can be accumulated and you can invest it. It is an economic and financial metaphor, although we rarely consider its economic meanings.

Becky, Tisha, and I have identified the top-cited scholars in the field of family literacy. Basically, we identified seven researchers whose work is routinely cited by family literacy scholars. We then examine one seminal article written by each scholar to explore its metaphors. We then track those metaphors to see how they change over time, and we think we're finding some interesting insights into the field.

Basically, we determine whether a given metaphor is maintained, refuted, or extended over time. The earliest piece we analyzed was Denny Taylor's (1982) and the newest piece was Kate Pahl's (2002). For example, one metaphor that shows up in scholarship conveys the idea that literacy learning is natural. If you look at Taylor's work, she uses multiple naturalistic metaphors. If you track the use of naturalistic metaphors over time, what is considered natural and what it means to be natural changes. In the early work, literacy itself is natural and children learn literacy naturally. Whereas, when you look at Luis Moll's work, the teacher is identified as a natural mediator between home and school. If you examine Pahl's work, you continue to find natural metaphors but they reference the geological notion of sedimentation. In her work, we are invited to attend to growth alongside established structures that are more permanent and enduring.

So, yes, I believe that the field of family literacy is changing as we learn more and continue to consider the range and breath of literacy practices in families and communities.

BOBBIE KABUTO: A SHORT BIOGRAPHY

Bobbie Kabuto, Ph.D. is Professor of Literacy Education and Department Chair of the Elementary and Early Childhood Education Department at Queens College, City University of New York. She was the 2019 recipient of the United Kingdom Literacy Association (UKLA)/Wiley Research in Literacy Education Award and the Senior Editor for the Garn Press Women Scholars Series.

Her research interests include the relationships among early bi/literacy, socially constructed identities, and language ideologies. She currently works with families of struggling beginning readers and writers.

Her work has been highlighted in journals such as *Reading Research Quarterly*, the *Journal of Early Childhood Literacy*, and *Early Childhood Research and Practice.* Her first book *Becoming Biliterate: Identity, Ideology, and Learning to Read and Write in Two Languages* was published by Taylor and Francis in July 2010.

LIST OF SELECTED WORKS BY BOBBIE KABUTO

Kabuto, B. & Harmey, S. (2020). Assessment literacy: Implications for the literacy professional. *The Language and Literacy Spectrum, 30*(1). DOI: https://digitalcommons. buffalostate.edu/lls/vol30/iss1/5

Kabuto, B. & Harmey, S. (2020). The biographic literacy profile: Version 2.0. In R. Meyer & K. Whitmore. *Reclaiming manifestations of literacies: Cultivating a discourse of meaning making.* New York, NY: Routledge.

Kabuto, B. (2020). Parental perceptions of learning disabilities. *Educational Forum.* DOI: 10.1080/00131725.2020.1737997

Kabuto, B. & Harmey, S. (2019). Editorial: Literacy in a global context: Educational policy, pedagogy, and teacher education. *Global Education Review, 6*(2), 1-4.[*Note: From Guest Edited Issue from Kabuto, B. & Harmey, S. (Eds.) (2019). Literacy in a Global Context: Educational Policy, Pedagogy, and Teacher Education, 6(2).*]

Velasco, P. & Kabuto, B. (2019). Transgenerational bilingual reading practices: A case study of an undocumented Mixteco family. In E. Ijalba, P. Velasco, & C. Crowley. From *Language, culture, and education: Challenges of diversity in the United States.* Cambridge, MA: Cambridge University Press.

Harmey, S. & Kabuto, B. (2018). Metatheoretical differences between running records and miscue analysis: Implications for analysis of oral reading behaviors. *Research in the Teaching of English, 53*(1), 11-33.

Kabuto, B. (2018). Becoming a bilingual reader as linguistic and identity enactments. *Talking Points, 29*(2), 11-18.

Olmstead, K. & Kabuto, B. (2018). Writing artifacts as narratives of emotion. *Language and Literacy, 20*(2), 102-124.

Kabuto, B. (2018). Family narratives of biliteracy. *Literacy, 52*(3), 137-144. *[Note: Recipient of the United Kingdom Literacy Association (UKLA)/Wiley Research in Literacy Education Award 2019.]*

Kabuto, B. (2017). A socio-psycholinguistic perspective to biliteracy: The use of miscue analysis as a culturally relevant assessment tool. *Reading Horizons, 56*(1), 25-44.

Kabuto, B. & Velasco, P. (2016). Taking a value-oriented perspective of biliterate families. *Multicultural Education, 23*(3/4), 20-26.

Kabuto, B. (2016). The social construction of a reading (dis) ability. *Reading Research Quarterly, 51*(3), 289-304.

Kabuto, B. (2016). Revaluing novice readers: Reclaiming families. In R. Meyer & K. Whitmore (Eds.). *Reclaiming Early Childhood Literacies: Narratives of Hope, Power, and Vision.* New York, NY: Routledge.

Kabuto, B. (2015). Transgenerational learning within families. *Journal of Family Diversity in Education, 1*(4), 45-65. Archived at: http://familydiversityeducation.org/index.php/fdec. *[Note: Fully Online Journal]*

Kabuto, B. (2015). The construction of biliterate narratives and identities between parents and children. *Global Education Review, 2*(2). Archived at: http://ger.mercy.edu/index.php/ger *[Note: Fully Online Journal]*

DENNY TAYLOR: A SHORT BIOGRAPHY

Professor Emerita, Denny Taylor is the co-founder of Garn Press, and a global scholar and activist. She was inducted into the Reading Hall of Fame in 2004. In 2019 she received Columbia University's Distinguished Alumni Award and also the NCRLL Distinguished Scholar Award.

James Paul Gee writes, "Denny is, in my view, one of the most brilliant and important scholars of sociocultural approaches to literacy in the 20th century—a field to which I contributed as well. Her work on literacy combines technical sophistication about language and a deep commitment to human dignity and social change. She has always worked at the intersection of human development both in terms of the development of language, literacy, and learning in children, but also in the sense of the development of more humane people, institutions, and societies."

Since 1977 Denny has been continuously engaged in research with families living in extreme poverty, and in regions of armed conflict and weather related catastrophes. The concept of "family literacy" originates in her doctoral research at TC, Columbia University.

Today, there are family literacy initiatives in most UN Member States established to build more just, peaceful and inclusive societies. Family literacy has become a conduit for many local and regional initiatives to address poverty and hunger, public health emergencies, gender inequality, and strengthen partnerships to address the United Nations Sustainable Development Goals.

Most recently Denny has used her evidence-based research on family, literacy and learning to focus on existential risks and science based macrostrategies for achieving the SDGs and human survival. Her many books span the sciences, and include novels and children's books as well as research texts. Accounts of her research on families, literacy and catastrophic events are available on her website at https://www.denny-taylor.com, together with many of her publications on family literacy in global contexts.

LIST OF SELECTED WORKS BY DENNY TAYLOR

From Family Literacy to Earth System Science: Denny Taylor's Research on Making the Planet a Child Safe Zone: Garn Press, June 2017.

Teaching Without Testing: Assessing the Complexity of Children's Literacy Learning: Garn Press, April 2017.

The Children of Sandy Hook vs. The U.S. Congress and Gun Violence in America: Garn Press, April 2017.

Split Second Solution: Garn Press, October 2016.

Great Women Scholars: Yetta Goodman, Maxine Greene, Louise Rosenblatt, Margaret Meek Spencer: Garn Press, March 2016.

Rosie's Umbrella: Garn Press, January 2015.

Save Our Children, Save Our School, Pearson Broke the Golden Rule: Garn Press, July 2014.

Nineteen Clues: Great Transformations Can Be Achieved Through Collective Action: Garn Press, June 2014.

Beginning to Read and the Spin Doctors of Science: The Political Campaign to Change America's Mind About How Children Learn to Read: National Council of Teachers of English (NCTE), June 1998.

Many Families, Many Literacies: An International Declaration of

Principles: Heinemann. May 1997.

Teaching and Advocacy: (with Debbie Coughlin and Joanna Marasco). Stenhouse, January 1997.

Toxic Literacies: Exposing the Injustice of Bureaucratic Texts: Heinemann, September 1996.

From The Child's Point Of View: Heinemann, September 1993.

Learning Denied: Heinemann, November 1990.

Growing Up Literate, Learning From Inner City Families: (with Catherine Dorsey-Gaines). Heinemann, June 1988.

Family Storybook Reading: (with Dorothy S. Strickland). Heinemann, July 1986.

Family Literacy: Young Children Learning to Read and Write: Heinemann, March 1983 (1st edition), December 1998 (2nd edition).

Toodle-oo Ruby Blue!: Garn Press, June 2017.

Rat-a-tat-tat! I've Lost My Cat!: Garn Press, November 2015.

Notable videos include: https://www.dennytaylor.com/news/watch-womens-federation-for-world-peace-international-featuring-dr-denny-taylor-family-literacy-in-the-time-of-covid-19-impacts-now-and-moving-forward

Podcasts: https://www.dennytaylor.com/news/2019/new-york-welsh-interviews-dr-denny-taylor

Research Report Documenting 40 Years of Research https://www.dennytaylor.com/news/2018/from-family-literacy-to-earth-system-science

AlterNet publication on Chomsky (first published by AlterNet in 2015) https://www.alternet.org/2018/04/heres-what-happened-when-professional-atheist-sam-harris-tried-and-failed-embarrass-noam-chomsky/

Originally published Language Arts Vol. 76, No. 3, Revealing Language (January 1999), pp. 217-231 https://www.

dennytaylor.com/news/beginning-to-read-and-the-spin-doctors-of-science-an-excerpt

Denny Taylor's curriculum vita can be accessed here: https://www.dennytaylor.com/curriculum-vitae

Most of her research is in the commons and can be accessed for download on her website: https://www.DennyTaylor.com

ANNE HAAS DYSON: A SHORT BIOGRAPHY

Anne Haas Dyson, Ph.D., began her career in education as an elementary school teacher at the El Paso Catholic Diocese in El Paso, Texas in 1972. In 1974, she moved to the Austin Independent School District in Austin, Texas, where she taught as a substitute teacher and, later, as a preschool teacher in a Title 1 Migrant Program and, finally, as a first grade and ESL teacher in bilingual programs.

Dyson received her Ph.D. in Education from the University of Texas in Austin, Texas in 1981. It was during her time at University of Texas, Austin that she connected her classroom teaching experiences with her doctoral work and became interested in the social and cultural worlds of childhood writers.

In 1984, she published her first book with her good friend and colleague Celia Genishi titled *Language Assessment in the Early Years*. Since this first publication, Dyson has published 12 books. Her most recent book is an edited volume titled *Child Cultures, Schooling, and Literacy: Global Perspectives on Composing Unique Lives*, which was published by Routledge, Taylor and Francis Group in 2016. Dyson's latest book features her collaborative global research project on children learning to write. In addition, Dyson has written over 100 journal articles and book chapters all regarding children's writing.

Dyson is Faculty Excellence Professor in the College of Education at the University of Illinois at Urbana/Champaign. Prior, Dyson has held positions at Michigan State University (2002-2006), the University of California, Berkeley (1984-2002), and the University of Georgia (1981-1985).

Dyson has been awarded numerous grants from the Spencer Foundation to study the social and cultural worlds of childhood writers. She has also received a number of awards for her scholarship and contributions to the field of education. Awards for her writing include the John Hayes Award for Excellence in Writing Research (2014, 2009), Janet Emig Award from the National Council of Teachers of English (NCTE; 2006, 2002) and the Purves Award from NCTE (1999). Dyson received the Early Literacy Educator of the Year Award from NCTE (shared with co-author Celia Genishi, 2012), the Distinguished Teaching Award of the University of California-Berkeley (1998) and the Promising Researcher Award for NCTE (1982).

In 2015, Dyson received a second NCTE David H. Russell Award for Distinguished Research (the first received in 1993). In addition, with Celia Genishi, she received the prestigious Outstanding Educator of the Year Award from NCTE. This award recognizes the distinguished careers of Dyson and Genishi and their major contributions to the field of English Language Arts.

LIST OF SELECTED WORKS BY ANNE HAAS DYSON

BOOKS

Dyson, A. H. (Ed.) (2016). *Child cultures, schooling, and literacy: Global perspectives on composing unique lives.* New York, NY: Routledge.

Dyson, A.H. (2013). *ReWRITING the basics: Literacy learning in children's cultures.* New York, NY: Teachers College Press.

Genishi, C., & Dyson, A. H. (2009). *Children, language, and literacy: Diverse learners in diverse times.* New York, NY and Washington, DC: Teachers College Press & The National Association for the Education of Young Children.

Dyson, A. H., & Genishi, C. (2005). *On the case: Approaches to language and literacy research.* New York, NY: Teachers College Press.

Dyson, A. H. (2003). *The brothers and sisters learn to write: Popular literacies in childhood and school cultures.* New York, NY: Teachers College Press.

JOURNAL ARTICLES AND BOOK CHAPTERS

Dyson, A. H. (2015). The search for inclusion: Deficit discourse and the erasure of childhoods. *Language Arts*, 92, 199-207.

Genishi, C., & Dyson, A. H. (2014). Play as the precursor of literacy development. In E. Brooker, M. Blais & S. Edwards (Eds.), *Sage handbook of play and learning* (pp. 228-239). London, UK: SAGE.

Dyson, A. H. (2013). The case of the missing childhoods: Methodological notes for composing children in writing studies. *Written Communication*, 30, 399-427.

Dyson, A. H., & Dewayani, S. (2013). Writing in childhood cultures. In K. Hall, T. Cremin, B. Comber, & L. Moll (Eds.), *International handbook of research on children's literacy, learning, and culture* (pp.258-274). Oxford, UK: Wiley-Blackwell.

Dyson, A. H. & Genishi, C. (2013). Social talk and imaginative play: Curricular basics for young children's language & literacy. In N. Unrau & D. Alvermann (Eds.), *Theoretical models and processes of reading, 6th edition* (pp. 164-181). Newark, DE: International Reading Association.

Dyson, A. H. (2013). Staying in the (curricular) lines: Practice constraints and possibilities in childhood writing. In M. Prinsloo & M. Baynham (Eds.), *Literacy studies, Volume IV: Literacy in education and at work* (pp. 107-144). Thousand Oaks, CA: Sage.

Dyson, A. H. (2012). Relations between oral language and literacy. In C. Chapelle (Ed.), *The encyclopedia of applied linguistics*. Indianapolis, IN: Wiley-Blackwell.

Dyson, A. H. (2012). Ethical worlds of school children's writing cultures: Individualism meets dialogism. In S. Matre, D.K. Sjohelle & R. Solheim (Eds.), *To find one's own voices, to express oneself and receive answers: Theoretical and analytical perspectives on textual work in the classroom* [English translation from Norwegian] (pp.93-100). Oslo: Universitetsforlaget Publishing House.

Dyson, A. H. (2012). The place of childhoods in school writing programs: A matter of ethics. In J. Larson & J. Marsh (Eds.),

The Sage handbook of early childhood literacy, 2nd edition (pp. 485-500). London, UK: Sage.

Genishi, C., & Dyson, A. H. (2012). Racing to the top: Who's accounting for the children? In B. Ayers, J. Siln & G. Boldt (Eds.), *Challenging the politics of the teacher accountability movement: Toward a more hopeful educational future.* Occasional Paper 27 [Online]. New York, NY: Bank Street College. (http://bankstreet.edu/occasionalpapers)

Genishi, C., Dyson, A. H., & Russo, L. (2011). Playful learning: Early education that makes sense to children. In B. S. Fennimore & A. Lin Goodwin (Eds.), *Promoting social justice for young children* (pp. 59-70). New York, NY: Springer.

Dyson, A. H., & Genishi, C. (2011). The buzz on teaching and community. In V. Kinloch (Ed.), *Urban literacies: Critical perspectives on language, learning, and community* (pp. 91-94). New York, NY, Teachers College Press.

Dyson, A. H. (2010). The cultural and symbolic "begats" of child composing: Textual play and community membership. In O. Saracho & B. Spodek (Eds.), *Language and cultural diversity in early childhood education* (pp.191-211). Charlotte, NC: Information Age Publishing.

Dyson, A. H. (2010). Writing childhoods under construction: Revisioning "copying" in early childhood. *Journal of Early Childhood Literacy*, 10, 7-31.

Dyson, A. H. (2010). Opening curricular closets in regulated times: Finding pedagogical keys. *English Education*, 42, 307-319.

Dyson, A. H. (2010). Childhoods left behind? Official and unofficial basics of child writing. In N. Yelland (Ed.), *Critical issues in early childhood*, Vol. 2. (pp. 159-176). London. UK: Routledge.

CATHERINE COMPTON-LILLY: A SHORT BIOGRAPHY

Catherine Compton-Lilly is the John C. Hungerpiller Professor at the University of South Carolina. As a professor in the College of Education, Dr. Compton-Lilly's research has focused on family literacy practices, particularly the literacy practices of children from communities that have been underserved by schools.

In her initial work, she documented the home and school literacy practices of eight of her former first grade students as they moved from elementary school through high school. In a current study, now in its tenth year, she is exploring the family literacy practices of children from immigrant families.

She has edited or authored eight books and has authored multiple articles related to family literacy in major literacy journals including *the Reading Research Quarterly, Research in the Teaching of English, The Reading Teacher, Journal of Early Childhood Literacy, Written Communication, Journal of Literacy Research* and *Language Arts*.

Dr. Compton-Lilly has a passion for helping teachers to support children in learning to read and write. Her interests include early reading and writing, student diversity, and working with families. She has a strong interest in teacher education and is currently documenting the exceptional teacher education practices at the University of South Carolina. She holds emerita status at the University of Wisconsin Madison.

LIST OF SELECTED WORKS BY CATHERINE COMPTON-LILLY

Compton-Lilly, C. (in press). Reflexive layers and longitudinal research: The Case of Christy. In M. Grenfell & K. Pahl (Eds.), *Language-Based Ethnographies and Bourdieu.*

Compton-Lilly, C. (in press). Revisiting development: Insights from a longitudinal research project. In A. Woods and B. Exley (Eds.), *Literacies in Early Childhood.* Australia & New Zealand: Oxford University Press.

Compton-Lilly, C., Kim, J., Quast, E., & Tran, S. (in press). Transnational literacy practices in immigrant families: A longitudinal study. *Journal of Early Childhood Literacy.*

Compton-Lilly, C., Papoi, K., Venegas, P., Hamman, L., & Schwabenbauer (2017). Intersectional identity negotiation: The case of young immigrant children, *Journal of Literacy Research, 49*(1), 115-140.

Compton-Lilly, C. (2017). Exploring literacy and identity at multiple timescales. In P. Albers (Ed.) *Global conversations in literacy research* (54-67). New York, NY: Routledge.

Compton-Lilly, C. (2017). *Reading students' lives: Literacy learning across time.* New York, NY: Routledge.

Compton-Lilly, C. (2016). The possibilities of longitudinal research: Lessons from a teacher and a researcher. *The Educational Forum, 80,* 466-478.

Compton-Lilly, C. (2016). A Closer Look at a Summer Reading Program: Listening to Students and Parents. *The Reading Teacher, 70*(1), 59-67.

Compton-Lilly, C. (2016). The development of literacy practices across a decade: Families, friends, and schools. In D. Appleman & K. Hinchman (Eds.), *Adolescent literacy: A handbook of practice-based research*. New York, NY: Guilford Publishing.

Compton-Lilly, C. (2015). Longitudinal studies and literacy studies. In J. Rowsell & K. Pahl (Eds.), *Routledge handbook of literacy studies* (pp. 218-230). New York, NY: Routledge.

Compton-Lilly, C. (2015). Reading lessons from Martin: A case study of one African American student. *Language Arts, 92*(6), p. 401-411.

Compton-Lilly, C. (2014). The development of writing habitus: A ten-year case study of a young writer. *Written Communication, 31,* 371-403.

Compton-Lilly, C. & Halverson, E. (Eds.). (2014). *Time and space in literacy research.* New York, NY: Routledge Publishers.

Compton-Lilly, C. & Gregory, E. (2013) Conversation currents: Family literacy. *Language Arts, 90*(6), 464-472.

Compton-Lilly, C. & E.B. Graue, with R. Rogers & T.Y Lewis. (2013). Agency, authority, and action in family literacy scholarship: An analysis of the epistemological assumptions operating in family literacy scholarship. In J. Larson & J. Marsh (Eds.), *Handbook of early childhood literacy, 2nd Ed.* London, UK: Sage Publications.

Compton-Lilly, C. (2013). The Temporal Expectations of Schooling and Literacy Learning Jermaine's Story. *Journal of Adolescent & Adult Literacy. 56*(5), 400-408.

Compton-Lilly, C. (2013). Temporality, trajectory, and early literacy learning. In K. Hall, T. Cremin, B. Comber and L. Moll (Eds.), *International handbook of research on children's literacy, learning and culture* (pp. 83-95). West Sussex, UK: Wiley-Blackwell.

Compton-Lilly, C. (2012). *Reading time: The literate lives of urban secondary students and their families.* New York, NY: Teachers College Press.

Compton-Lilly, C., Rogers, R. & Lewis, T. (2012) Analyzing epistemological considerations related to diversity: An integrative critical literature review of family literacy scholarship. *Reading Research Quarterly, 47*(1), 33-60.

Compton-Lilly, C. (2011). By the book and behind the glass: Teacher self-regulation in one reading intervention. *Language Arts, 88*(6). 429-438.

Compton-Lilly, C. (2011). Time and reading: Negotiations and affiliations of a reader, grades one through eight. *Research in the Teaching of English, 45*(3), 224-252.

Compton-Lilly, C. & Greene, S. (Eds.). (2011). *Bedtime stories and book reports: Connecting parent involvement and family literacy.* New York, NY: Teachers College Press.

Compton-Lilly, C. (ed.) (2009). *Breaking the silence: Recognizing the social and cultural resources students bring to the classroom.* Newark, Delaware: International Reading Association.

Compton-Lilly, C. (2007). *Re-Reading families: The literate lives of urban children, four years later.* New York, NY: Teachers College Press.

Compton-Lilly, C. (2004). *Confronting racism, poverty and power.* Portsmouth, NH: Heinemann Publishers.

Compton-Lilly, C. (2003). *Reading families: The literate lives of urban children.* New York, NY: Teachers College Press.

WOMEN SCHOLARS SERIES

Negotiating a Permeable Curriculum: On Literacy, Diversity, and the Interplay of Children's and Teachers' Worlds

Negotiating a Permeable Curriculum: On Literacy, Diversity, and the Interplay of Children's and Teacher's Worlds is part of the Garn Press Women Scholars Series. Originally printed in 1993 in the National Council of Teachers of English (NCTE) Concept Paper Series, *Negotiating a Permeable Curriculum* revisits Dyson's powerful concept of a permeable curriculum, a socially constructed learning space created by teachers and children.

Negotiating a Permeable Curriculum is a timeless piece as it is relevant to current moves in education with the implementation of the Common Core State Standards (CCSS). In 2010, the CCSS were released as a set of standards devised to create national benchmarks of student knowledge and skills in literacy and math. While not specifically mentioning curriculum, the CCSS explicitly outlines what should be taught from kindergarten to grade 12 and, therefore, it has had a major impact on establishing a national curriculum and assessment system led by private, corporate companies.

Challenging the standardization of learning, Dyson ask readers to push back the "curricular curtain" to wonder about the complex social and intellectual work in which children engage when they become writers. The emphasis on becoming focuses on how learning to write is always a dynamic state, as children learn about themselves while they learn about written language.

In *Negotiating a Permeable Curriculum*, Dyson provides concrete examples of the social and cultural challenges learning to become writers entails. Dyson highlights how teachers can enact a permeable curriculum so that the worlds of teachers and children come together in instructionally powerful ways.

Teaching without Testing: Assessing the Complexity of Children's Literacy Learning

Teaching without Testing: Assessing the Complexity of Children's Literacy Learning by Denny Taylor is the second book in Garn Press Women Scholars Series. This book revisits Taylor's seminal and influential work based on her Biographic Literacy Profiles Project. *Teaching without Testing: Assessing the Complexity of Children's Literacy Learning* is a timely book that challenges the scientific assumptions of standardized testing in developing effective instruction to meet the literate lives of all students.

Through detailed observations of student learning, Taylor encourages readers to consider alternative ways of assessing children's reading and writing based on observable literacy behaviors. Supporting a humanistic perspective to the education of children, Taylor argues that standardized and diagnostic methods of assessment and teaching, based on test-driven, cooperate-led accountability practices, have detrimental effects on children and result in the de-professionalization of teachers.

Time in Education: Intertwined Dimensions and Theoretical Possibilities

Time in Education: Intertwined Dimensions and Theoretical Possibilities is part of the Garn Press Women Scholars Series. It explores the intersection of literacy and the construct of time within education through the scholarship of Catherine Compton-Lilly, who highlights the complexity of studying learning. In particular, she focuses on how and what people learn over time within school-based structure, which entail established power structures that define who we are as learners, privileging some learners and marginalizing others.

Catherine Compton-Lilly presents a theoretical kaleidoscope of learning and literacy over time and illustrates how understandings of learners and learning shift as educators cast their gaze through different theoretical lenses. She asks how people reconcile, or strive to reconcile, complementary and contradictory framings of learners—a dilemma often faced by educators and parents.

Specifically, Compton-Lilly proposes that time acts as a constitutive dimension of people's experiences that significantly affects how people make sense of their worlds by exploring the temporal affordances of three highly influential theories: Jay Lemke, Mikhail Bakhtin, and Pierre Bourdieu. To illustrate the temporal potential of these theories, she draws upon data from a ten-year case study of one student and his family. Attending to how people operate within time provides important insights into longitudinal processes including identity construction, literacy learning, and becoming a student. These insights are important not only to researchers who attempt to make sense of the experiences of children and teachers, but also to educators who must seek ways to acknowledge and effect the longitudinal trajectories of children.

www.ingramcontent.com/pod-product-compliance
Lightning Source LLC
Chambersburg PA
CBHW062114020426
42335CB00013B/966